When I Was Comin' Up

When I Was Comin' Up

An Oral History of Aged Blacks

Audrey Olsen Faulkner
Marsel A. Heisel
Wendell Holbrook
Shirley Geismar

Archon Books
1982

Printed in the United States of America

Library of Congress Cataloging in Publication Data

When I was comin' up.

  Life histories of elderly black people in Newark,
N.J. from tape recorded reminiscences collected as a
project of the Rutgers Graduate School of Social Work.
  Bibliography: p.
  1. Afro-Americans—New Jersey—Newark—Biography.
2. Newark (N.J.)—Biography. 3. Rural-urban migration—
United States. 4. Afro-Americans—Southern States—
Social conditions. 5. Southern States—Rural conditions.
I. Faulkner, Audrey O.   II. Rutgers University.
Graduate School of Social Work.
F144.N69N48   1982   305.8'96073'074932 [B] 82-8738
ISBN 0-208-01952-9   AACR2

To our Historians, in admiration of their faith, their courage and their strength.

Contents

Acknowledgements

This manuscript results from the combined efforts of many people in the Rutgers University community and the black community of Newark, New Jersey.

We appreciate the financial assistance given us by the National Institute of Mental Health.[1] Our special thanks go to Marie L. Blank, Assistant Chief, Center for Studies of the Mental Health of the Aging, NIMH, for her strong support as we set up our research shop and gathered data in the difficult times of the early seventies. Mary Harper and Tom Anderson of NIMH were especially helpful, and Barry Lebowitz has continued to give us technical assistance and imaginative consultation on administrative problems.

Bill Twyman, Executive Director of the Fuld Neighborhood House, gave most generously of his assistance in the original design of the project. We still mourn his sudden and untimely death, and we sorely missed his good counsel as the project progressed. We hope this book would please him—he, too, came from a rural Southern background, and had lived through many experiences similar to those of our Historians. Ida Bell, who succeeded Bill as the Director of the merged Friendly–Fuld Neighborhood House, made the agency's full resources available to us, often at the cost of cramped space for her own program.

The Board members at Friendly–Fuld Neighborhood House supported us and interpreted our intent and our procedures to the neighborhood and the city leadership. Many members of the Board extended themselves greatly to make us feel welcome and safe. We could not have carried out the project without them, and we gratefully acknowledge our debt.

Conrad Graves, presently Chairperson, Department of Anthropology, Sociology and Social Work at Keane College, was always there

---

[1] Grants #MH-18051 and #MH-27894

when we needed him. Chester Jones, Chairperson, Planning and Community Organization Sequence, Rutgers Graduate School of Social Work, and Wynetta Bryant, now of Syracuse University School of Social Work, helped us gain understanding and insight. Jackie Mirkin, of the Elizabeth School System, and Phyllis Peterman, of Rutgers–Newark, helped us with many problems, and made their resolution a joyful experience.

Margaret Moore, one of the Grand Ladies of Newark, served as our Program Director. She later became the Associate Director of the Newark Office of Elderly Affairs, where she continued to be a staunch friend to the project. She has passed' since this manuscript was completed; we hope she, too, would be pleased with it.

We cannot praise too highly our Family Consultants (the Listeners). Stanley Flamer, Lona Berkeley, Peacolia Simms and Esther Dotson did a superb job of collecting the histories. More than that, they were friends to the Historians and to us. Their kindness, their good humor, and their dedication to the community and the project will remain in our memories for a lifetime.

City, county and state officials aided the authors, the Historians and the project. Mayor Kenneth Gibson, who created the Newark Office of Elderly Affairs, helped to create a political climate in which life improved for our Historians. Bernard Gallagher, then the Director of the Essex County Office on Aging, championed the cause of our Historians and their elderly contemporaries. James Pennestri and Ron Muzyk of the New Jersey State Division on Aging made it possible for us to carry out our commitments to help the black community find funds and personnel to continue social services when our project was completed.

The two research projects of which this collection of histories was a part, spanned the years 1970–1981. During all this time, the Administration of the Graduate School of Social Work at Rutgers has actively supported our research. The project began under Dean Werner Boehm. Morris Siegel, Miriam Dinerman and Ralph Garber continued to provide administrative facilitation of the highest quality. Our special thanks go to Dean Harold W. Demone Jr., for actively assisting the first author in obtaining a sabbatical to finish the manuscript. Associate Provost Jean Parrish was also consistently helpful.

Ludwig Geismar and Isabel Wolock of the Social Work Research Center helped us with the interview guide and trained the Listeners in techniques for using the guide.

Iris Bauman, Administrative Assistant in the Institute on Aging, managed all the details associated with creating a manuscript. More than that, she brightened our days with affection and good cheer.

Barbara Saper and Rochelle Kornfeld served as Administrative Assistants in the early days of the first project. Bessie Millotis and Terry Moffet typed and assembled the final manuscript with forbearance and understanding.

This book is characterized by collective authorship: the real authors, of course, are our Historians—the black men and women of Newark who shared the stories of their lives with us. We thank them for this generous act. The "formal" authors are not listed by importance of contribution, but by the order in which they joined the project.

Audrey Faulkner was responsible for the design of the project, and for the interview guide. Marsel Heisel joined her in the efforts connected with the collection of the data. Shirley Geismar edited the tapes—a massive job which she carried out almost single-handedly. These three authors were responsible for the first chapter. Wendell Holbrook had the primary responsibility for the research connected with the final chapter on the historical backdrop, and for guiding our interpretation of historical events as they affected black lives. Audrey Faulkner and Shirley Geismar assisted in that research, and the final chapter is the product of the efforts of all three.

Husbands Maury Albertson, Don Heisel and Ludwig Geismar comforted us in our trials and rejoiced with us over our successes. They also cooked our dinners and washed our dishes on occasion—an inestimable help to harried authors.

We thank all of those who helped us make this a better book. The errors and omissions rest with us.

AUDREY OLSEN FAULKNER
MARSEL A. HEISEL
WENDELL HOLBROOK
SHIRLEY GEISMAR

1

Introduction
Collecting the Life Histories

One of the most amazing demographic phenomena of the twentieth century has been the movement of hundreds of thousands of Southern blacks into the Northern cities. This mass migration, begun about the year 1915, changed the ethnic composition of geographic regions within the United States and eventually altered the face of the large cities of this nation. The country's institutions and way of life were greatly modified by this voluntary exodus from one region and resettlement in another. This change affected individual black lives as well, for it catapulted a rural farming population, kept outside the mainstream of American life by a rigid social system, into a rapidly changing urban environment. Here the mode of life often was determined by slum conditions and a livelihood had to be found within an industrial setting.

This is the story of that folk movement, told in the language of the people who took part in the great migration. They are old by now, and their reminiscences are sometimes rambling, sometimes clothed in the blur of nostalgia, and sometimes incomplete (especially in regard to specific dates) because of fading memory. They provide an invaluable picture of the Southern black society that was; of the manner in which that society survived; of the individual reasons that prodded Southern blacks to leave their homes for the trip North; and of the early days in a Northern industrial city, Newark, before the wave of Southern blacks transformed it.

The biographical material does not end with the early days of migration, however. Many individuals describe the living conditions that they found and the ways in which they managed to earn their livelihood in the new land. Some contrast the Newark of today with the city of the twenties, others examine the differences between themselves and the black young, and all of them comment upon their old age and the changes that have come about because of it. These biographies document the variety to be found in turn-of-the-century black society.

They have been gathered from individuals born in the North as well as in the South, from at least one person who spent his youth in both regions and can tell of the contrasts, from middle-class and working-class blacks, from men and women, from the urban and the rural. We do not claim to have completely represented black society or even to have aimed at that remote goal, but we have tapped into many of the different groups that made up Newark's black population in the early twentieth century.

There was a certain urgency attendant upon gathering these life histories, for we could hear the ticking of the clock. With the death of this generation of blacks, the best source of knowledge about the historical period within which they lived will disappear, never to be retrieved. And so the gathering of individual biographical material became one of the more important tasks of our social work project, which, in addition to collecting data, was also sponsoring services to elderly blacks in Newark.

Funded by NIMH in 1970, Rutgers University in conjunction with Friendly-Fuld Neighborhood House, set up offices in one of the public housing projects that dominate the Central Ward, the black heartland of Newark, New Jersey. Locating the older people was an essential element of the program, for the project was conceived as an opportunity to serve elderly blacks and at the same time gather information about them.[2] It is important to note that this research was designed as a study of intra-group differences in life styles, attitudes, interaction, and responses to services, not as a comparison of black with non-black elderly people. We felt there was no place in this project for the insertion of a white, middle-class group that might be taken as a "norm" against which to measure "deviations." The material that was gathered is a description of one group of aged blacks, and we maintain that such a description cannot start from a position that asks: how are they different from non-blacks? Such a starting point would imply a concept of deviance, whereas we assume the existence side by side in this country of a variety of life styles that have been developed to meet different life experiences.

Relatively little is known about the black elderly and the sub-

---

[2] Services of an out-reach nature were offered to the aged black population and the impact of these upon the mental health of the recipients was measured. The staff also collected data on the attitudes, life styles and social functioning of the population. Other aspects of the Rutgers–Friendly Fuld Aging Project have been published elsewhere.

groups among them. (For that matter, very little is known about any ethnic, racial or language sub-group of aged people who do not spring from mainstream America.) Housed as it was in the midst of the black community and eventually integrated into the daily lives of the old who lived there, the project was in a unique position to gather information. We realized, however, that this opportunity carried with it a twofold responsibility: informing the general public about the lives of the aged blacks and the historic movement in which they took part, and helping those who provide services to the community to understand the cultural backgrounds, the patterns of living, and the attitudes that motivate the black population. This volume deals with the first responsibility that we have outlined above—that of relaying little-known information about the lives of aged black individuals, people who were directly affected by the migration of blacks from the South.

We called the people who allowed us to record their life histories "Historians" and those who were employed to do the recording "Listeners." The Historians and other old blacks who received services lived in an area of the Central Ward of Newark dominated by high-rise public housing (one building specifically set aside for the elderly) and ramshackle private rooms and apartments. Some of the Historians were from the group of elderly people who received project services, some had been located in a house-to-house survey done at the time the project was established, and some became known to the staff after they became acquainted with the people in the area.[3] Selection of the Historians was made from individuals who seemed to typify the elderly of the area, those who visited the project's offices, who used the services that were extended to them, who joined the clubs and the shopping tours, and who answered the questionnaires on life styles, interaction, self concept, etc. In other words, every effort was made to contact people who were characteristic of those the staff had gotten to know so well. Thus we feel fairly comfortable in stating that, while these life histories are not from a representative sample in the statistical sense, they are from a cross section of the population inhabiting the two census tracts in which we worked.

---

[3] A door-to-door survey identified those households in which old people lived. (Old was defined as being over sixty years of age, and in the case of individuals aged fifty-five to fifty-nine, those no longer in the work force.) From this information a random sample of both research and control groups was drawn up. This initial grouping for purposes of research was helpful in choosing the Historians whose recordings are in this volume.

One additional factor determined who would be included. Since life histories were collected by tape-recorded interviews, those who were selected had to be verbal and willing to share life experiences with us.

Because of the necessity to create an open and accepting atmosphere for the interviews, the Listeners—those who contacted the prospective Historian, formed a relationship with him or her, and received permission to record—were black, and sympathy and acceptance were two of the most important attributes a good Listener could possess.

Some Listeners were selected just to do recording while some were from the project staff and carried out other assignments as well. Some were Master of Social Work students from Rutgers University. With one exception (a native of the West Indies) all Listeners lived or had lived in Newark, and a few who were in their early twenties had been reared in the South.

The Listeners were asked to establish an easy rapport with those who agreed to be recorded. These were not to be traditional interviews, nor was there to be a traditional client–worker relationship. The biographical material was to be recounted spontaneously by the older individual, with only an occasional prodding question from the Listener to make sure that all areas of life were covered or that unclear material was explained.

Listeners were told to think of their assignments as opportunities to hold conversations with older friends in the social atmosphere of their home. The central themes were to be what life had been like for the Historians in the past and what it was like for them at present. The Historian was to go at his or her own pace, talking about subjects he or she recalled. However, the Listener was to encourage covering the following subjects: childhood joys and sorrows; courtship and marriage; educational experiences; making a living; having children; losing family members; migration; onset of old age. More material was offered about childhood and youth than about family life, middle or old age. This might be explained by the Historians' reluctance to talk about highly personal aspects of family life as well as the older person's tendency to recall better that which happened in the early stages of life. Although less material was gathered about adulthood, the biographies allowed us to get a good picture of the entirety of the Historians' lives.

We wished to explore the manner in which our Historians coped with crisis. Despite the difficult lives many or most of the old blacks had experienced, they proved themselves to be resourceful and good-humored, with an enormous vitality and independence, perhaps better described as a sense of being able to take charge of what was happening to them. It is clear that these strengths were still there after a lifetime of oppression. The Listeners were asked to concentrate some of their questions around crisis situations, but it proved to be almost impossible to get much information about episodes that the Historian would recognize as a crisis. Perhaps this is because they had so constantly lived with situations others might call "crises" that they did not label them as such. They simply did the best they could under the circumstances, not accepting defeat, never terming it defeat, and never reacting to it as such.

The Listeners were also asked to pay particular attention to attitudes regarding being black in a non-black world. Consequently, there was an attempt to direct the conversations to such subjects as relationships with non-blacks, what non-black society had been like for them, and the specific effect of black identity on day-to-day living. Not all the biographies deal with this question, but where the cue was responded to, material about both Southern and Northern society as well as the psychological responses to minority status was obtained.

The Listeners were trained by staff of the Research Center of the Rutgers Graduate School of Social Work. Trial interviews were undertaken, group critiques were held to improve techniques, and constant supervision was given when actual recording was underway.

There was almost no limit to the amount of time a Listener could spend on an individual biography, since the maximum had been set at forty hours. The Listeners were told that as long as both parties were comfortable and new material was emerging, recording should continue. In actuality no one took all that time. Some Listeners returned for ten to twelve sessions, while many were content with two or three. In some cases a good deal of time was spent establishing a relationship before the tape recorder was produced, and this was accepted as a necessary step. Where problems were encountered, the training staff or directors of the project were always on hand to help.

The Historians from whom these biographies were gathered were born, for the most part, in the thirty years between 1880 and 1910. Thus the historical period that shaped their lives is bounded by the last two decades of the nineteenth century. This can be translated in the following manner: in 1910 their ages ranged from infancy to around thirty; at the end of World War II they were predominately middle aged, and in 1970 the youngest member of the group became sixty years old. Moreover, other data from the project revealed that more than three-fourths were born in the Southeastern part of the United States, with Georgia, the Carolinas and Virginia heading the list. Most of them came to Newark while in their early thirties, meaning that a great many spent their childhood years in the South.[4]

The city in which our Historians live is the largest in the state of New Jersey and has undergone a recent dramatic demographic change: the black population of Newark has become the actual majority of the city. Together with the Puerto-Rican population they outnumber English-speaking whites. A black mayor, Kenneth Gibson, has been in power since 1970.

The Historians live in the Central Ward, an area abounding in redevelopment projects. All the symptoms of decaying urban centers—drug addiction, disease, crime—are here.

In the areas where there has been redevelopment, box-like public housing units dominate the skyline. The housing project in which the Rutgers–Friendly Fuld offices were situated is like the others: the units rise from concrete courtyards and asphalt playgrounds that intensify the heat of summer and add gloom to the winter. No greenery softens the landscape. Around the buildings lie half-razed areas with vacant lots, lonely apartments and ramshackle buildings. The riots of '67 burned out the shopping area that once surrounded the housing project. One grocery with limited stock and highly inflated prices, one family cafe and a few summertime vegetable-peddlers are the only nearby sources of daily necessities for the 1,300 families who call this place home. There are no dry-cleaning establishments or laundries close at hand. Stamps cannot be bought here, nor can money orders be obtained. One must travel at least six to eight blocks—a difficult and slow trip for the elderly—to find a viable business area. Liquor is the one item which is readily available. A generous number of taverns, blinking their signs, ring the housing project.

One of the high-rise buildings has been set aside for the aged. Its courtyard has concrete benches set in a concrete lawn. The doors of this building are locked and manned by resident volunteers, for they have learned to be wary of the outside world. In the other high-rise buildings, where the elderly live among people of all ages, the tenant must face constant fear in unlit hallways and deserted stairwells. In these homes the lame and the heart-damaged and those confined to

---

[4]Average age of migration was 32.2 years.

wheelchairs have to manage the many floors with elevators that are often inoperative. Attackers are more swift and agile, and the aged must be constantly on the alert to defend themselves. Ingenuity and suspicion are the elderly's coping devices, and some spend days of solitude behind triple-locked doors.

In 1967 a riot propelled the city of Newark into the national news. That July millions of dollars of property were destroyed by racial rebellion, twenty-three blacks and two whites were reported to have lost their lives, and twelve hundred people were arrested. The National Guard and the New Jersey State Police moved in and occupied the city, and many businesses, thought to be temporarily closed, never opened their doors again. Mention of the riot is made here in order to identify and explain the rebellion which is touched upon in almost all of the life histories. These elderly blacks were caught in the middle of the eruption, and their biographies contain many passages outlining their reactions to it. Their attitudes toward the riot are almost without exception negative.

Blacks who grew up in the South at the turn of the century learned a bitter lesson from their earliest years. In order to survive, the lesson went, you must give up your rights. In addition, you must accompany the sacrifice with a bland expression turned toward the outside world. Only by understanding this compelled behavior, the cornerstone of black existence, is it possible to understand the attitudes and actions of that generation.

Times are changing, and the young black is involved in a struggle to change society, perhaps eventually to rid it of rigid racial barriers. The aged black population whose histories are included here grew up in another era. It is often difficult for younger people to understand this. During the project's tenure a conference was convened to assess the particular case history of an elderly woman with six children who had worked as a domestic in the South. The woman had been poorly paid and exposed to many indignities throughout her working career, all of which she had accepted without overt verbal reaction in order to continue supporting her family. In the Mental Health Assessment Form of the project this case was to be evaluated in the following terms: was putting up with these conditions to be considered a positive or a negative experience? Initially the younger members of the staff assessed the experience as negative. However, after conferring with the older staff members they moved toward a positive evaluation of the case, indicating that they began to view the woman's behavior in a different light, seeing it as the sacrifice of her right to express anger to assure the welfare of her children.

It is this kind of sympathy, forbearance and reassessment that we hope to foster through this volume. As one student excitedly exclaimed after conducting a test "listening" session with her grandmother, a woman who had lived in the student's home since childhood, "I never knew what kind of a person my own grandmother was!" What is so often forgotten is that we are dealing with a unique individual with judgment, perception and a viewpoint, with evaluative facilities sharpened by long years of experience, and with a past personal history sometimes breathtakingly admirable in its casual assumption of courage.

These biographies do much to demolish the negative images of old Southern blacks that are current in our society. Political apathy, the absence of anger, docility, lack of initiative, family disorganization— these and many more stereotypes are refuted in histories that have been recorded by real people from the Central Ward of Newark, not cardboard caricatures of bygone times. Their biographies form the first, and major, portion of this book, followed by a brief chapter examining some historical data relevant to the personal histories.

A migrant woman's work in a Newark political campaign should be viewed against the social constraints that had kept her voteless in the South. The wonder of her interest and participation can only be grasped after the total picture of disfranchisement and educational deprivation is understood. The strengths of many of the black families and the large number of dominant fathers talked about in the biographies must be seen against the Southern backdrop of hopelessness, deprivation and lack of opportunity. Against that backdrop, how remarkable it is that so many families were cohesive! The overriding concern for her children's safety that impelled one Southern woman to journey North and work as a domestic, bringing her boys there one by one as she painfully gathered the pennies necessary for the journey, must be seen within the framework of her social position in the South, a position that kept her illiterate, frightened and isolated. The initiative, courage and selflessness she exhibited is above anything one might have expected from the product of such a crushing environment, and runs counter to prevailing stereotypes of unquestioning docility and humiliating acceptance. And so it goes. The resilience and fortitude of the elderly blacks of Newark can be appreciated best when placed within the context of the general history of the time. After working with our Historians and getting to know them well, we have come to the conclusion that to be old and black, to have survived the conditions detailed in the histories, and to have managed to live out your days in reasonable charge of your existence is to be an individual with more than ordinary strengths.

The names used in these life histories, and some details of the circumstances of the Historians' lives have been changed in order to protect their privacy. When such changes were made, we were careful to maintain the spirit of the Historians' recall.

2

Scared of Everything When I Grew Up

I didn't have no contact with white folks when I was comin' up. The people all around me, the people in the neighborhood, had 'em. But I was scared. You know how come?

We couldn't live in the house. We had to go out and stand in a pond of water up to our waist all night to keep away from the white folks. They would go to our house and bust in. And we had to run away to protect ourselves. We couldn't come out of the water till the next day.

I was scared of everything, scared of everything when I grew up. I don't know how in the world I grew up—I don't know.

All of my children I had down South. And their father died. I prayed to God to let me get my children away from there. The white folks was so mean to us there. If my boy done something they didn't like, they'd kill him and me too—all of us, you know. They'd blame you because you race bein' black. They'd catch him and hang 'em up on a tree and come to the house and get you, too. You cain't help yourself.

I didn't come North lookin' for flower beds, but I did come here not wanting my children to be killed like they was bein' killed down there.

My mother had all them children, and we had one room. That was down in Georgia, in the country. My mother had ten of them, but I was the oldest. Quilts spread down on the floor so them children could sleep. Her and my father was in the bed, one bed. And all of us children was down on the floor, one quilt, keepin' warm.

My father left my mother sometime when I was a child. Then she had to raise us all by herself. I remember the last time I saw him. He come by the house one day, one Sunday mornin'. Oh, I don't know whether it was a weekday or what. But anyhow, he laid a joint of meat up on the gatepost, and kept on walkin'.

He was a peaceful person, wasn't fussy at all. He was a Methodist preacher and I'd go to church with him. I 'member he carried me through the pines to church, and I was a little afraid. My mother wasn't converted till after I was grown, but I was converted when I was a child.

I don't know how old I was when my father gone, but I was big enough to look after the little children while my mother go to work. The white folks want you to stay in their house all day. And she had to stand there. Work all day for thirty-five cents. Hang all their clothes out on the line for thirty-five cents a day.

They felt sorry for her and they cut the vegetables down and give 'em to her. She had on a apron around her with a string, and she'd take up the corn and tie it around. They'd go in the smoke house and get up old skins and things they didn't want. Oh, we had a time, honey, hard times. We didn't eat like we should, you understand, 'cause white folks don't give you but something they don't want themselves.

You know, they had what they call a meat tit. In that you put them meat skins. And we had a little patch outside the yard called a garden. I would put some of my meat skins in that pot and boil them and go out to that garden and crop some of them onions. I would make that pot of soup good and put some corn meal in. I had to feed all them children with that stuff. I'm like, towards eleven or twelve years old. And I had to see that the children get something to eat or they would perish to death.

I hate to talk about it, but it's true. The Lord knows its true. My mother did what she could, but she had too many children. She couldn't take care of them all by herself and stay at home when there wasn't nobody big enough to work.

When school time come she had to borrow books and we paid thirty-five cents a month. Give you thirty-five cents to take your teacher and me thirty-five cents to take my teacher. And all right, maybe you just couldn't do it. I couldn't do it. If she didn't give me the money, I couldn't go to school. The teachers wouldn't allow her to send us to school 'cause she didn't have the thirty-five cents.

So I didn't have much schoolin'. My mother wasn't able to pay thirty-five cents for all of us to go to school. I can spell my name and know a little readin'. When she could get that money she send me, and that's what I did to the third grade. That's as far as I got.

When I went to school on many a day, a piece of corn bread was in the bucket. I had to get off from the other children 'cause they would see. They had mothers and fathers. Mine couldn't take care of me. I get off on a log by myself and eat the corn bread. It tears my heart. I didn't know nothin' and I never learned. She had to borrow everything. So that's what we had to come with.

My grandmother was sick, and I went to her sometimes 'cause she didn't have nobody to stay with her. She had a cancer, and my aunt wouldn't stay home with her. She liked to run around. I had to go there and wash the floor and feed her. I took the clothes and washed them better. She wasn't able to get out of bed. She wasn't able to do nothin'. I'd cry for my mother to let me go and see my grandmother, 'cause I loved her.

My grandmother got so sick my uncle went and got her. Put her in a wagon and rolled her down to his house and that's where she died.

My grandmother is dead and gone but she would tell me more than my mother would. She would sit down and talk to me. She taught me—she said, "Never let a boy put his hands on you." She said, "It's dangerous." She told me that and I believed it to her grave.

I was a child. I didn't know what nothin' was. When I was men-struatin', it scared me to death. You know what I done? Went in and sat down in a bath of water. I let the blood run out of me. That's right. And I went and quick took off my drawers, washed 'em out in back and hung 'em up on a bush. Let 'em half dry and put 'em back on. I felt wet. I looked down there, and it was all bloody again. I said, "Lord, I don't know what happened to me. I'm crazy."

You know, children know today what's happenin' to you. They see a woman and she's pregnant, they know you pregnant. I didn't know all that junk.

My grandmother told me, "Don't never let a boy put his hands on you and don't never let a boy kiss you. Two things you don't never let him do." So one day I was comin' from church, walkin' up the railroad tracks. That's when I lost my shoes there—dollar and a quarter shoes. I had on a three cent dress. We didn't have no clothes, nothin' like you all have today. This boy was runnin' to catch me, on the other side of the fence to catch me when I got over. But I know my grandmother told me, "Don't never let a boy put his hands on you 'cause you will have trouble, and I don't want you no trouble. I want you to be a good person." And I run, run, run until I run down. I jumped the fence, put my leg over the fence, my one leg over, and he grabbed that leg and dragged me over the fence. I cried all night long, and I told my grandmother that's what the boy done to me.

So she went to my mother's house, told my father what this boy done to me, and he got a switch and whipped me. Went around their house, to that man's porch, and told that boy if he ever seen him near me again, he'd beat him to death.

And that's what happened to me. I was green, honey. People was raisin' children then, but they ain't raisin' them now. They get everythin' they want, and that they don't want. I didn't have money to go to stores and buy stuff like folks have. I was never lazy, and I always raised my children and cooked for them. I didn't go out to these white folks' house and leave 'em with a quarter to buy a hot dog. I cooked their food on my stove. You don't go to no whitey's house for food. When I leave you here, you come from school to my house and clean up my house. That's what you have to do. The white woman told me, "Why don't you let me get you on relief?" I said, "Long as I can manage, I don't want relief. I don't want no welfare. I don't want nothin'." I said, "The girls havin' babies in school, and the mother lettin' 'em do it. Let 'em go ahead; the welfare's takin' care of 'em." "Oh," I said, "Lord you be with me. I try to take care of myself."

These young girls, just runnin' around with these boys and men. I tell you, we didn't get even a chance to *play*, honey. When we were big enough, we had to go in the fields. I had to chop cotton, pick cotton, pick peanuts up and stack 'em around. That's what I had to do. All of us had to, big children. We had to go to the fields, sun-up every day, and come out, sun-down. We didn't go like you go eight hours here and you finish your days work. Leave early in the mornin' with our breakfast sometime in the field and dew in the grass.

You know, my husband come to ask my mother for me. I didn't know what it was. All them children there with my mother—I didn't want to leave my mother.

I don't know exactly how old I was when he come. I was no baby, but I don't know how old. Maybe a teenager. He come to see another girl, Annie, and I was at the house when he come. Her mother let her court in the dinin' room. Whew! My mother wouldn't let me court in no room with no boy. No, sir. No, Lordy. I didn't go in there, in that room. I was in the kitchen cookin' dinner. And he come back there. He made like he wanted a drink of water 'cause he heard somebody in the back. It was me.

And when he come back in the kitchen, asked me to give him a drink of water, I poured the water. Got the dipper. Had a dipper and a bucket, and I gave him a glass of water. I didn't know he was lookin' at me.

He had left his mother and father long time ago, and he wasn't

livin' with them. He was livin' back in Alabama somewhere, I don't
know where. But after then I got a letter from him. I said, "Why did
he write me when he goin' with Annie?" He just kept on writin' and
writin' and writin'. He had an uncle there, didn't live far from us.
And he write to his uncle to talk to me. That I was the only girl that he
see'd that he thought would make him a wife. Well, his uncle talked to
me a long time and come down to my mother's house.

He said, "My nephew liked you."

I said, "No. He don't like me. He like Annie. That's where I
seen him at. I don't go out with no boys."

He said, "Well, you better latch onto him 'cause he's a good boy."

I said, "I don't know. I ain't ready to go nowhere."

Then I had to go outdoors, and he see'd I was barefoot, had no
shoes. Didn't have them till I was grown, honey. Had all hand-me-
downs from folks that were white.

Well, he wrote me and just kept on writin'.

His uncle say, "Well, give me two words in my letter, and I'll
write to him and tell him."

"I don't know," I said. "That boy come East. He done been all
over the world. I'm a young woman, and I don't intend to spoil my
life. He's a boy done left his home, his mother and father—maybe
that boy ain't no good. I don't know if he's any good or not.

When he came back to Georgia, he went to his uncle's house, and
his uncle brought him down. We was in the cotton patch, barefooted,
and the purslane had done blackened my foot like a lookin' glass. You
never seen that. Purslane is somethin' that growed on the farm. You
wade through it and gets dew on your foot and then it turns black.
You can see yourself in your foot. All of us was sittin' in the field, my
mother and all of my sisters and brothers, workin'. And we picked
that cotton.

He stayed in the back there, talked to my mother. I didn't know
it was him. That's when he asked my mother for me.

Then he come on down where we was, young folks pickin' cotton.

He said, "Uh, Lucy?"

I said, "Yes?"

He said, "I, uh, asked your mother for you."

I said, "For what? *For what?*"

He said, "To marry."

I said, "To marry who? You out there in Alabama, where all of
them good lookin' woman is. You come here to a country girl like me?

You don't want me.'' I was always outspoken to folks, and I thought he was makin' a fool out of me.

I said, ''You know you don't want me. I know you don't.''

He said, ''Well, I decided that I want a wife, and a country woman is the best woman to make a man a wife.''

''I'm no goin' to marry you. No, don't marry me. Go and get a fine dressed woman, sportin' woman, smokin' cigarettes.''

I thought that was a disgrace to catch a woman smokin' a cigarette. I didn't know what nothin' was. Nothin'. And you know what? He just hung around. He'd come and I didn't have a chair to sit on in the house. He'd come with his mother's buggy and horse to my mother's house and unhitch the buggy and come on down to see where we was.

''Well,'' I said to myself, ''My mother got so many children I ought to light up some on her. But I don't want to leave her here with this burden either. I don't want to leave her, and she got nothin' to give me.''

So my mother said to him, ''When did you intend to marry Lucy?''

He said, ''The minute you say, that's when.''

She said, ''Well, you done been out in the world. This is all of Lucy's world. She don't know nothin'. So there ain't no need foolin' yourself, make like you want to love her and treat her like a dog. 'Cause you could let her be treated like a dog, let her be with her mother and sisters and brothers.''

He said, ''No, I wouldn't never do the likin's of that to her.''

And my mother said, ''If you marry her, y'all gonna have a place to stay?''

He say, ''Yes, ma'am, we gonna have a place to stay.''

So I got married. I just felt like it. I wanted to make a life for myself, so he carried me to town on that day. But-uh- I didn't go home with him, 'cause I wanted to go back to my mother. I went back to my mother without him and he didn't come along.

I stayed three weeks at my mother's house. I stayed so long his mother told him, ''How come you married and don't bring your wife to my house to see me?'' His mother told him to come get me. Told him don't come back to her house without me—she wanted to see her daughter-in-law.

When that horse and buggy drove to her house that night, I was in it. My heart kept goin' like this. And I cried, honey. Oh, God bless

us, I cried! I didn't know what a man was for, a bit more than a dog.
Not as much as a dog 'cause a dog got sense.

And my mother-in-law says, "Well, I'm goin' to bed." And she
got up and go down. She might as well have shot me with a pistol.

And he started taking his things off that night. I had one gown, a
nightgown. I had long hair, nice hair. I braided that hair, put on my
gown and I sit up there in the corner of the room. He called me. He
said, "Come here, Lucy. Come onto the bed." He said, "I ain't
gonna bother you."

I was scared to death 'cause he didn't talk to me like a man talk.
And I didn't know what a man had to do, like folks do now. And I
stood there in that corner.

So I sat on the bed where he was, and he reached out and grabbed
me. I screamed—I screamed murder.

I said, "Don't do that."

He said, "I ain't gonna hurt you. Don't you know why you
marry? So you can have some children."

I say, "But I don't want to lay down."

He say, "You got to lay down. I'm your husband, and you done
been up all night now."

He grab me and I went fallin' on down, fightin'. And that's when
I knew. I was brought up dumb, ignorant, crazy. I might a knew, if I
had been flirtin' and flyin' around with other folks, and everythin'.

I said, "I didn't have it, and I don't want it now."

He had a bottle of vaseline under the bed, on the floor, and I
didn't know it.

I said, "Oh, no. You ain't puttin' none o' that stuff on me! No
man!"

Now you know I'm old enough to be your great-great grandma,
and I wouldn't tell you these things if it wasn't true. But I just want you
to see how the world is today, how it's changed, and how it used to be.

Women now ain't got no pride in theirself. They just go around
with dresses up to here. I got a housekeeper and she come here with her
dresses so short, and she's a married woman. Twenty-two years old!

My mother-in-law asked my husband somethin' the next mornin'.
I don't know what they was doin', talkin' about.

I told my husband, "Maybe, now you marry me, you see another
fine woman come along. You throw me in the gutter for her, and I
don't want that." I wanted the man to be a husband for me if he's
gonna be, and that's what I got. I got a good husband. Till the day he

died he was a good man to me. And I tried to be a good wife to him.

I didn't let him work all day and come home and find my house messed up. Just after I had the baby, the baby messed it up. Who needs cribs? I laid that baby on the porch, lay him on a old coat. I'd have his water hot between his coming home, and his supper done and everything. He'd come in the house, get his wash first, then sit down and eat. Go out there and lay down with his paper. When I go to church Sunday, he carried that baby.

He moved me in a little log hut. And all the houses close together, they had to wash clothes down where they was. He didn't want me to go down there to wash no clothes. He put a tub down in my yard, and I washed out there. I didn't have to go down.

Course, when I see he comin' in the evenin' I'd cry, 'cause I didn't want him to bother me. That's true, I didn't want him to bother me. But I overcome so far, thank God.

I didn't work at all down there. Only my little patch I had, tryin' to make some money to get here with. I prayed to God to let me get my children away from there. I was pregnant when my husband died. And my oldest boy, he was goin' to school. I wanted that—I didn't want them to be like I was. I had some old laced leggings on my legs. Put them around my legs to keep them from tearing up my dress down there. I made all the clothes and things, 'cause I wasn't able to buy 'em. And a man gave me a mule. I would plough until 12 o'clock. Take that mule out, give him three heads of corn, put him back in the traces and go plough again. When my son came home from school, he would change his clothes and go out there and plough. Many a day I fell on my knees and asked God to help me, to give me the strength to get my children away.

And I came here in '24—'23 or '24. I know it was one of them— don't know exactly. I got here and made enough to get them, one at a time. I didn't bring them all at once. The baby didn't have to pay no fare. The oldest boy, I got him when he was about sixteen. I had to get him alone. My other two middle boys had to stay down there until I got money enough to send for them.

I sent for them and somebody put them on a boat. They was little; they didn't know. And I didn't know, 'cause my mother got somebody to put them on a train and boat, or somethin'. When they come up here on the boat, bein' children they took them off and put them on the trolley car, and put them off on the street where I lived at. They walkin' by the street. They knowed the number where I lived.

So when they was walkin' by the numbers, they found it. My oldest son was sittin' by the winda, and he raised the glass, and he said, "Here I is. Over here."

When I first got here, there was a lady come from down South and she's a friend of mine. She had a flat, a straight-through flat. And she let me sleep in her living room with my baby. Her husband was a preacher. And after a while I said, "I have to go get me a room for myself." I had to leave my baby all day by hisself, 'cause I didn't have no man to take care of him. I didn't want no man. I would stay with no man, 'cause I was tryin' to raise my children and I said if I raise my children all kind of ways, you won't have no respect for me.

There's a Jew lady lived next door to me, and she took care of my baby until my boys come. She would make soup and feed my baby, and all. I was so grateful to her 'cause she was a nice person. I don't care who it is; if you're nice, you're nice. Some people say I ain't never seen a nice white person. Yes, I have. You have love in your heart, you see a plenty of nice folks in the world. But if you got hate in your heart, you won't love nobody and nobody loves you, and that's pitiful.

I never remarried, never, never. I was a widow woman, and I never had a whole lot of drunken men hangin' around my children. I said, "Your daddy's dead and buried. There ain't no need of my tryin' to make another father. What if he didn't like my children?" A man did write me a letter once from Florida. He wanted to marry me, but I didn't want nothin' from no man. That's the only thing that kept me back—my children. I just love my children. Maybe I wouldn't have loved them so much if their father had lived with them, but he died and left them alone. So it wasn't nothin' for me to do. I tried to get them out from down there to make a better home for them. When they got grown they could work and make a livin' for themselves. And that's what I've done, and that's what God has spared me to do.

I always did day work, workin' in somebody's house. 'Cause I didn't have no education. I couldn't get no nice job or nothin' like other folks. And it was hard to find a job, 'cause I didn't know how to go about it. I was from down there, where you worked from sun-up to sun-down. You didn't get no hours work, like they did here. There was a office where you could go to find work, but you had to go and sit all day to get a job. When they sent you out in the mornin' you worked for twenty-five cents an hour.

There was an employment office on Morrison Street, and the

lady's name was Miss George. I heard about it—somebody told me to go down to her. In that office you had to take a chance of gettin' work. When I told her all my troubles, she take an interest in me and tried to help me. I told her I would like to get more money if I could, because $2.50 a day was no money for me. I was roomin' then, and I had got three rooms on the third floor that I took for my children to come. She gave me a job and give me $3.00 a day.

I was in a strange country. My baby sister, I knowed her, and I knowed the woman that I room with, but them was only folks that I really knowed. I didn't know the family where I went to work every day. Twenty-five cents an hour. I would work from eight o'clock in the mornin' to sometimes eight o'clock at night to make them extra quarters. I could take a quarter and get enough pork chops to feed me and my baby. No, I didn't have to feed him 'cause he stayed with the old Jew lady next door till I come home. She done fed him. A loaf of bread was eight cents and a pile of fat back was eight cents—not like it is now.

One day I was goin' to work and gettin' on the trolley. It was rainin', and a automobile skid that was comin' beside the trolley, and it just swept three of us away, just like that. I was hurt the worsest. The man who hit us with the car took me and carried me to Martland Medical, the city hospital. They examined me there and told me I didn't have no broken bones, but the man that hit me knowed I was hurt 'cause I couldn't, couldn't move. So he carried me back home and took me upstairs like I was a child. I laid on that bed *nine weeks*. There wasn't but one of my boys here at that time, and the baby. The little ones was home yet. They hadn't come. The Jew woman called a doctor—he was a German doctor. He came to see me and said I had to be on that board, because my back was injured but it didn't show up as a broken bone. Then I contracted double pneumonia when I was down, and that man had to get up at night in his pajamas and come to my house at two o'clock in the mornin'.

My big boy had gotten hurt then, too. He had gotten a little job in a grocery store and he had got his hand caught in the meatgrinder. The man told him not to come back to work. My baby was with the Jew woman. She kept him while I was workin'. I was payin' $18 a month for three rooms on the third floor. Colored folks couldn't get no house to live in then.

I said, "Well, I don't know if I'll ever walk again."

But the doctor come and give me so much medicine and so much needles. I didn't know whether I was livin' or dyin'.

Another doctor come. They hit the woman downstairs on the second floor what got hurt, and they signed a paper for her. When they come up to my house (I was hurt worse than the other woman) they said, "Miss Benson, we from Public Service. You was in a accident." Then they took all my history and after they taken it, they come over to the bed and asked me to sign a sheet of paper.

I said, "I ain't goin' to sign nothin'."

They said the woman downstairs signed. I said, "I ain't got nothin' to do with nobody but myself. I've got children, and if I don't support them, nobody else will."

I said, "I ain't got nobody to give me a piece of bread. I've got to work for what I get."

One woman I worked for, she was nice. And my landlady, all the neighbors was nice to me. My landlady said, "Miss Benson, you better go down and get on relief." I said as long as I can make it, I'll make it—don't worry. Things was cheap then. You didn't make much money, but things was cheap. And I got along as well as you could expect.

I talked to my sister, and she and her aunt lent us some money so I could send for my mother. My mother come up here and stayed with me until I could kinda get around. The woman where I worked at, she give me aid, brought me food and stuff. And then my boy's hand got better so the man take him back. When he worked he brought a little money home, so I got along the best I could.

When my mother come up here, you know, I didn't know what to do. I was in a strange place, strange folks. When I see my mother, I come to pieces. She waited on me until I got up. That's the time I was draggin' on two crutches. I drug on those crutches long before I could even go back to work.

I had four accidents. The car skidded was one; a bus accident was two; and I come out of school rehearsal one night and the car—the man turned or somethin'—I don't know—my knee hit the thing and both of my knees was skinned and burned. I didn't go to work for I don't know how many days. Then, when I was walkin' up the street where I lived, I fell on this broken thing and I had to go to the doctor. I've had those marks and bruises on me—it's terrible when you sick and can't get well.

I had two operations. After the first one I come on home and every year I'd commence to gettin' sick again. I said, "I don't know what it is." Livin' here with all these children. See, I got a little one family house for cheap money, and I went and moved there with my children. I stayed in that house until my son got twenty-one years old. I give him a birthday party in that house, my oldest one. Then he went out, they caught him messin' around, and they wanted to get married. I said, "They can't be nothin' but married." But I told him to wait a while. Then my second boy was workin' down at Treat's, the big hotel downtown, washin' dishes, gettin' $15 a week. So this boy married this girl, and he got this crippled boy and two little babies. They were born in my house. I had five rooms upstairs, and that's where my grandchildren was born.

Then the little boy got so sick, he went to Martland Medical. I sit up there with him, night and day. I didn't go to work then; I was crazy about my grandchildren, like any other mother. I sat there so long until they come at night and put a blanket over me, just like they covered him. When the doctor come by, he said, "You must go home. The man wants to scrub the floor."

But I said no. He was so sick and so little, and they got those long needles and stuck them up his knee. I went home to get myself cleaned up and get a little rest. When I got back the nurses had him covered up. When I walked in that hospital that evenin'—he was the oldest baby—he was all covered up. I cried like a baby. He had to be buried in the clothes that he was in.

His father was on welfare that time. You couldn't get no work. None of my boys couldn't get no work.

All my children were livin' with me at that time. My oldest son was the only one that had a family, and we didn't have no money to get no house. You know how you try to help the children the best you can. I tried, I tell you, many a day.

Then my son had to go in the army. His wife left him and took the children. Well, my grandson always been crazy about his grandma. I was on the third floor and I went to the winda—and he was down there, cryin'. That broke my heart. My son went over there and tried to get his wife back. But she wouldn't come, and he got tangled up with another woman. He married her, but the children didn't like her. So they stayed with me, and I had my children and those two—I raised them all up. He'd work and give me a little money for the children, but I don't say that that would take care of them. I went to work right after that first operation. I have set out there many a day on the steps six o'clock in the mornin', waitin' for my second son. He'd go to work and he'd carry me to my job to save me the car fare.

The lady would leave me the key under the mat, and I would go in her house and do that wash and most of the ironin'. That's what I had to do. That's when I was strugglin'.

In '25 I was operated on, in St. Michael's Hospital. In '36 I went back for another operation. I'm miserable woman. I laid up in the house one day and I cried. I've cried all my life—I don't know how I've got so many tears left. Times I would get better, and then I would go right on back to my work. I didn't lose no work.

The first operation my stomach was so sore. I cried all night, and when I got up in the mornin' I went to the bed and kissed my little grandchildren. I said, "You all take care of my little children, 'cause I'm goin' to the hospital, and I may not come back."

When the door opened at St. Michael's Hospital I was sittin' on the steps. They said, "Who are you?" I told them and they said, "Well, you'll have to wait. The hospital ain't open yet." I asked will it open sometime today, and they said, "I don't know." I said, "I want to see a doctor. I'm sick and I ain't goin' home."

The nurse let me inside. I sat in a high chair. The nurse said, "You're in so much pain." I said, "I've been holdin' in so long—I can't tell you how long."

When the doctor come down he took me in that room, examined me, and said, "She's got to have an operation." I was a young woman then. The doctor said, "You go home and when we get an empty bed we'll send for you."

I said, "No, you won't. I'll sit down here on the floor." I wasn't in the ward or nothin'. I said, "I'll lay right here down on this floor until somebody comes." I meant every word I said—my stomach was like this. And that's where I laid, on that floor in the chapel.

So the sister went down and told the priest, and she whispered to the other sister. She said, "That woman's sick. We'll have to make room for her." They carried me downstairs, took another woman out there, and they put me in that bed. And they operated on me the next mornin'.

They cut me and they bandaged me up this way. I was no trouble to them. They would bring me food. I would eat a little bit and send it back in the tray. I told them I didn't want it. I didn't bother them.

All the while I was in that hospital there was Christian literature to read. The other women in that room would cuss every word they said. They boy friends would bring them fried chicken every night, and they would talk all night long. I laid up in the hospital until I got in a rollin' chair, a wheel chair, and they carried me downstairs and I went home.

I had a little money. I always tried to keep a little money because I didn't know what was comin' up. So I had a little bit for after the operation. I pulled through it all right. I know I didn't have to pay for no operation 'cause the doctor told me that—a widow woman with four children.

The second time the doctor called up to the hospital; he wanted me to go there. They put me in the hospital that night. I was near gone. Dr. Williams was deliverin' a baby and come as quick as he could. My son run me up to the hospital, 'cause he said he don't want no ambulance comin' out this time of night.

When I got there the nurse, she said, "She don't need no operation."

When she said that, I said, "What's the matter with me? The doctor sent me here. Why he send me here?"

She said, "I don't know."

That time Dr. Williams come in the door. They took x-rays. They operated on me the same night.

But I tell you, I've been too sick in my life. I'm still sick. I was so sick this week here—I don't know how I'm livin'. My housemaid was here, and she held me up. I can't take that much sickness many more times before I have to be gone. My friends call me, and I was too sick to talk. I told them, "Don't call me. I can't talk no more."

You know, I've always had faith in the doctor. He was goin' to do what was needed to be done. I don't worry about that. And then I gained my strength and went back to work.

Then in 1957 I had a son that died. He was the baby. That's the one I brought here. I raised him, and when he got big enough he went to school, finished high school. He was very smart in school, worked at the post office until this accident happened.

To tell you the truth, now, I don't know just how old he was when it happened. 'Cause you know, things go and come, and I don't know. I forget. I got the age down. I got the children's ages down. My oldest boy, he's goin' to be 64, that I know. The other ages, they sort of mixed up. The older boy is a little older, and second boy is close to the third boy. Maybe I got it wrong.

Anyway, he was in a accident in Virginia. He was ridin' a horse, and the horse throwed him. He was sick when he come home. He come home and the doctor found he had some broken ribs and they punctured one of his lungs, and he had lung trouble. He went to Verona for care. When he got out of Verona he come back home to me, and went back to work, and he lived pretty long time after then. But they took them ribs out. That lung was operated on, and he didn't have but one half.

I wasn't workin' at that time. I had arthritis so bad. All them accidents I had with them automobiles—the doctor said that's where it come from. They say anythin' to get your money.

When the baby was in Verona his brother carried me to see him every Sunday. My mother was here. She was stayin' with my sister some and my brother. She was sick. She went from my brother's house to the hospital, and she was in one hospital and my baby was in another. She was in Martland Medical and he was in Verona. At the same time. And that was a pressure more.

And when she died I wasn't able to go to Georgia for the funeral. I went to see my baby every Sunday and every Wednesday. He was a sick boy and I wouldn't leave him.

You know, when I come here people wasn't allowed to vote in Georgia. But I voted here, put the first colored man in office. I had to go around with a paper and pencil to get voters. I would go to the voting place. They was strict then. You want to tell me how to vote—you got to stay so many feet away from me. I worked in this man's campaign, and I can remember the night when they got the votes counted.

They had me on the platform as a speaker, but I didn't have no education. The man told me, "You just get up and speak your mind, 'cause you've got just as good sense as anybody else." I got up—the mayor and everybody was on that platform. I ain't never been bashful, I ain't never been scared of nobody so I didn't care. I told them I was sorry for one thing—that I wasn't born and raised in college. But I said, "I thank God for the mother wit that I'm born with. I know what is good for people and what ain't good for people. I can't make nobody do nothin', but we all know that what's good for one is good for the other."

Honey, the men on the platform was carryin' me out like I was a baby. The man said, "You may not have been to college but you know more than all these folks that went." I got a letter from the mayor, personal, my own self. I couldn't understand it 'cause I didn't have no schoolin'—just went to the third grade.

I tell you, I always voted up until I got the stroke. I went to the polls and I had to walk with a crutch, but I went right on until I couldn't go without somebody helpin' me everywhere.

Yes, I helped put a ward leader in office. I don't know. I don't think I've done so bad in my life time.

When I was a child I said when I grow up I hope to be a good singer. I always wanted to sing. I liked to dance too. There was a dance called the Shoe-Along and the Cake Walk and the Charleston, and all of that. I was home tryin' to do those things. My father come up to the house one night and caught me singin' over the fry—fryin' some eggs. And he took off his belt and hit me. I got a scar on me now where he hit me. 'Cause he was a preacher and he didn't think I should be singin' and dancin'. And now, you know that's terrible you go to a habit and you know you ain't supposed to do it—you shouldn't to it.

I wanted to be a singer, and I was a singer and I'm glad. I had a good voice. Now I'm sick so I don't sing but I used to. Took my grandchildren and my children with me. People come from all over, Connecticut, Pennsylvania, everywhere, to hear me sing.

I got my recording right here now. I was the secretary at the convention, the Union Vocal Convention. And people would come and say they want to hear the secretary sing. We had officers and everything. We used to go all over in busloads, telling people to sing. We went to Hartford, Connecticut, every first Sunday in July. The best was me, you know. I had a quartet. My baby, my oldest boy, is bass in one of my quartets on that record there. I been secretary of this same convention forty-five years. I cherish singing yet. I didn't sing for to be singing, for someone to think well of me. I'd sing for what's in my heart.

You see, I went to church every Sunday. I carried my four boys to church every Sunday with uniforms in my bag. And we would come back on the trolley cars. I would say, "Go home and eat your dinner and stay in the house till I come." I went out, right there, on Sheffield Avenue, and washed dishes for white folks for twenty-five cents an hour, and they'd bring me home in the evening after I done cleaned up everything. Oh, I worked hard.

I was converted when I come here, and I knowed that God would take care of me. And that's what he done. He's doin' it up to today, and you know, I'm an old woman now. I'm old. Yes, I is. I ain't worried, and I don't beg nobody for nothin'. I don't go out there, makin' like I'm young. I never drink nothin', smoke nothin'. I wasn't better than nobody else—I just didn't do it, that's all.

I think I worked twenty some years, but I don't know if that's

right. My second son was doin' pretty good there and he helped me
on my rent. My granddaughter was workin' and my grandson was
workin'. They helped me a awful lot. I been stopped work a long
time.

I get Medicare. I get a little welfare. They give me $31 on welfare
and $84 on Medicare. Everyone tells me they don't give me enough. I
know the lady who works at the welfare. She's the one who knows they
wasn't treatin' me right. She told me the other day, "They ain't
givin' you enough money." I told her, "There ain't nothin' I can do.
I can't fight nobody. I can't go down there and tell nobody nothin'. I
ain't got nothin' to do with that." She said, "That's the reason they
don't treat you right. Old folks what need money, they don't give it to
them."

They raisin' the food so high I can't get a decent meal. The lady
called me yesterday from somewhere, I don't know where. Asked me
did I want some things. She got a letter in the bank from me that I
needed some stamps—food stamps.

I asked her how could she get a letter from me and I can't even
write. She said you will understand.

I said, "Listen, I don't understand what you're talkin' about. I
have nobody to put in line to stand for no stamps, and I don't get that
much money to give money to get stamps for somethin' I ain't got.
When I go to the counter and buy soap, I ain't got nothin' but stamps
to get it with and they won't give it to me."

She said, "Maybe you can understand. The problem is the little
money they give you. They want to get it back in those stamps. You
can buy canned goods with that."

But I don't buy canned goods. I don't eat that stuff. I buy my
own vegetables and cook them. I make my own pies and cakes.

She said, "If you'll allow me, I'll come and talk to you. Stamps
will go farther than money."

I said, "They won't go farther than money. If I need something
it takes money to buy it 'cause they won't take it."

She said, "I'll come up and investigate you. I'll come up to see
you anyhow."

I said, "Come on."

I can't get up on my feet. I can't wash my things. I'm here by
myself and the doctor said, "If you fall you can't let nobody in the
house. Somebody needs to come and get you up." He said, "If you've
got to walk, walk with this thing, this walker."

I'm tellin' you. I talk to this lady at the welfare, and she sent me a letter. I have to come down and explain. I told her, "I can't come nowhere and explain. You'll have to do what you want to, honey. There's nothing I can do. You in power."

I did appreciate her enough to call her when I got the letter. She goin' around a whole lot of things—I had to come down and this thing or another. I ain't able to do nothin'. When I go to the doctor, they almost carry me out of the house. That's the reason I leave the door open, 'cause I can't get up to open it. I got a walker but the walker sometimes don't be where I is. And I can't get it so easy. I felt like the doctor was mean, sayin' I had to use that walker. I felt like I could drag around and I wanted to help myself. I never been a lazy person in my life, from a child, not lazy. No, no.

That money they give me ain't enough to take care of me, but I ain't goin' to say another word to them. I told that lady from the welfare she could do anythin' she wanted. It's alright by me, 'cause God's goin' to take care of me and her too, at the end of time. And she has to know it when it comes. 'Cause He only lets you suffer to know what you have done to me. Each one of us is His children. I been converted and I'm a child of God. I been a church woman all my days, and I have never fell away a minute of my life. I never took no stuff from anybody, and I don't give it to nobody. I treat you sweet like I want you to treat me. That's all I ask.

I been in the Presbyterian Hospital twice. When I first had my stroke I went there. And then I had to go to the Old Folks Home. Nursin' Home—they don't want nothin' but money. They get that money and talk to you like a dog. The old people up there can't talk, can't hear, they's blind. Them's the kind of people they want there, that can't tell nothin' on them. You're not supposed to have a bit of sense in that home. But you know, God gave me a stroke but left me with sense. And I thank Him for it. The nurses come and talk to you like you is a baby. I was there a long time. I'd have been there longer, but the nurses hit me, and I told them they got no right to beat on me. I don't take no beatin'. I said, "If it wasn't for me, you wouldn't get no money."

Those old people. They just call, "Nurse," all night. That's a pitiful condition, I tell you. The nurses sit up all night, playin' poker, cussin' the sick people, hollerin' at the people. And the poor people, can't do nothin'. They treat those old folks so bad.

I said, "I didn't come here to die. I came here to see if the Lord is ready for me to get better. I've got a bed I can lay in to die myself. I don't need this bed—I didn't come in here to die here. I want to be treated like people.''

The nurse said to me one night, ''Miss Benson, you get out of that bed.''

I said, ''I can't put on those shoes when I go to the bathroom. How can I go to the bathroom?

She said, ''I mean for you to go to the bathroom.''

I had on this little short gown. I got up there about two o'clock and went on into the lobby. I had a dime, and called my oldest son. When I got down to the lobby all of a sudden she came and said, ''What are you doin' out here?''

I told her I wanted to go home. That woman grabbed me and took me up to my bed.

She said, ''You can't get out of here this time of night.''

I said, ''The cops can get me out of here, any time of the day or night. That's what I know about the law.''

My son come up there and brought me home. Then I had to go back to the hospital. But not the nursin' home. I've been sick a long time. I'm old enough to have better care than what I had, but I thank God for life.

I'm old—too old fashioned. I'm old, ugly woman. I know it. If they live, they'll get old and ugly one day.

I live with my granddaughter now. She went out a while ago. You know, she can get on a piano at church and do anythin'. But she will not do it. All that money was put on her for them lessons. She graduated and threw all those things away. That's no good. That hurts you to think of it. When she goes to her job, meets her nurses, they just like she is.

She's a nurse for ten or eleven years now. But she ain't got no respect. You must have respect, I don't care what you say. That's all I ever had. I didn't got no schoolin' but I had respect.

I got a grandson too. If he had the chance he would have been as big a man as anybody, but he didn't have the chance. 'Cause they didn't spend the money on him that they did on their daughter. He was so sickly. He's been sick all the time, but she never been sick, never.

I went to the hospital. Who put me in? My grandson. Who got the cash money for me when I was in the hospital? He got it. Who painted my flat? She didn't fix nothin'. After the ambulance come and got me, she wanted to pay it. I said, ''No, you don't pay.'' I paid the ambulance everytime. I paid, every time. That opens the way in my heart for him.

He comes in the mornin' askin' how I feel. She wouldn't ask. I don't care if she stayed here twenty-four hours a day. That's bad, honey. I said they ain't nursed—they ain't out for nothin' but the money. They don't care nothin' for those poor sick folks.

I try to make it pleasant for my grandson to come to my home. He tries to do everything. He goes to the store and buys me food. Asks me what I want him to bring. She won't, and she makes good money. I ain't talkin' about no pennies.

My granddaughter sassed me out one day. I said, "Well, let everything go. My daughter-in-law will come down and wash all my curtains in my house." You know, if she was a good granddaughter, she wouldn't let them go, would she? She goes to work at eleven o'clock at night and comes homes at seven in the morning. She has all them days.

She's got a nice job, makes nice money. And she goes. I worry about her. I never did the things she does 'cause when I was young I saved every penny I had to raise my children. If I hadn't of saved, where would they be today? Put them through high school and everything to try to make somethin' out of them.

My son was here. He comes to see me every weekend. This is my oldest son. But he wasn't here for so long. He was in the hospital four weeks. They had him in the hospital, and nobody told me. That's what broke my heart. I didn't know it till they got him out, and he walked through that door. I called his wife, and she said he was workin' late. She went to see him everyday, but they don't want me to know.

Somebody jumped him in the saloon. He had blood clots in his head or somethin'. Then he lost so many days work 'cause he wasn't able to drive his car. Got to go back to court tomorrow. But he's OK now. He's goin' huntin' today. He'll just keep on goin' till the Lord takes him, I reckon. He does construction work. You know, anythin' he can do for me, he'll do it. His wife is one of these fancy ladies— that's why I didn't want to live with them.

You know, if I get sick in this house and nobody in here, I don't worry. They don't have to be here. Once the Lord gets ready for me, He's goin' to come. I hope when He comes for me I'll be ready to go. No, I ain't goin' to fight God when He comes. If I've lived the life I've lived, I won't fight. I got this old and nobody don't want me now.

You know, in the South white folks don't like you even when

you're young. They don't like no black folks. They'd kill 'em all, down there. They'd cut off their ears and cut off their toes and string 'em in the streets on a rope and hand 'em across the street when you're comin' into town.

It was a hard time, growin' up children then. The white folks all runnin' through the woods, singin', "Nigger, be ready when I come, 'cause I'm comin' again. Won't be long." With this little bell ringin', and Niggers just runnin' out in the bushes to hide. At night they couldn't see a one. "Ah, here's one. There's two."

The reason I hurt so bad when my husband died 'cause I had nobody to help me with the children. I had to bring them away 'cause them white folks would kill 'em.

3

Work Made Me a Lady

I was born in North Carolina, 1910. There was fifteen of us children, but they didn't but four live to get growned—four sisters. I had four sisters and eleven brothers, but I don't remember 'bout any of the boys because I was a baby. My mother said when she was having children, in those days, they was having diptheria and sore throats, and it was hittin' boys more than girls. They'd get six or seven months old and then they'd die.

I would have lived with my momma if she'd a lived; she was still farmin'. When my momma taken sick I was just old enough to do a little work, to take a hoe to the field with them. I mostly was sittin' in the field playin', but before she died I had gotten old enough where she had gotten me a hoe for my own self. When she died I was grown enough, old enough, to really go out in the field, and stay just as long as my sister stayed, and chop cotton along with her. The hardest for me was—I wouldn't say it was really a hard time, but I was the youngest and when my mother died, my oldest sister raised me, my sister and her husband named Lou.

I had one sister who come up over me before my mother died. She was the last one that grew up with me. She had peculiar ways. Right now if I go down there we don't get along too well. You're walking on glass when you're with her. You don't know what you're gonna say that's wrong. Everything you do is wrong. Me and her used to fight. She'd fight me because I was small and she was five years older than I was.

This incident happened before my mother died. My mother was going to sell cotton. Nobody bothered about doors or anything. We were just two kids, girls there. She would go twelve miles to sell a bale of cotton. My momma always left us with plenty of food. She kept a flour bag of that full for us, meat and stuff. But everytime my mother would leave, my sister would kill a chicken and fry it, and we would eat that whole chicken and it didn't make us sick.

That day she didn't kill a chicken; she started on the sugar. It was late in the afternoon, and about time for my mother to come home. She got a tall glass and filled it up half full of sugar, and with water, and put some sugar and water in my glass. She was sittin' there, eatin' her damp sugar with a spoon. I asked her for some more. She said, "You don't get anymore; you don't need it." We got to arguin'. We were sittin' at a long kitchen table, she at that end and I at this end. She kept on eatin' her sugar and talking that big talk, and I just threw that glass, and hit her right here! First time I ever hit her, 'cause I was afraid of her. She'd whip me. I wouldn't never tell Momma, 'cause she'd whip me again when Momma left. That day when I hit her with that glass, I left the table. Fact, I left the premises! Went down that road runnin', she right behind me. I wanted to meet my momma, 'cause I knew she was on the way home. But she was late. My sister was beggin' me to stop runnin'. "I won't hit you," she promised. We had run a long way from our house. Finally I got so tired I had to sit down by the side of the road.

I said, "You're going to knock me in the head with a rock."

She said, "I'm not goin' to whip you. Let's go back home."

"I'm goin' to tell Momma everything you've been doin'. I'm tired of you beatin' on me," I said. About half an hour after she carried me back, Momma came home. She would call us when she came up in the yard. She always had a bag of candy for us, with chocolate drops. I love them today. So she come on in. I was still sulkin' at my sister. I had my mouth stuck out. I wanted Momma to see that something was wrong with me. My sister kept shakin' her head for me not to tell. I looked like I was goin' to cry.

"What's the matter?" she asked. I told her everything. How my sister been whippin' me, and cookin', and fryin' a whole dozen eggs and eaten them.

She said, "All that's been goin' on. Why didn't you tell me?" I told her that sister said if I told, she'd whip me. "Is she the momma? What am I, if she's the momma?"

I didn't know what she was goin' to do. She changed her clothes. She didn't whip with no strap. You know what a dogwood tree is? Well, that's what we swept with. We'd get a bunch of them and tie them together. She went out there and got a limb from that pile. She got my sister first. I was standin' back there making faces and gigglin'.

She said, "I better not hear of you cookin', with all the food I leave for you, and whippin'. I'm the grown lady in this house."

When she got finished, she said, ''Come here, young lady. I'm not whippin' you for eatin' it—I'm whippin' you for not telling me! You could have been dead, eatin' all that stuff!''

From that day to this, my sister didn't cook no more. And, she didn't whip me no more neither. My mother broke up all that stuff. Eatin' all that food—we could have died. My sister's a good cook today. She sure did cook a lot of food.

I have never been real happy in my life, I don't think. I was raised motherless. And my father died when I was a baby. I ain't never seen him. When my mother got in bad health, my sister had to take me. Course my sister was nice to me. I couldn't tell no difference. I just switched from one mother to another. My brother-in-law was nice to me, too. I wouldn't think of him as a father. Course I didn't know nothin' about fathers since he died when I was a baby. My sister was older than the fourteen of us. I don't really know how much. In those days the older people didn't know how old they were. They wanted to keep them home to work. I heard my mother say so. My sister really didn't know how old she was until she wrote the census in Washington. Lady sent her her age, and she was older than she thought she was.

My mother couldn't read or write, but you couldn't cheat her out of a penny. She could get on the ground and make marks. She could count down to the last cent that anybody owed her, but she didn't know to write her name when she died.

My sister didn't have no other children while I was living with them. I was the only one. I had close friends around who'd come and play Saturdays. Sunday, we'd go to Sunday School and come home and eat our dinner. I'd either go to my friends' house to play or they would come play with me. I wasn't lonely. I don't ever think my sister spoiled me. I didn't suffer for nothin', but I had work, too. I never had anything handed to me on a silver platter. I had my chores to do 'round the house. When I went to the field, I made my way. I don't think I was spoiled.

See, the farm was my brother-in-law's farm, and my sister's. I had to work. I had to get up in the mornin' and churn the milk and take up the butter, put it in cold water, leave it sit to come back that evenin' and fix it. I'd make it out in pounds. We had a butter thing you put it in—mold—and I'd pat the butter in the mold, just as tight as I could get it, and I'd twist that stick up and it'd come out with a pretty design on it. On the top. Sometimes I'd make four or five pounds of it. And then my sister would take it, and she kept it in the well. She had a bucket and she'd put that butter in the bucket and laid it down in the well. And the butter stayed hard till peoples comes to buy it.

When I was goin' to school, my first thing was to wash up, eat my breakfast and churn the milk 'fore I went. We didn't go but about four months a season. We went about four months in a span, and spent four months on the farm, because we had to come out and go to the fields in the summer. I had to walk a mile to school, and that road, when it rained, wasn't nothin' but mud. I had to come from school a lot of times barefooted 'cause I had on my good shoes and I didn't want to ruin them. I'd pull of my shoes and carry those and walk home barefoot 'cause I could always wash my feet.

We had the school in one room with a little potbelly stove sitting right in the middle of it. And the children was all 'round the walls of the school. This set would come up and get warm and they would move back, the other would come. That's how we kept warm. The girls had to bring the wood for the stove. The boys would go out and cut the trees down and chop them up to fit the stove. We girls had to bring it and put it in the schoolroom. And then we'd go back and get the chips and things from the wood, and put all that in the schoolroom.

We got our water out of a spring in a bucket. The neighbors kept it cleaned and boxed it 'round. Spring water's good. It's cold. It was so clean and cold 'til it's blue lookin'. It was so deep—that's why they kept it boxed in, because the small children might go in there and drown. A spring can go deep and a spring can also move. A crawfish keeps a spring, and if you make him angry he'll go and move it. As long as that crawfish likes that spot and stays around there, they tell me, in the bottom of that spring, you'll always have water. If you go in there too much, he'll put the spring underground and move it on somewhere else. We had a large spring in our pasture, and our cows would drink out of it. We got some watercress growin' in it, and people discovered it was good to eat, and they'd go there and pick it. I think they got that crawfish mad. He moved that spring, and we never did find it. They say he takes it underground and moves it somewhere and makes the water come back up. But we never did find it. It just dried up. I said the crawfish had more sense than the grownups.

When we got six years old we all went to school together. We just had one big room and all the grades—six grades—was in that room. One teacher did all that; she had to cope with those different ages and different mannered children. She whipped them 'cause she had some very mean ones in there. We had a boy one day that was goin' to tackle her. The other boys got up there, and if he hit her they was goin' to get him. It was goin' to be a free-for-all right there in that room!

She was a good teacher. She was paralyzed on one side all the way down. She was older woman, but a good teacher. She learned me everything I knew, that one teacher did. She lived about twelve miles from us because that's where her father lived. She'd always have a room to stay down by us until Saturday. Then somebody would pick her up and take her home.

If it was bad weather we'd close the door and keep it closed. We'd get out our lessons and we'd have our lunch—we had to take lunch. Sometimes we'd have little plays—the teacher would fix them up for us. I never got a whippin'. I had some girlfriends that was talkin' and they wouldn't mind her, and she was over there with that switch.

We'd finish gettin' our lessons for the day around 4:00. Then we'd have to get up and straighten up the schoolroom for the next morning. I told you about the water. We had to bring our water up to the school from that spring. We had a bucket and a dipper and when we had to go home, we had to dump that water. Had to wipe out that bucket and dipper and everything till it was dry. Then we'd close up the school and we'd start our long trip back home. Four o'clock she let us out.

I think the school went to the seventh grade there, and then we had to go to the city. But I didn't go—I didn't finish nothin' but the fifth. We didn't have no kind of programs or anything, but just went there to learn how to read and write, and like that. One reason I didn't care about graduatin' from school was you had to go away from home for more. I was in the country. I never liked to stay away from home. My sister asked me did I want to go, and I told her no, 'cause I didn't want to be away from home. Ever since I got grown and been by myself, I got to lookin' back on it, and see if I had of gone, I could have gotten better jobs and things. If I was able to get an education, maybe I could get a job that wasn't so hard in my older days.

I had some friends and cousins that went to school for a long time; they went to college, whatever kind of college it was. They got to be a teacher, but didn't go long enough to be no real good teachers. They wasn't in but a year or two before they were teachin'. They teach in the rural part, in the little, small school houses. They made the money, what little money they was payin' them. They didn't pay teachers much in those days. We didn't treat the teachers specially. We was just nice to them. Nobody looked up to them, but kids was afraid of them. They whipped children and sent a note home with you, and you'd better give it to your parents and not throw it away—regardless of what you did. Then your parents might punish you too.

I never did have it real hard on the farm. I had plenty somethin' to eat and I had clothes to send to my cousin's children, you know. If it was summertime, then after I would make up the butter, we'd get the house cleaned up and we went into the fields. We worked so long and then my sister takin' in washin' and ironin' and we'd work till it got real hot in the field. We would come back home and we would cook our dinner.

We had a well in the yard, and it wasn't no fun drawin' water. I had a lot of water to draw for the washin' and ironin'. A lot of wells got a handle that draws up, but ours you had to pull. We didn't have a pulley on it. That was very hard, 'specially if you had to pull up a lot of water to wash with. I wasn't with them when they dug my brother-in-law's well; my sister wasn't even married to him. He built his house when he was a young man. His father gave him that piece of ground—gave all his kids land. I didn't see running water till I went to the city. I liked it 'cause I didn't have to draw it. Just go there, turn on the faucet, and there it was.

At night, after we ate our supper, I'd get my lessons. I never went to bed until I got my lessons. If it was winter time I had to bring in all the wood for the big, old fireplace, too. My brother-in-law cut it. We'd just pile big, old logs on the woodpile, pile 'em up, and he'd cut it. And then I had to bring all that in and stack it in the house.

Night time come and my sister would piece quilts, quilts, quilts, and I would just sit there, you know, without a thing to do, if I didn't have lessons to get. I never could piece 'cause I couldn't use a thimble. It kind of just stuck my fingers up so much. In the bad weather, all winter, she'd piece those quilts. She had quilting frames hangin' up in the house—her husband hooked them up. When she wasn't usin' 'em, she could pull them up and hand 'em on the ceiling. She'd put that quilt in there, and she would sit there and piece away until way in the night. I'd sit up there and read. I didn't have nothin' else to do. I'd just sit up there and read my books and keep the fire goin' for her. She would piece and piece those quilts. My sister could do most anything. She just had a head on her that I didn't never had. She could take a crochet pattern and look at it and make it. I couldn't do that. She showed me, but I couldn't sit that long. I can't sit that long now. Um-um. I got to be moving about. She made me piece up a whole quilt one time, tryin' to learn me how to use that thimble, and when I got through, my fingers was raw. So she didn't make me do it no more.

When I first married, I didn't know how to make a biscuit, because my sister wouldn't let me cook. 'Cause when she was making biscuits, I used to stand around and watch. And when she made chicken, I used to stand around and watch. But she didn't let me cook at home. When they kill hogs in the fall, they would make two or three of those big, old cans of lard, and that had to carry them until they kill hogs again, from one season to the next. She said that I'd waste up her lard, and she wouldn't teach me. I couldn't ever get to the lard can at home without her knowin' 'cause she was home all the time. I learnt myself how to cook. The first meal I made was a disaster before I got it straight—but I finally learnt how. It was a long time before I could make a good cake—a long time—but I finally got it together.

We didn't have no holidays—we didn't hardly know what a holiday was. We'd celebrate the Fourth of July, and Christmas Day, and New Year's Day. Those are the only three holidays that we really knew about. For Christmas we'd sit around and eat fruit. My sister would cook up stacks of cakes, pies, and make ambrosia. And she used to make a big, old jug of apple cider. That's what she'd give her friends when they come in for Christmas. We'd always kill our hog, and we had plenty of meat—she'd cook hams and chickens and stuff. The neighbors, they'd come by, because she was a pretty good cook and everybody would come to get some of her food during the holidays.

Those days I would have liked to have more time for play. As long as I didn't have it, I took it as it come. I had Saturdays. We'd get out there. We had an acre, almost, of yard to sweep. We had to get a brush broom and sweep that yard. Then a crowd of the kids would come and we'd play ball or somethin' like that—jump rope—in fact, we didn't have no rope. We'd go down on the creek—big old creek right below our house—and the boys would cut up a vine, a long one, and that's what we'd jump rope with.

We'd have a good time. Boys were nice to girls in those days. It was summertime. Grapes was in season, old wild grapes, that grew up and down the creek. We'd go up and get a bucket and gather up those old sour grapes, and we'd come back and sit down and eat 'em. Plums—we had a big plum orchard on our farm, and then we'd get plums and blackberries, and stuff like that. We used to pick back there, my sister and I, and she'd can them. She'd can a lot of food and fruits that we ate during the winter. Apples—she had a big apple orchard, and she'd make apple jelly, and pear preserves, and black-berry jelly. She'd can blackberries, and peaches, and we'd have pies during the winter. We'd pick peas in the summertime and shell them and put them out and let them dry, and she'd put those peas away, and we'd have them for our vegetable in the winter. Oh, we did a lot of things on the farm.

In my hometown you didn't have a meetin' in the same church every Sunday. You'd have a meetin' at our church this Sunday; the next time you'd go five or ten miles. They didn't have one church the whole month, like you do here now. When we got ready to go to church, we didn't have no automobile. My mother didn't have no wagon, no mule of her own. We had to walk where we had to go when she was livin'. My brother-in-law, when I went to live with him, we took the buggy. If we went to take a crowd, we'd hitch up the wagon and a team of mules, and we'd put straw in the back. He'd put boards across the seat, the wagon bed, and we'd sit up there with umbrellas over us, and that's how we went to church, in a wagon.

When I was courtin'—I had a boyfriend always when I got old enough—we would see each other in church. Place was so small we couldn't talk about nothin' what everybody didn't hear. And, when we got back home, he couldn't see me. People didn't have living rooms then, but we had something in those days called "company room." Even had a bed in there, but that was for company. Nobody sit in there but the preacher when he come to preach at the church, and if we had other company. But anyway, we'd sit in there, courtin', our kind of courtin', the door'd be open, and if you'd talk too low, they'd want to know what you're talkin' about.

We didn't roam the streets like womens do now. Miles of differ-ence between us and girls of today. Nothin' like that when I come up. Why, I never heard a boy curse the whole time I was courtin'. Or say a nasty word. But the boys now don't care what they say or where they say it at or who they say it to. A boy go with a girl now, he gonna take her around the corner somewhere. They didn't do that when I come up. They was nice to you.

So I was raised on the farm, and I had to do a lot of work. I learned how to take care of myself and work for myself and not be out in the streets. I wanted to work; it made me self supporting. I didn't mind tacklin' no job that I know was an honest livin'. I don't know how to explain it, but I do figure it made me a lady. I've been takin' care of myself for a long time. That's all I ever knew. That's all I ever wanted to do, was to work and make my own money. When I was married I worked. I don't like to ask the man. When I want to spend money, I have to have something to spend of my own.

So I stayed on the farm until I was about eighteen years old. At that time, I moved to the city and I went to work doing housework. And I've been working ever since.

I married real young and of course that didn't work. I met my husband—well, I was working with his sister, at the YMCA. She introduced me to him and we married. He was young and I was young. My sister and her husband thought that would be good for me, and I did too. I didn't have no mother or father. I always wanted a husband, a home, a place to call my own, and two or three children. I never did want a whole mess of children, just two or three. But my husband was too wild. I just married a wild boy. He wasn't ready to settle down, and I was. We was together, we wasn't together, we was together—and I just didn't go back anymore. It didn't work, and so I just stayed away. You can't marry and still do the things you did when you were single, I don't figure. You have to sacrifice some things. You can't be a married man and still be out there courtin' somewhere. 'Cause I figure if you want to do that, you should have stayed single. I said, "Well, I'll get me a older one. Maybe I can make it." He was worser than the young one. Both of them drank too much. I couldn't stand it.

I had some friends liked to drink too much but I didn't go out with them much. I never did like to run with that heavy drinking crowd, because you could get in trouble. But I had friends come and visit me and I'd visit them. I just didn't run around with them. I didn't do it. I never did much entertainment. I always have been homey. I'd go out sometimes with the girls to a club—they'd have clubs, meetings—I'd go there sometimes, but I went to church most of my time. I wouldn't say I was very religious, but I was raised up here to go to church, and I never did get away from it. And I still do. I didn't even drink a drop of whiskey 'till I was married the first time. My husband gave me a drink. Made me sick to death.

When I separated from my husband, the time was real tight. I didn't know much about alimony, and I didn't ask for anything. The happiest days I remember was when my daughter graduated out of high school and got a job and went to work and got off'a me. I wanted her to go to school and learn as much as she could—more than me, see. And she went. And when she graduated, that was a happy time for me. 'Cause so many girls don't make it.

I wasn't strict with my daughter like they was with me. I let her go to the movies by herself. And go downtown and shop by herself. I just give her the leeway. I had confidence in her. And she didn't deceive me at all. Lot of girls, when I come on, the mother was so tight on 'em, it wasn't a good idea.

I can say one thing about my daughter, she never give me any trouble. She went to school in Georgia, and come up here by herself. She got an aunt, stayed with her and got a job. She wanted me to come and visit her, and I come in '57 for two weeks and I've been here ever since. I was goin' back, but she was the only child I had, and she told me, she said, "Momma, you're so far away from me." She said, "If anything was to happen, I may not have the money, right away, to come and see you." "Stay here," she tells me, so I stayed. I got this job about a week after I was here, and I liked the people and they seemed to like me. So I just stayed on.

My daughter was roomin' with two girls. "Chillun," one day I say, "You know, if I get me a job I'd make it where I'd save my money and go back home." So one of the girls said, "Miss Cooper, are you experienced?" I said, "Sure, I worked down South." So she said, "I think I know where you can get a job right now." She went to the phone and called, and this lady told her sure, she wanted somebody. Told her to bring me out there, because she knew my daughter. And my daughter takin' me over there, put me in that job. She hired me, and I stayed there until '66. They said I wouldn't. "Aw, you'll never stay there. She have a girl every week."

When I first started workin' for them I felt funny, 'cause I never did that kind of work, lived in a house with white people. But later, I felt just like I was goin' home when I went back to work 'cause she was nice to me. She didn't act funny towards me; she treated me in a way just like one of the family. She wanted me to sit down and eat with them, and I wouldn't do it. I would go to the counter. So she had a table built in the wall. It was a shelf like. She had a man come there and build it. I could fold it up when I'd eat. She said, "If you won't eat with me, I'll have to make arrangements for you to be comfortable." I had no complaints with her; I enjoyed workin' for her, I really did. That's the only job I had till I went to Woodbridge Day School. I don't believe in runnin' from job to job. You don't get anywhere, I don't think. I like to get used to people when I work for them. If I enjoy workin' for them, ain't no need for me to quit. You got to work, anyway. That job wasn't too easy, but the Woodbridge one wasn't easy at all. When you got to work, you got to work.

I felt lonesome and sort of out of place when I first started there for about two months. She would go out in the neighborhood and tell the girls (she had got acquainted with them), "I've got a new girl here. You come over and see her because she's very lonesome. I'm thinkin' if she don't find nobody to talk to, she's goin' to quit." And I got a friend there. She still is. She lost her leg last year. She's at home; I go to see her.

My lady told me I didn't have nobody there to cook for but the children; she'd take care of her husband's cookin' 'cause he didn't hardly come home for suppertime. He was workin' in a department store in Philadelphia, and he gave me all my coats and suits. Everytime he brought her a coat, he would bring me one. They would be sort of defective, they couldn't sell them, so he'd bring 'em home. Sometimes I didn't see him in a week. He'd go before I got up in the morning, because he had to go to Philadelphia.

The boy was already goin' to school when I started, kindergarten. His little friend was takin' him. When his sister was old enough, her friend was takin' her. I enjoyed bringin' them up. The little girl was one year old when I began there, and I done raised her up just like my own, almost. She would come to me instead of her mother. I got a letter the little girl wrote me. They was sweet children. They're doing fine—big now. I think the boy's in college. I haven't seen them in quite a while. I go to visit her just like I visit my sisters. I'm gonna get the bus and go to the seashore if I feel well enough this summer, while she's down there. She has an apartment she has a lease on; she uses it in the summer.

When I first started there I had to work on Sundays. I was just off on a Thursday. When the children grew up they would get what they wanted, so I told her, "You don't need me here on Sundays. I'd like to go to church." She wouldn't agree to it, so I quit.

That Thursday, when I went home, I took everything I had, but she didn't know about it. I didn't go back, and the phone ring on Monday morning. She said, "What's the matter?"

I said, "I quit."

She said, "Why?" and I told her.

She said, "Get on the bus and come out here. Let's have a talk."

I said, "I done had a talk with you. I told you I wanted Sundays off, and the children can wait on themselves now. You didn't need me

on Sundays. You said you did. And I just left. But, I'll come out there
and talk. I don't have nothin' else to do."

I got on the bus and went out there. She was smokin' one cigarette
after another. I talked to her like I talk to my sister. She said, "I
realize you want to get out among people. That was very selfish of
me, 'cause my children are grown up. I really don't need you on
Sunday. You can have Sundays off."

I settled that part of it. But another thing made me apply for
another job.

I knew the children was growin' up and she wasn't goin' to need
me. The boy made a crack one day that I caught. He said, "We're
growin' up, and we won't need Hattie everyday now. Momma's
goin' to keep her about three days." I went on and applied me for a
job. I gave the lady two weeks' notice, but she didn't believe me.
When the time come, she really believed I meant business; she hasn't
had nobody since. She don't know today that the little boy said that.
I'm glad he gave that away. She wasn't tellin' me, and she should
have told me. I might have considered stayin' on there and workin' like
that for her. As she was doin' undercover, I wouldn't have worked for
her for nothin'.

I had to go to school a month before I got the job at the Consoli-
dated State School, you know, for the retarded children. They taught
us everything. I put my books and notes up on the shelf. They taught
you how to do different things. If one got sick, how to do turning.
What to expect from a kid like that. Just what you should do if he
hurts you, or is hurtin' himself, or somethin'.

There's a lot goin' round on T.V. about the children and how
they're treated, how they're unclothed, and no shoes on, but it's not
the attendants' fault. I worked there and I know. You can dress one this
minute and look around, and another kid will pull that one's clothes
off, shoes, and tear 'em up. It's just impossible to teach those children
clothes stay up on people. You can't do it because some other kid
pulls 'em off, or he pulls 'em off himself. They don't know any better.

I had around seventy some boys. Sometimes they would take one
or two out, or bring one or maybe three in his place. They was goin' and
comin' all the time. We had to take count every morning to see if someone was missing. When we'd go off in the afternoon we would count
'em, too. If they got away, they would get away from the night crew.

Sometimes we would have a good number of staff, but they would
go and come. You'd think you had a good staff and tomorrow they

wouldn't show up. The truth about it, if you have seventy retarded children, you need seventy staff, one to a child. If you can afford it, but they couldn't. At least they needed two to every ten kids. Sometimes it's one. I have been there with that whole group by myself. Nobody showed up, but me and the kitchen girl, the one that feeds. She'd have to try to feed and have to try to help me to watch, and sometimes the supervisor would come out front to help. It requires a lot for that kind of child.

I think we had about three boys that could have gone away to a training school, because they helped us. See, we had to do all our own moppin'. My job was hard. We had to do that moppin' before we left the boys, and leave everythin' spic and span for that night crew. About three boys, if they wanted to—nobody compel them to do anything— if they felt like they wanted, they would get the broom and sweep the floor for you and dustmop it. And some of 'em would watch the children, or take them in the bathroom and put them on the stool for you, and stand in there. 'Cause you'd have to stand with them. You can't take those children in that bathroom and leave. Somebody got to be in there with them at all times. If you don't take but one in there, you got to stand right there with him. Now somebody got to be watching this crew out here in the playroom. They could hurt themselves in the bathroom. They do so many things. They turn on the hot water and scald themselves. They stick their head down in the commode. They don't know any better. Now, those three boys we had in our cottage, sometimes they'd take them in there and set them on the commode for you. And they'd stay there with them. But, even so, we had to watch them, too. We couldn't just put the children in their hands. We had to go back and forth, peek in the door, see what they were doin'. So that's just the way it was. But I think those three could of been trained, if they had any parents. I didn't never see the parents come and see those three boys. Finally, they transferred them out of our cottage and put them into another, so I don't know what happened to them.

I liked to work with those boys. I just liked those boys. We did everything for them. We had to feed 'em. We had to bathe them. Sometimes we'd bathe one kid—I call them kids but they're not kids— four or five times a day. They didn't even know how to go to the bathroom. They didn't know nothin'. You just doin' the same thing all day long. But you can get used to it; I think I got used to it. No need to call them sometimes. Just had to go to 'im and take 'im to the table, take 'im where you're gonna take 'im, 'cause he didn't know his name.

See, somethin' like that is pitiful, but you get used to it.

When I first went there, all of them was sick. They had ate somethin'—the night before the girls had give them somethin' they didn't have no business to. They always did that. Just about every child in the building had diarrhea. And I said, "I won't be back here in the morning." I come back home at night and said, "I'm not going to work in the morning. I'm not going back." I went on and on like that for about a month. I wasn't going back. And then I got used to it. Just like comin' home, goin' to work in the morning. In a way I knew what to expect, 'cause my daughter had told me. She had done the same thing when she first started to work. She told me how it was going to be, and I said, "Well, if anybody gonna make it, I'm it." So I did.

I'd be there now if I hadna' got sick, got sick leave and had this heart attack. Now, when I had to go away, I went there and toll them about it. I had been out a long time, and I thought that the doctor would give me permission to go back to work. Everytime I would ask him, the doctor would say, "No, you can't go to work now; you can't go to work now." He just kept on like that.

I said, "Listen, I got a job. They can't hire nobody in my place. I can't hold that job because they need somebody to take my place. Can't I go back to work?"

He said, "No. You'll never go back to work, now. That's what throwed you."

I said, "Well, why didn't you tell me that before now, so I could get me an extension of absence?"

And he said, "Well, that's what throwed you, that job. I don't want you back on a job."

So then I went down there and told them.

They said, "Well, Miss Cooper, you don't have to retire. You can get a leave of absence just as long as you want, because they likes you in that cottage. And we had good reports on you."

I said, "Well, I'm sorry; the doctor said I can't work. I'm holding up a job somebody can hold. I won't be back."

Then I went up to the cottage. I said, "Well, boys, I won't be back."

"Hey," when I walked in the back door, "Miss Cooper!"

Them that could talk, they wanted chocolate.

"Miss Cooper, Miss Cooper, Miss Cooper."

I went and laid one on the counter. And I said, "Miss Cooper won't be back now—Miss Cooper's sick. She won't be back no more."

I think one or two sort of halfway realized, 'cause I had one or two that had pretty good understandin'. They looked so sad, but I couldn't go back.

I never been back again for a visit. My daughter don't have a chance to take me. I didn't have a one that would recognize me now.

Didn't work there long. I went there in '66 and I had to leave in August, '68.

Durin' the day now I don't do nothin', just stay home. I walk my grandson to school sometimes, and the lady upstairs walks him and picks him up. I have to get out and exercise, though. That's all I do, when I feel like it. I have high blood pressure, and this heart condition, arthritis, and poor circulation with the blood. Sometimes I could stick a pin in my fingers and I can't even feel it. The doctor gives me medicine, but I don't ever think he gives me enough.

You know, I wish I was able to work in a day nursery or somethin' like that. Pick me up a little change. But I can't.

I don't think so much whippin' nowadays is necessary. The more you whip a child, the more stubborn and rebellion they get. I think a child is supposed to be taught. Cuddle him up to you, settle him down, get his attention, and then teach him. You've got to give them what they're supposed to know. You can't just do this one time and stop. You got to continue to do that.

A mother can't wait until the father comes home if she gonna punish a child. You get him right then. Do whatever you're goin' to do, punish him or spank him or whatever you goin' to do. But the time father gets there, he done forgot it.

I think when a child does something bad, he should be spanked. I figure like this: you've got to get some sort of understandin' from that child. If you let a child do what he wants to do his whole life, you ain't never goin' to be able to control him. I think you should chastise that child. I'm goin' to say this. I don't know whether it's goin' to get me in trouble or not. The policeman can get your child and they can beat his brains out with those billie clubs. If they can beat him when he gets grown, I figure you could at least spank him at home 'cause you're not goin' to kill him—and let him know that he's doin' somethin' wrong that you don't approve of.

The lady that I worked for in West Orange, she told me one time, "Hattie, I don't know how you lived down South."

I said, "What do you mean?"

She said, "You speak your mind."

I said, "I spoke my mind down South too." When they hired me I did my work. If I got a job with an old devil, where I saw me and her wasn't goin' to get along, I quit. Never had no trouble on no job.

I never did work for any mean peoples in North Carolina. They always treated me nice. I had my work to do and I did it. The thing about Carolina work and this work is, it wasn't as long as this work. You'd go about workin'—when I was down home—at eight o'clock; you was workin' till about two—or two-thirty. Then you was goin' home. And it wasn't as hard as jobs in the North, not as hard as here.

When I went back down South to see my sister, I saw that the city was larger, and it looks like there are more peoples in there than it was when I was down workin'. The South has sure changed. It's much better. Those people down there, they have beautiful homes and clothes. When I was there the colored wasn't allowed to ride in the bus with white people. Stuff like that. All that broken down now. You go in stores now, and you see colored boys and girls runnin' 'em, just like up North. Everything has changed. They have better houses than they had when I first started doin' day work. And the rent is cheaper than here. Cost of living is cheaper. And they can get more help there than we can here. Now, my sister's on welfare, and she gets her old age pension too. Sounds better for older peoples than here, because I can't get welfare. They won't give it to me 'cause I live with my daughter. I'm having a pretty hard time because I don't have but $110 a month to live on.

I wish I could move back down South, but my daughter won't do it. She wants to stay right here. But I'd rather be on a farm right now. I don't like the city. The farm is healthy. You can have more room out on the farm, and you can have more fresh food on the farm. I like gardening and I like to raise my own stuff, chickens, eggs, and stuff. I love the farm better than the city any time. It's a good life. Anybody ever lived it, they wouldn't want anything else.

Now Newark is gonna soon be a ghost town. They're tearing it up and burning it. Yeah, they tell me a lot of people are leaving here. I'd go right now if I could get my daughter to go. She doesn't like it here, but she got a lot of seniority on her job, and retirement stuff, and she got to work for so many years for that, she said she's too old to go back home and start all over again. So she's gonna stay here.

The riots—I think it's awful. Nobody give you nothin'. I don't know what white people think. I think it's ridiculous. Why should we burn up our homes, the only places we have to live? A gang of hoodlums! Burnin' the house down—they don't care if you're in there asleep, they burn you up too. I don't approve of it. I don't think it's all colored—there's colored and whites burnin' down the buildings. Regardless of who it was, they didn't get us anything but a whole lot of empty lots.

There's discrimination, all right. There'll be discrimination as long as we live. I don't really think the demonstrations did any good. There'll always be somebody that'll look down on us as Negroes, and we're not supposed to make what the white make or live where the white live or do things what the white does. There'll always be somebody here like that. The riots didn't help anything. Just look around. There used to be nice stores. They burnt all of those down—they still burnin' that down. When they burn down food stores, they just makin' the groceries higher, groceries get scarcer and scarcer, food is goin' up. They only thing to do is just pray that they'll stop, and see they're hurtin' nobody but themselves.

To tell you the truth, I think the world is gettin' worse. The murder—you can't go nowhere without gettin' killed. I think the world is comin' to an end.

Read your Bible. We haven't had no real bad weather since I came. It's gettin' warmer in the winter. That's a sign. It's somethin' to think about. People are goin' on with the same old routine. In Noah's time, too; that's the way peoples livin' right now. You see more people in the bars on Sunday than you do in church. That's the worse thing in the world, havin' these bars open on Sunday. A Christian's not supposed to go in that bar at all. Even my preacher goes in there and drinks. I didn't see it, but smellin' it, I did. That's hypocrit.

Newark will soon be a ghost town. Here's one lady that wants to get out of it so bad, I don't know what to do. I might leave it, one day. I'd go right now, if I could get my daughter to go. I would like to go back to my home.

4

Nine Luzianne Coffee Boxes

When we first come to Newark it was tight. That was in 1962. We come from Virginia. Work got scarce down there, and we couldn't get nothin' to do. You know how you manage—you save up a little money to travel with. So we saved up a little. First come, it was my husband and myself. Well, we roomed, just roomin'; didn't have no house like we got now. Things got so tight I would run and do days work. My husband did scuff around and start to paint. He painted here and there, tryin' to make a dollar. I would go to the 'ployment office in the mornin's and try to get somethin' to do. Some mornin's I would get somethin' to do, and then some days I wouldn't.

The days that I did work I always tried to save a penny or two for the next day so we could have sump'n to eat. You understand? And then he started workin' construction. After that we got along pretty good.

So then I went back. We saved up enough money to go back, and I got my daughter and her children. She took a room right there into the same building that I was livin' in. That building is torn down now. So after she came it seemed like it was a little tighter on us, and it was. I was payin' $12 a week for my room, and then we had to pay $13 for her room. That made $25 a week for two rooms. And then we went on and scuffed and scuffed.

And then in '65 I was taken by a heart attack. And then my daughter got sick. She was in Virginia. She had gone back home. She got sick so I went down and I took four children. I got them and come back up here. We went to Welfare for a little help. They wanted to know how long the children had been here. Said they couldn't give them no support unless they been here a year. We didn't get nothin' for about five months, and when he did give me a little, it was something like $75 a month.

After then seemed like I got worser off sick, got high blood pressure and heart trouble. So my daughter she come, and she got two of the children and left me two. I was sick, but I could work. So I worked in a plastics factory, makin' Christmas gifts. I would go long in June or July, and I would work till they laid me off every season. I worked there, season after season.

Then I had a little accident with my back, a car accident. I'm disabled to work. I can't even mop my floors. If I cook I've got to sit down. You see these childrens in there I watch? I don't lift them. I won't take no small ones 'cause that keeps me goin' all the time. I keep about five. When they come from school they come here.

Before that accident I wasn't sufferin' with my heart as bad. Now I have to have those niglycerines 'cause it gets so bad sometimes. I can lay down and I can feel seems like my whole body is shakin'. I have to hassle for breath. Then I'll take one of those and I will quieten down. Sometimes I have to go 'mergency room of the hospital.

My husband, he's off from work. It ain't goin' to be long before that little 'ployment compensation is run out. Then what we goin' to do? I'm disabled to work; he can't get no job. If I was able to work and go and do like I used to, it wouldn't be so tight on me.

See how we do it. When he draws 'ployment, he save so much from this week and so much from the next week, and that's for to pay the rent. Then I go get a little baby sitting. We git food like that. Then every time he can go out and make a little change he always put that in food. That's my situation, and it's rough.

My daughter, she works. But how can she help me, with six children? She lives on the second floor. Right under me. Part the time it's tight on her. You know how it is—sometimes they run out of shoes, run out of different things. It takes.

She takes care o' the children by herself. But the children, wherever they get sleepy, that's where they lay down. If they're up here, they go to bed here, and if they're downstairs, they go to bed down there.

I don't charge her for taking care of them. I got that little one over there. I can't charge her 'cause, see, he's mine.

You know, when we was farmin' we took in my cousin boy with us. He was around eleven years old. Now he's in South Carolina. He have three children and a wife. So I wrote him and I told him about things. See, I don't want to worry people with my problems. So he kept on writing and asking me, "Momma, how you doin'?" I told him I'm gettin' along, and he said he's comin' up here. He came on Friday and went back on Monday. He come with his wife and the baby. The other two children he left with his wife's mother. I enjoyed it. We talked and talked. He told me, "Don't worry. Everythin' will be all right." I said, "The Lord has it in His hands. I know He'll take care of things." He said, "You's right."

He was drinkin', and I told him, "Look, these here beers you drinkin'. It's all right, I guess. A person that want a drink is all right. But don't overdo the thing. 'Cause you know the Bible tells us no drunks, no gamblers, no backsliders will enter His Kingdom. I'm not goin' to tell you nothin' wrong to do 'cause you feel just like you's my son."

He says, "I am your son. My mother didn't do but one thing for me but born me and give me out. You took me in. I would go from this place to that place, this place to that place. You the only one that took me in and give me a home. And wherever you be, I'll call that home as long as I live."

He stayed with me until he was 20. Now he is 32 years old and still calls me Momma. And he calls my husband Daddy.

When we took him in we was rentin' a farm on halves. All that year we lived on $7 a week. There was four of us. I planted me a garden. I had cabbage, tomatoes, corn, butter beans, snap beans and peppers, peas and carrots. The only thing we had to get from the store was flour, sugar, coffee. Sometimes I would pick up somethin' like extry for Sunday dinner, like stew meat, fresh pig tails, stuff like that. I had over 200 layin' hens and we had killed nine head of hogs that year.

A whole lot of peoples would come by and ask me for vegetables from the garden. My sister, she come one Saturday, and she stayed all day with me. I had picked butter beans. We talked, and we cooked and we ate. Seemed like I enjoyed her so much. I love all my sisters and brothers, but there's one that you is real close to. So this mornin' I was sittin' here, readin' a old letter that she had wrote me a long time ago. It was in 1959, right before she went to the hospital. I couldn't get to see her when she was in the hospital 'cause I was sick myself, so I told my husband I'm goin' to try to go home next week. He said, "Anytime you get ready to go, I'll try to make a way for you to go." That was Tuesday. That Wednesday I got a card that said she was dead. They told me don't worry, 'cause she left this world singin'.

So I went down to the funeral. It wasn't snowin' here, but when we got to Maryland it was. The snow was so bad we couldn't do but twenty miles a hour. When we got there I said there was eight of us— she made the eighth and now she's gone. I went in the house, and it looked to me like I should see her sittin' there, 'cause I would always come and she would grab me and say, "I'm so glad you come." When we'd go down we would take her 'round with us, different places, 'cause she loved to go. She did love to eat bar-b-que. We'd get some, and we'd sit in the car and eat it. My husband would say, "Now you know you all ain't got a bit of business with the bar-b-que. You all got high blood, and you'll be grumblin' and feelin' bad before the day is gone."

I'd say, "Well, maybe it won't hurt us."

Then we'd go down to see my Aunt. She's 96 years old. I enjoyed her.

Anyways, we goes down to my sister's funeral, and they was over a hundred cars. They was puttin' her in the grave, and cars still was comin'. And they was flowers, the whole church was nothin' but flowers. Reverend Hawkins, the pastor of the church we all belonged to, he preached. But she was a member o' the church down there where she was buried, at St. Matthews.

See, when you is down home, wherever you was baptized at, that's the place they carry your body to and have your funeral—the first church you join. Like my sister's husband, he passed away in December. We had to go down home. They carried him to Mount Sinai. Although he come a member of a church over here in Brooklyn, his membership was in Mount Sinai back home and she had him shipped back. That's the way they do down there. Wherever you go to be baptized, that's where they carry you back.

Momma was a member of Chimin' Bell Chapel Church. Daddy was a member there too. The whole family was a member there. We lived around that church for years and years. When my little brother Jackie died, they buried him in Chimin' Bell Chapel.

I remember from my childhood when I was nine years old. I was real sick, had tonsilitis. I suffered for so much with it; I couldn't go and play like other childrens did. My mother give me a dose of castor oil, and it stroked me. It give me a light stroke—a paralysis.

She said the next morning that my mouth was twisted and my right hand was twisted over. They called the doctor because she didn't want to move me. When the doctor came he give me some kind of medicine which would grow the bone, 'cause see the bone was already 'flicted. It was so many drops she had to give me. If she give me one drop over, the doctor told her, it would kill me, so she was very careful. When she didn't drop it, Grandmomma would drop it. But

Grandmomma was so nervous that she and her both together would give it. I seen her pour it back into the bottle and get another glass and drop it all over again.

Grandma would be 'round the house with me. She just left her home 'cause Aunt Dodie took Grandpapa over with them. Grandma told Grandpa, "I'm goin' to help out. I know I ain't able to do no more work in the field, but I can stay 'round the house and help cook and wash and do like that." So that's what she did, and she stayed with us until I was twelve years old.

I got so I could sit up on the side of the bed. I was weak. I was so sick on my stomach and moanin'. I would just vomit—ooh—and vomit. The doctor told her to give me a little snuff on a broom straw, 'cause a little snuff on the tongue in the mornin' would help settle my stomach. That's the reason I started dipping snuff.

My mother would sit me on the porch, and I would watch the other children. I would see my daddy comin'. You know how money was in them days. And Daddy was sharecroppin' with these here white people. We had to move from one farm to another farm, 'cause some of these old white people would take everything that we had, wouldn't even leave us a penny for Christmas. So there was me. I was the sick one in the family. Daddy would come up on the porch. He would pet my hand, and he would put a piece of candy in it. He'd tell me to put it in my mouth now, 'cause Daddy didn't have but one penny. Said, "Don't let the rest of the children know."

The sun would get on that porch. Mother would come out and move me to a shady part. She was so lovely; she was so kind. In my 'fliction she never scolded me. She didn't act like she would ever get tired of waiting on me. I'd just set and watch the other children. I had no games, nothin' but a baby doll that I'd play with now and then.

After that I got so I could creep around. Long then, Daddy got a crutch. I don't know how he got it—must have got it through the doctor. So I used it under my left arm, because I couldn't stand nothin' touch my right side. It was like dead or something. If anything touched that, it was just like somethin' crawling.

I remember the day I put my crutch down. That was the most wonderful day in my life. But I still couldn't walk good. I always drug the right foot. I had to learn all over again how to walk. I had to learn how to write and eat and everything with my left hand, so that's why I'm left handed today, I guess.

Momma didn't ever put no hard work on me 'cause I was

gainin' my strength back. When I was twelve sometimes she used to put me in a chair and I would wash dishes. Or I would sweep a little and help out with the baby. Then when I got thirteen, I just went on about my business, just like everybody else did.

At that time, I was goin' to school, and some days I could, some days I couldn't. But when I was fourteen I had to stop school on account of my mother. She was taken with sugar diabetic, high blood pressure, and arthritis. She suffered from heart trouble, too. I was in the eighth grade. One mornin', the first day of school, Daddy says to me, "Your momma's sick, and somebody's got to stay and take care of her 'cause you know I can't take care of the house and work too." So I cried that mornin'. Then it seemed like something would take you and say, "Don't cry. You'll make it." So I went on and pulled my clothes off, laid my books on the sewin' machine, and went on into the kitchen washin' dishes. Still, they was tears in my eyes. I said to momma, "My future is cut up, because these days that I'm missin' now in school, I'm goin' to need them one day."

My oldest sister was goin' to college, learnin' to be a music teacher. But there are some people can't do as good as other people do a job. Some peoples can come in and clean a house and it will look nice, and some can come in and clean and it don't look like they even touched it. So that's the way that it was with my sister.

Daddy come back to the house. He sat down and talked to me. He said, "Willie, I want you to go to school just like the rest of 'em, but you see how it is here. Ain't it no way I can make it. Your momma's on the bed, and nobody to pass her a glass of water. I can't be to the house all the time. You know there's work in the field to be done. When Momma get better I'll send you to school."

Momma was sick then about six months. She wasn't able to do a thing. I didn't go to school none at all that year. When Christmas come she was able to sit up around the house and tell me what to do, you know, in the food line.

That Christmas was wonderful to me. You would decorate your house with this here paper you twist, crepe paper. And the top of the loft you would have a big veil, any color you wanted. I had pink and blue. That was the front room. And then you would go ahead and clean good, and cook like cakes and pies. We had 'tato pies, coconut pies and chocolate. All different kinds of cakes too. Daddy would kill a pig and he would bar-b-que him in the yard. And we would cook up a whole lot of collard greens. During that Christmas my mother's two

brothers came down to see us, and they was talkin' about how good
the food was. They say, "Who cooked it?"

Momma said, "Willie cooked it."

They said, "You's makin' a good cook out of her."

Before Christmas Eve we would get out there and sweep that big
yard just as clean—and then the children was gettin' ready for Santa
Claus and wouldn't do nothin' bad, help with little things. When
Christmas mornin' come, that would be a happy time. They would get
doll babies, and horns, and harps—different things Daddy told Santa
Claus to bring.

My brother, the baby boy, Clifford, got up that mornin' and he
was sick. He had a sore throat and high fever. Daddy said, "Well, it's
Christmas mornin'. I don't know where I can get a doctor." So there
was an old doctor. Daddy got in his old T-model Ford and went for
old Doctor Brown. He came that mornin' and told Daddy, "He got
the diptheria. I got to quarantine this house."

My mother's brothers told him, "We're a long way from home.
We plannin' to go back next mornin'."

Doctor said, "Well, I got to give you a needle."

So he give them a needle, and then Daddy had us all vaccinated
for the diptheria. We used to have a lot of company, but that time we
didn't have too many because the house was quarantined. Then after
Clifford got up, Daddy said this is Old Christmas. Old Christmas is
for the animals, such as the mules, cows, the trees and all. It is the fifth
of January. All the animals bows twice on Old Christmas. At twelve
they bows on their knees and thank God. Even the trees bow their
heads. That's what Daddy told us. He said, "That's for the
animals." Well, that Old Christmas, we made a big dinner for
Clifford, being that he wasn't able to eat and like that before. We
made six cakes and some pies and killed four chickens. We enjoyed
that as much as we did the regular Christmas.

Momma was gettin' around 'bout that time, but still no hard work
could she do. She couldn't eat nothin', no meat, no cake, nothin'
sweet at that time. Her legs was swole 'cause she had this here ole
arthritis, they called it rheumatism then. She would creep around—
sometimes you'd catch her out in the yard feeding her chickens,
gathering her eggs, and looking out after her little stuff around there.
But moppin', cookin', stuff like that she couldn't do. No washin' or
ironin'.

My sister was going to college at that time. Her room rent—board and room—was twenty dollars a month and Daddy had to work. He had a little job on the outside, like a little carpenter work, in order to git that twenty dollars.

Momma went on then about two years. She got so her legs went down and she could go 'round, do her housework again. But in the field, choppin', pullin' up 'baca plants—Daddy didn't let her do none o' that.

I didn't never go back to school. I felt in a way in my mind that I had been cheated. But then I looked back over it all and I said to myself, I don't know whether I been cheated or no. Because there comes a period in everybody's life that you got to lean on somebody, the way Momma leanin' on me for to be helped. Just like now, I don't know whose hands I'll fall into for to lean on somebody. I'm gettin' old, you know, and I don't know what day the Lord goin' to come in and call me. But I know them days are comin' to me where I've got to lean on somebody. Might be on my daughter, grandchildren, or a friend, but, see, we don't know how our lives stand with God.

After that Old Christmas we went back to work, 'parin' tobacco beds and sewing canvas to go on the beds and things like that. And shellin' peanuts. We had twenty bags. Them bags stood up that high. We had twenty bags to shell, for ourselves and the landlord, ten bags for Daddy and ten for the landlord. We was doin' that on account o' the crop. We planted them in the ground. See, he had twenty acres of peanuts, and it took a bag to the acre.

Fact, the first thing I can remember about sharecroppin', Daddy rented a crop on a big farm; it has a lot of houses on it. We was just tenants. We growed corn, cotton and 'bacca. I wasn't six years old, 'cause we didn't go to school yet. My sister would have to babysit while Momma was workin' 'cause she was the oldest one. Along cotton pickin' time Momma would 'get us a little bag and put it on the side of us and tell us to go way up on her row and pick cotton. 'Cause we couldn't carry a whole row by ourselves. So that's the way she done.

It was a big house—six rooms, big rooms. And a little shed room on the porch makes seven. We had a pump there to pump our water. And they 'lowed so much around the house for your garden—your 'tater patch—and there was a chicken house, barn for the 'bacca, pack house, and a barn for the corn. It has a partition between the corn so you divided it. On this side was the owner's corn and on that side was the landlord's. When you pulled it, you had to go in the field and break it off the stalk. Then you put a cart load over here and a cart load over there, and that divided it.

We dug a hole under the house and played in it. Momma would come up from the field and we'd be under there playin', makin' mud cakes. When I was seven that time, my sister was taken with the typhoid fever, and about a week, two weeks after that, my brother, he was taken. So the doctor come out and quarantined the house. But Grandmama, she come in anyhow and she stayed. Only two children came down with that fever. Jackie—his real name was John but we called him Jackie—he died less time than a month. That was a time. Momma was cryin'. Daddy was cryin'.

I was seven years old but I can remember. They hadn't got no coffin for him. A man came. We didn't have no bathtub or nothin' like that. Momma had a little old foot tub. The man got him some water and that rag and went in there and give him a bath all over. And put his clothes on and laid him out on the same cot, one of those little old folding beds Momma had. Laid him out on it. 'Cause his eyes was open they put pennies there to close 'em. That man what brought the coffin put the pennies on his eyes. They didn't no embalming 'cause long then they didn't embalm people.

After that Daddy cleaned out a place in the front room, and they put his body in there. Momma had every mirror wrapped up in a white sheet, and Daddy stopped the clock. I didn't ask them why they did those things.

He stayed in the house two days after he died. The third day about ten o'clock Daddy took a spring wagon, one horse wagon, and carried his body to the grave on horse power. There was some man there on the farm, and he was a white man, and his name was Charlie Joe, he carried him to the grave. Momma was cryin'; Daddy was cryin'. I was cryin' too. When they was puttin' dirt over him, I said to Daddy, "Why you all puttin' dirt over him? Ain't you goin' to take him back?"

Daddy said, "Come here. I want to explain somethin' to you."

I had a white handkerchief and I was wipin' tears. I was tryin' to keep them from puttin' dirt over him. Everytime when they put him in the hole and start puttin' dirt over him, I went down and told that man, "Don't put dirt on my brother."

Daddy called me and said, "Now, look, he's dead. He don't walk no more. He ain't even breathing. The Lord done took him home."

I said, "No, Daddy. This is his home."

He said, "Uh-uh. The Lord took him with Him." And then he

said, "That's that old body. He don't have no breath in it. That body got to go back to the dirt but his soul has done gone."

Grandmomma, she come and take me by the hand and took me back to the surrey. My granddaddy was right there, standin' beside the surrey. And she say, "They had to do that. They had to take him away. He couldn't stay at the house because he was dead."

And that was the first member of our family that I remember dyin'.

Then we moved in the second house. I remember that Daddy bought his own mule. If you had your own mules you wouldn't have to pay for no fertilizer. At that rate, the white man had all the fertilizer paid for and still Daddy would get half of the crop.

The following year we moved. I don't remember the name of the place, but I know it was close to the town where we was. That was the year that Daddy turned in and sold his team of mules. See, he had moved with a different man, and this landlord already had mules stationary to that place. So that's sharecropping. That year went along smoothly. A girl they named Violet—I was seven at that time—she didn't have no place to stay and she was only fifteen, so my mother took her in.

Everything went along smoothly that year. Along about June, the crops was so pretty, so green, and it was the first day of June 'cause Daddy had put in one barn of 'bacca.

We lived right on a stream of water. It run all the way around—I don't know how far it went, but I know it went a long ways. Daddy used to take his poles at twelve o'clock and go down there while the mules was takin' it easy and sit down and fish. I used to go with him.

One day he was down there, fishin', and I pulled his worms out and throwed them in the stream of water.

He said, "What did you do that for? Don't you know I can't fish?"

I said, "The fish is in the water. They can eat the worms there."

He got angry and run me to the house. Well, it was rainin' then, and it kept rainin' and rainin'. It was three days where it steady rained. The fourth day it was still rainin' and the dam busted down there where you cross over. The water come up and was runnin' all through the house. Momma got us; she was standin' in the water in the house when she put our clothes on. And Daddy and Uncle Jeff went and got a canoe from someplace, and they put us on the canoe and took us to dry land.

We stayed with our grandma and grandad. About a week and

Daddy went back and found the water had thrown the house, and the leaves of the 'bacca was all washed off the stalk, and the corn was done drown. The cotton was drown, too. He had a hog. I don't know how she got out, but she got out and swimmed up on dry land. That's where he found her, with nine little pigs. He brought her back on a truck. He had built a little box and put those pigs in.

That year we didn't have nothin'. The house was wrecked inside. All the chickens washed away. So the boss man, he was right good. Told Daddy, "What 'bacca you got and that you got into the barn, just go ahead, grade it, sell it, take the money for your family. Because we couldn't help that. That's the Lord's doin'." He was real good, a good landlord.

So then we started another crop. Momma said, "Supposin' another flood comes?"

Daddy said, "We have to look to the Lord for that."

So we stayed there another year, and that year we came out good. And during the summer, Momma went to her cousin's, 'cause her cousin was sick. Momma didn't take none o' us children 'cause Grandma was with us. Her sister come pick her up, Aunt Dodie. And Aunt Dodie's husband trotted that mule all the way—it was twenty miles. When they got there they was all settin' there, eatin' dinner, and Dave Moore's daddy says, "Dave, that mule is swellin'. She got the colic." Momma says that Dave Moore's mother took a old greasy apron and one got on one side of the mule and one got on the other side, and the mule was still swellin'. Then they toll my mother, "You all better got ready and let's go."

And Momma said they all got on the surrey. And Momma said that mule was gruntin' every step and they went across the swamp bridge, and the mule was gruntin' so much. When they got almost to Greenville—we lived on the other side—when they got there, almost where the concrete streets is, the mule fell and busted wide open.

Daddy was on the way, 'cause he had a old mule. Grandma told him, "You better go get Georgia, 'cause it's gettin' dark and I'm kinda scared for her."

So when Daddy got there, the mule was already busted, layin' on the street. And the law took Dave Moore and locked him up in jail for trottin' that mule like that. He pulled time.

You know, he had a pretty good crop. They moved his wife out. A crowd of whites come and moved into his house and took over where he left off. They just took over his fields and cleared all that money during that year. Momma said it was a shame.

So then we moved to where I had the stroke. And then when I got better I would have to go to the field, chop a half a day, chop cotton, corn, peanuts and 'bacca. Chop a half day, till 'round about 11:30, and then I'd go to the house and prepare dinner for ten. At that time I was the age of fifteen. And then it come along, them Hoover days. That's when President Hoover was in the chair, and people was starvin'. You would work for ten cents an hour. You could go out and work, hire yourself out to a farmer, and end of the week, if you made four dollars, you had done somethin'.

I remember that we would sharecrop with a man they call Bill Curtis. He was law in a big town nearby. He was a policeman. At the end of that year he took everything that we had; didn't even leave my daddy one dollar.

After that, I remember that time when Aunt Annie and Uncle Leroy come down from Mason—see, that's our home, where I was born. He come down and didn't have nothin', no nothin'. Nothin' to eat; the children didn't have a change of clothes. See, that old landlord had took everything. And Daddy went and was tryin' to rent them a place around us. Which Mason was a hundred and some miles away.

My uncle got there on a train. He sold his chickens off the yard to get his fare to come to his brother—that was my daddy. And my daddy and him was walkin' from place to place, tryin' to find him some place to live. And they couldn't find him no place.

Now, at that time, my mother help a old white man they called Old Man O'Brien. She helped him kill hogs. And she was tellin' him about her sister-in-law with fourteen children and they didn't have no place to stay. He told us, "Well, I've got a place that I would rent him. I'll send my truck to get the furniture."

My mother told him it's over a hundred miles, and he said that that don't make no difference. He said he would supply him with money, but how much I don't know. So the truck brought his furniture and his children. And when they got there they didn't have nothin'. 'Cause my mother, she'd divide her food with them, and she divided her clothes with them. That was what you call them Hoover days.

I remember the time that we didn't have meat on the table. Daddy goes to the pen and killed a hog. He said he'll kill every hog that he had before his children go hungry. At that time no one was even buyin' those hogs, things was so tight. So my daddy was just trying to provide for his family.

Daddy was good to his family; he would provide for his family. Talkin' about a father now—he was a father to his family. Because he seed that we had food in the house. He seed that we had clothes. He seed that we had shoes on our feets. The only time I felt needin' for clothes was along in them Hoover days. He couldn't get them. I seen he and Momma sat up nights during Hoover days, by the fireside, wonderin' what they was gonna get and how and whether they was gonna make it.

Then we moved a couple more times, and at that time my daddy got on his feet. When we were movin' in the Lawrence place, they was an old gypsy woman come in. That old woman told Momma, "Aunt, you movin' in on fortune." She said, "You give me a dollar, and you'll have good luck."

Momma give her a dollar and she read the palm of her hand. She told her that before the year's out, she'll have good luck. Then she took that dollar and throwed it in the fire, and burned the money up.

That year went on and on. When school time come, the principal asked Daddy could he drive the school bus. It seemed like that was a blessin'. That helped out a little bit. And seems like people would come that year more than they did any other year to pick us up to do work for them in the fields, like choppin', by the day. And that was a little money comin' in.

Momma said, "That old gypsy lady was true. We is havin' a little more fortune this year than we did last year."

It seemed like everythin' went along smooth. And long about September Momma's brother, the one we called Uncle Donald, come to live with us. He got him a job and give Momma so much a week for to cook his food and to keep his clothes clean. Momma told him, "I don't want to charge you," but he said, "I feel like I want to give you somethin'." See, his wife had left him with his family.

Now some people had told Daddy that there was an old white man who had lived in the house before and had died there and his money had never been found. So Daddy said if there is any way that he could find the money, he was goin' to find it and take it for his own use.

So my uncle moved out into a little biddy house where he worked, moved out from us and moved in there, and 'bout two weeks after he moved in there, you know, we found the place was haunted—our place. We all was up one mornin'—Momma wasn't able to do nothin'—and Daddy told me, "Willie, you get up and put your clothes on and get one of your mother's aprons, come on up to the house, 'cause we're goin' to need you this mornin' to help with the hogs.''

Momma said, ''You better go ahead.''

I said, ''Momma, I ain't made the boys' beds yet.''

She said, ''Go ahead on. You'll straighten them out this evenin' when you come home.'' And she went upstairs and was goin' to straighten and she said she heard somethin' tellin' her, ''You come here.''

Momma said she looked, she just thought it was somethin' or other, and she looked again.

It said again, ''You come here.''

Momma said she turned around and come back down and went back to her room and set down. Well, she didn't pay no mind. Then one night we was all settin' and we heard somethin' fall in the hall. Oh, it made such a noise. And Daddy, he looked. He said, ''Well, I don't see nothin'.''

And Momma said during that year she went to the house and she thought it was some of the children comin' 'round the house. Momma said, ''Sonnie?'' That was my brother's name. She said, ''Sonnie, is that you?'' Momma said the thing didn't say nothin', just walked right on, and she knew that it ain't none of the youngins.

That fall, along about October or November, Mr. G. come. He had one of those underground ''tredgers.'' I know you hearin' talk of them. It's one of those 'chines they dig money with, the money which peoples bury. He had one of those 'chines that would find the money, and whenever you find it, you would dig down and git the money. 'Cause Daddy had said, ''I know a man that's got one of them 'chines. The next time the moon get right, the next time it get full, we will search for it.'' So Mr. G. came, and they went all around the house and searched the yard. We would see a little girl out there in that yard; she would have a little white dress on and she would be turnin' around. And Daddy said, ''That's where your money could be.''

Well, they searched around and searched around. And the thing brought them back into Momma's room. I know you've seen these here fireplaces. You know, there's all those bricks layin' out in front of it. That's what we call a ''half.'' Well, that 'chine went right down there. When it did, Mr. G. told Daddy to git us all in there.

Daddy, 'stead of lettin' us go in another room, he put us all in Momma's room. He said he didn't want nobody to be runnin' 'round 'cause if anybody would run he couldn't git the money. So he brought us all in there, and he took a blue chalk and went around and drew a ring, and told us none of us don't come out of that ring. For if we do, we break that ring and then he couldn't git the money.

Then Mr. G. give Daddy a book; they call it the sixth and seventh chapter of Moses. How he got that book we don't know. He showed Daddy where to read at and how far to read. He told him that if he don't have the money by the time he finished readin' those verses, they wouldn't git the money. When he started to movin' them bricks the first thing come in there was a rat—wasn't a mouse. The rat stood up there, and you could see that rat's moustache. Ooh!! I was so scared. Daddy was readin' and shakin' his head for us not to say nothin' or either move. After that came two roosters. They was fightin' and just bloody. You could see the blood around the neck. I was sittin' there and lookin' at them just like I'm lookin' at you. I wanted to holler so bad I didn't know what to do. The next thing was a old woman and old man, come in the door, looked around, and they went on, out of sight. The last thing—I heard somethin' hit the back porch. It was a big bay horse. She come there and stuck her head in the door, whickled twice, went right on through the hall, and jumped off the front porch. I was so scared I could hear my heart beat.

This time Daddy didn't have but one more verse to read. And Mr. G. had the bricks up and they was a box there. It was a wood box, and they had made a lid to slip over the top of it. Inside they was nine "Luzianne" coffee boxes; they stood up that tall. You see a two pound coffee box? And honey, they was dollars and dollars of paper money in them boxes. Then they was four more came, and that was full of fifty centy pieces, dimes, quarters and nickels. He had one filled up to the top with pennies, but they couldn't use it, because it was too old or somethin'. I don't know how much money there was there, but I know that Daddy took and divided it half and half.

So Daddy and Mr. G. caught the train with suitcases and come to Washington, D.C., and I guess they had it changed there. I don't know how they done it. But I know when he come back he didn't go right head then and buy him a farm. He waited a year and then he went to St. Michaels. Yes, we farmed on halves another year. If Daddy had went ahead and bought him a farm, them folks would of suspicioned. So Daddy went a whole year and then he went down to St. Michaels and buys him a home. We lived in a old house where was already there. It was a great big farm there, and then it seemed we lived a little better.

And Momma said then Daddy could take her to the doctor and buy her medicine and give her the treatment then as she should have. Seemed like when she started takin' her treatment, seemed like she sort of cleared up a little bit. She said she felt better. She had to go once a month, and they would put her on electric table for this here arthritis.

Yes, Mamma was better but Daddy wouldn't allow her to work none. Now, 'long 'bout puttin' in 'bacca time, she would creep around the house and put the cabbages on and try to fix dinner. She didn't have nothin' to do but just put them on and sit on the porch, keepin' wood in the stove. And when she got ready she would make up her corn bread and put that in the oven and bake it. So I would say that we was good livers. Them was the happiest days, the best part of my life along then. I was with them, workin', helpin' them. I didn't have no worrations. I didn't have no problems of my own. All the problems, all the troubles, my parents had all of that, all them headaches.

Peoples was all mixed up in St. Michaels, white and colored, but they didn't go to school together. They was segregation. There was one little ole white girl, her name was Janet, that would come up there evenin's when she come from school. She would bring her paper and pencil. And we would get off to ourselves. She would go over the lesson that she had that day. She would do that every evenin'. It seemed like I learned more from her after I stopped goin' to school than I did the whole time I was at home. 'Cause I had to work and I didn't have time to get my paper and pencil and stuff like that. And she would write me letters, you know, and send them through the mail, and then I would write her back. She was about a year older than me, a good friend, real good.

She lived right 'cross the field from us. You could see her comin'. The children around there used to say, "That old white cracker. Why do she visit you so much?" Well, I told them that we were just friends. But I didn't tell them what we were doin' because she didn't want nobody to know it. And she would say, "That is our secret," and so I kept it as our secret.

And when we got older, she would tell me about her boyfriends, and I would tell her about mine. And she would ask me, "Willie, what difference is it in white and in colored?"

"Well," I told her, "I don't think that there is no difference—there no difference in God's sight. If there was, then we would die and you all would live. But we all have to die. To God it don't make no difference."

She said, "You is right about that. I wonder how would it feel if a colored boy went with me and a white boy went with you?"

I said, "It wouldn't make no difference. Because God give the colored nature and He give the white nature. The only difference that there is, is in the skin."

And so, whilse us got on that subject, we talked and talked.

And she says, "I don't know why folks are like that. I wonder why the whole world can't join together? Y'all go to different churches; we go to different churches. We all pray to the same God. Why can't we all be together?"

I says, "That's the way we is, down here. Up yonder, it ain't no separatin' up there. Anyways, that's what I hearin' people say."

And she say, "Well, why are they separatin' down here?"

"Now Janet, now you are askin' me somethin' that I don't know."

And we went on and talked 'bout this thing and that thing. And she say, "I wonder what is up there in them clouds? Have you ever sat down to yourself and wondered?"

I said, "Yes. They always told me that heaven was up there."

She say, "Do you reckon that there is a heaven up there?"

I say, "Peoples die, and they go away from here and they don't come back."

She said, "They don't go away—they put them in the ground."

I say, "No. That's the old body that they put down in the ground. But the Bible tells us that breath goes back to God that gives it."

She say, "Do you wonder if that is so?"

And I say, "You know that the Bible ain't told nothin' wrong, Janet."

I was friends with her up until I got married. Her daddy had his own farm. She didn't do nothin' but help her mother around the house. You didn't never catch her in the field workin'. She didn't have to work, 'cause her father had tenants on their farm and they just had a little place around the house. Her daddy didn't have to tend over five acres. That's all they done.

You could see her comin' across the field over there to my house. Sometimes I would be workin' and she would come across there, with a great big ole fruit jar full of ice water. I would chop out there till the end of the row, and we would sit down and we would talk and laugh and eat strawberries off the ditch. We would sit down under a tree and I would rest a while like that and talk, and then she would take the jar and carry it on back to her house.

Most of the other white girls was friendly, but she was the only one that would take time to sit and talk. The rest of the old white girls around there, they would speak to you. Sometimes I would be passin' and they would say, "Hey, Willie!" and then keep on about their business. But Janet, she would always come in and talk like that.

We strayed away from each other when we got growed. After that I ain't seen her no more.

Those days we was busy workin'. On Sundays we would go to church. And on Sunday evenin', after we come from church, we would have little cookouts and sit out and eat barbeque ribs and eat ice cream, cakes and pies. In the summer they would plan things like that. We would bring them old great long baskets full of food. We children would be playin', and the old folks would be cookin' and talkin'. Along then they didn't have no liquor or nothin' like that. And we would go to ball games. Daddy would take us all in the car. Momma, she didn't care nothin' about it much, but she would go just to be with we children. And sometimes they would be sellin' ice creams and snow balls there. Different little old boys from one neighborhood would play the other neighborhood. So that is the way we did. That was the fun we got along them days, and seems like them was the best.

And some Sundays you didn't go no place like that. Aunt Dodie would come, and everybody would sit and sing Christian songs. I used to lust to hear Uncle Charlie sing because he would hoot that song. And we would stand in the door while they were singin'. They would come out and it would be hot long 'bout then. Seemed like you could look and see them lazy old larks in the sky, it would be so hot. And they would come out and get some chairs and sit around outdoors around the tree, drinkin' lemonade. By and by you would hear them say, "I got to go in now, 'cause work tomorrow." That would be on a Sunday. Seemed like it was good livin'.

Now, we didn't never work Sundays or Saturdays. Long the time when you were puttin' in 'bacca, if that patch wouldn't hold until Monday, Daddy would get up early that Saturday mornin' and he would go over the field and we would put that in. But excusing that, we didn't work on Saturdays. That was the only kind of work that he would ask us to do on Saturdays, 'cause we had to get our clothes ready for Sunday.

Every Sunday, before we made a fire in the stove, or made a bed, or put on any clothes, he would call us to the front room and have Sunday mornin' prayer with his family. He was tryin' to serve God, and he wanted us to serve Him too. He would get down and he would pray. We'd have a song, then we would have scripture readin' in the Bible. After that, we'd have another couple of songs. Then, he would tell us go on about our work.

Daddy was not baptized till he was 41 years old. See, Momma was sick and we hear her father died. That day at twelve she got a telegram—special delivery it was—for to come home. So Daddy took us all in the car. They done carried Granddaddy to the funeral home and had him embalmed and brought him back to the house. Momma was cryin' and Daddy had hold to her. Durin' that time they carried him to the church that he preached at. Granddaddy was a preacher and he was 88 years old. It was in March. Reverend Berry, he was kind of old too, preached his funeral. When the hearse rolled up in the yard, a storm broke out. Granddaddy told them before he died don't take his body on no hearse, take him to church on horse power, but they didn't do that. They say it looked bad. So they took him on and they buried him. And when we came back, it was rainin' too. It was rainin' so bad, and Daddy was drivin' across the bridge. You know, one of those old plank bridges. It went across the road, and the boards was floatin', it was so bad. Daddy come on home then, and that Wednesday night he went to church, to prayer service. Daddy got right up and went to the Mourner' Bench and said, "God, help me change." He said God was with him in that storm, and God would be with him always. So he was baptized. That changed his life. After, he joined the choir, and they made him a deacon in the church. He said that him and his household was goin' to serve the Lord as long as we stayed under his roof.

Momma been a member of the church before Daddy. When we moved near Chimin' Bell Chapel Church and School, when I was still little, she went and joined and was baptized. In a pool full of water they baptized her, and she believed she would get better. After it seemed like she had a change, you know—it come a change into her life. You seen a person look like he's down, but when you come into Christ seem like your spirit will be lifted up. She was still sick, but seemed like her spirit was lifted up. She sung, she praised the Lord up until she died.

She said she felt a lot better after Daddy give her that medical treatment when we was livin' in St. Michaels. She went on, about maybe twelve years, and then she was taken with a heart attack. From the heart attack she had a stroke. She stayed in the hospital a month or more. And then she passed.

I would go every day to see her when she was in the hospital. It was about two miles. Sometimes I would walk, and sometimes my husband would take me. We was married then, and we was workin' a farm on halves. I was thirty-two then, when she passed. And after they buried her, it didn't seem like I could go on. And I asked God to give me strength to go on. She always told us to pray and ask God to help us. She would tell us, "One day, I'm goin' away and leave you. You won't find nobody is close as I am to you." And I said, "Why my mother talkin' like that?" My sister said, "She don't feel good. She knows she ain't got long to live."

So my mother's sister died. And then my mother. They was only six weeks apart when they died. And in that summer, long about June, I was taken sick too. You seen people with sugar in the blood, but I had salt in my blood at the time. The medicine and the treatments doin' me good, and they brought me home the fourteenth day of August. It was the same hospital that my mother died in.

In the hospital I felt a fear, bein' it was the same place. Ain't you never felt a fear? I had that feelin' that she would come where I was, but I didn't see her. So when I come out of the hospital I came home. I wasn't asleep, but I was just dozin'. And I could feel her presence. Ain't you never felt like there was somebody near you? Well, that's the way I felt when I first came home.

After that I went on and on and lost weight. I lost 70 pounds. All my clothes, they wouldn't fit. So my sister come, the one that died last April. She says, "I'm the oldest, and I come to give you advice. All we do is try to meet her one day."

And then I got to sayin' to myself that God took her. After then, seemed like it was upliftin'. Ain't you never been so burdened down, it seemed like a person would come in and jus' say one word of courage and that will uplift you spirit towards God? I was. I was only thirty-three years old, and that's the time I turned to God. One mornin' I was sick there and seemed like somethin' said, "Pray," and I started to pray, and it seemed like somethin' was carryin' me. I couldn't get a hold of myself. When I did get straightened out, it seemed like somethin' was tellin' me to turn, meet Jesus half way. So then I turned to God. So I've been tryin', treadin' that narrow path. I knows we all can't be perfect, 'cause you know the old flesh is weak. We got to pray,

I say, to keep the devil off our backs.

My daddy told me to trust in the Lord. I have a letter here. That is the last letter he wrote before he died. He said, ''Willie, you know you always have been the sickly one in the family. But you pray and ask God to help you. Only trust God and talk to him.''

And I do just what he told me. You know when I was living on Runyon, here in Newark, and one mornin' I was on the bed then sick, and they was somethin', seemed like it come right through that window. Somethin' come through that window and it jumped. It was in the form of man, had a tail like a cat, and it had on these here brown Florsheim shoes, and that thing was blazin' away. It was a gray headed man, and the robe he had on wasn't white, it was gray. I said, ''Lord have mercy,'' and that thing went well away.

Daddy called me on the phone. He was up North, in New York. I tells him 'bout it. Daddy tells me, ''Pray. You ain't prayin' hard enough. You've got to give up, and turn soul and body and heart— give it all to the Lord. You'll find out you'll be better.''

That's what he told me on the phone, and I'll never forget that man. He was a good father. We went to his buryin'. He died one night in the house by himself. We went to his funeral and buryin' and come back. I was sittin' in this here room and asked God why did he go. He peered back through that door and looked at me and smiled and went right away.

So I said, ''Well, I don't know what's comin' next but I'm goin' to try to serve God.''

When we was at the funeral, my little grandson had to see a doctor. We was takin' him home from the office and he says, ''There's a white rabbit.'' My husband gets out of the car to help the boy into the house. I said I wasn't gonna get out 'cause t'was already dark. Sittin' up there in the car and this here same rabbit comes by again, and that rabbit had wings! It didn't frighten me right away.

When my husband come out I told him about it. He got in and stepped on the starter and it ground. I said, ''What ails the car?'' After a while it started. He come out of the lane and got there on the highway and cut the engine off. He said, ''I'm goin' see would it start.'' It just started right on up. I told him when we got goin' that I believed that was a token.

You know, sometimes you'll see those tokens before people pass away. I seen a token, a great big, black bear, reachin' his mouth into a shuck of corn—and then my momma passed in three days. That was a token. It used to frighten me, but now it don't bother me at all.

I prays and ask God to help me along. If it weren't for prayers I would have done been gone on, I think. My life changed, I think, on account of my mother. After all that grievin' I tried to take it easy and I said, "I want to meet her one day," and I prayed, askin' Him to let me see her face one day when my life is over. Just like I'm askin' to see my sister. Her funeral was in April. And she was in the same hospital that my mother died in. She was singin' this song, "I'm searchin'," and after she sung that song, she dropped her haid and never another word. They stretched her out on the bed 'cause she had the last breath gone out o' her. Now I want to meet them when my life is over.

So that's why I tries to do the best I can. If I do wrong, I don't know—I knowed these here little biddy things you do will keep you out of the kingdom of heaven. But I fight against them things and ask God what are the right things to do and the right way to go. 'Cause when I walks through my neighborhood and goes to church, I want this little light of mine to shine.

5

The Master Called Me to Preach the Bible

My father didn't recognize that I was goin' in the ministry 'cause I didn't have no knowledge of it myself. But my mother. . . I remember one Sunday afternoon. We was to a service, and it was a man preachin'. I went out the door, and when I came back she looked at me and she said she could see the ministerial call all in me.

And she said to herself, "Lord, my Clifford is goin' to be a preacher. I can see it on him. I may be dead, but my son is goin' to preach before he die."

Well, I didn't never thought that I'd be able to stand before the audience and tell them what the Master said they should do—as a minister of the Gospel. I did serve as a deacon on the board of my church for twenty-one years. I would have been there right now if the Master hadn't called me. I can't remember how old I was when I started thinkin' of the ministry—can't see that point clearly now. But when I started thinkin' 'bout it, it was four years before I made it known that the Master had called me. And in that space of time I could see myself nice in the Spirit, standin' round on the communion table, all dressed in white, breakin' the bread and passin' around the wine. And that Spirit stayed with me until I made known to the people that the Master had called me to preach the Gospel.

See, I always thought that people ought to live together as children of God. Whatever comes up to you, there ought to be some way that you can thrash it out. I had that desire. In my childhood days sometimes, in the community, I run in contact with boys, you know, as boys do, have misunderstandings. Sometimes we fight, which I never liked. Ought to be a way to do it without fightin'.

My father didn't have no land of his own, worked as a sharecropper. I had to spend my time workin' on the farm, only finished the fifth grade and started the sixth. I ain't never liked to chop cotton too well, 'cause it pull my neck in a crank when you're holdin' the hoe, you know. But at housin' time, when we was pickin' the peanuts up out o' the ground, shakin' them off and puttin' them on the shelf, I liked that pretty much. I wasn't too well with the cotton; crawl too much on my knees. Sometimes some stalks was higher than others and we pick it just like this when it gets high. Most of the time we get on our knees. I have picked up as high as 230 pounds of cotton a day. I remember kids, they talk about three hundred pound pickers. But every day I picked over 200 pounds. I ain't never been called one of them champion pickers. It just seemed like I did it on my own merits. I ain't never been known as a "real" cotton picker.

With my father, they never has been an hour or a minute that he did somethin' mean that I couldn't take it. I never did run off, stayed 'round there until we come to be reconciled, I and my father. I knowed he was my father, I was his child, so we ain't had no whatcha call cat-down, or somethin' like that. I was close to him. When he passed, I was lookin' at him on the bed.

The school we went to was a little place, set near the railroad, out in the woods. It was one big room school. All the children around come to that school. Crowded school.

Three of us went—my folks had three children to live. Now her, my mother, was named Ruby Anderson before she married my father. When she married my father then she was a Carter, Ruby Carter. My father, his name was Samuel Jackson Carter. My brother, his name was Arnold Carter, my sister was named Jennie Carter, and I, Reverend Clifford S. Carter, now.

And we went to the school out in the woods. When it was cold we had to go out in the woods and get those lighted notches, we call them, break them up and make a fire for the school. Notches come from pine, out of pine trees. The tree lay down, the main meat part of the tree rot off, and then you've got the heart there. When you strike a match to it, it's just like paper almost.

See, I come along in that day. And I stayed on the farm until I was twenty-one. And I married on the farm. The farmin'—that's what you might say the main, important part of my life. Because I know more about farmin' than I do the cities. Now you take the farm. It is a good place, I can tell everybody that. It's a good place for to live, providin' you can get in the right county. What I mean by that, I mean if you can get the equipments and the place that you can provide a good farm for yourself, you can raise what you want, and you can pay the man how much rent he say he wants you to pay him. Then the rest of it go to you for to pay on your bills.

Sharecroppin' is different from rentin'. In sharecroppin' you've got to pick out the whole field of cotton, you've got to shake up all the peanuts, and then it's all got to be ginned out or thrashed out. Then here come the time of sellin' it. You've got to pay for the fertilizer, all that seed, and everythin'. And you got to give him one half when you sell it. All those bills comin' out of your part now. And his part come clean. You got to pay for what happened there on the farm—all that got to come out of your half. That's the advantage that they have in sharecrop most o' they do in rent-a-crop.

Now, some landowners, good landowners, they will give you more opportunity to do something if you is a sharecropper. Around in my area, in Georgia, there was white landowners, more so than there are others. Mighty few blacks owned their own farms. Couldn't even hardly name them, mighty few. All those farms around there was owned by whites, them big farms. What little farms was owned by the blacks is just enough for them, entirely. I'm telling you just like it is.

I remember when I first started to farmin', was just a kid, I remember that I did a job there one day that the overseer thought I wouldn't be able to do. The overseer is this here man who brings down the message from the boss man. Stands 'tween you and the boss man. You got a overseer when you don't have no land of your own. See my father wasn't a sharecropper but he worked as a sharecropper, didn't have no land of his own. And the overseer takes the message from the boss and pass it on to you.

And I remember one time I was workin' an old mule there and the old mule was skittish. I came that night, just about dark—you work till sundown. This ol' mule all at once he made just like that. When he did all I could do to keep him from fallin' out. I got right down off that mule and give that mule a good whippin'. That's what stands out to me till now. And the overseer said I did a good job, 'cause I was just a young one, just beginnin'.

I enjoyed farmin', enjoyed farmin'. Stayed with my mother and father till I was twenty-one. Got married. The married life was fine. At first we stayed on the same farm down there. The name of the farm was Smith's farm, and we shared crop with the Swansons—they owned the land.

We stayed on that same farm my father once lived. He died in 1913. I didn't stay there all the time. After a time we moved 'round, you know, to see if we could find a better place. That's the nature of farmin'. When I take over I try all I can do to make farmin' what I thought it should be. That is, to raise and cultivate what was allotted off to me as my share.

We canned up stuff for the winter—did right much of that. I raised practical all the meat that took us through the year. Sweet potatoes. All like that.

To keep sweet 'tatos for to set them out next year, we just plow them up and lay them out and let them dry out some. Then we make a circle and that's considered to be the hill. Get some pine straw and put up there and salt the sound 'tatoes, those that didn't have no cuts on them. Then take some corn stalks and put up like that, and just fill it all up with dirt. Keeps it up long comes spring time. Time come to rebale them, get youself, make a long bed, set out you plants in there.

In this day and age they got a potato house built, where there's steam heat and a certain temperature, all year long. You see them in the store now, they come from places like that. But in that day that's the way it was kept.

I raised seven children to get grown. When I got to the place that I needed help on the farm, then the children would come to help me out. Besides there was other people to help. It was one of those kinds of farms. You could go out and hire them to bring their men to give you a boost up.

Some of the children went to school, and some didn't go too long. Didn't none of them leave the farm until they was of age, twenty-one. I got three boys in the city, right here. And three girls right here in Newark. Then I got one down there in Georgia. He's followin' public works, workin' on a golf course and all that.

Those twenty-one years as a deacon for the Burnin' Bush Baptist Church down there, there couldn't a member in the church around in that community could have come up and lay hands on me about anythin' wrong. In those years if I saw one or two out o' line, and the news begin to spread in the community, then it's time for some action to be taken.

I go to them and ask them, "Those rumor which I hear concernin' you, are they true or not true? If it is, I would like to know, because there's alarm in the community. I'm here to rest alarm and get the facts."

And anybody 'round home can come up and tell you this evenin' that Reverend Clifford S. Carter was a man that kept a' servin' his community. The whites can tell you that. The whites can tell you this evenin' 'round my home that Clifford Carter is a man who tries hard to stand up and be counted as a man.

The blacks in my community, them that drink and gamble, they had respect for me, and have it there now. One time this man got drunk in this little town. Now, I was in town too at the time, and I saw him when the other brethren take him out home. Well, durin' the week he came to my house.

Said, "Deacon, they tell me I was in town drunk. And I don't know how I got home."

I said, "You don't?"

"No, I do not."

I said, "Well, I'll tell you how you got home. It was some friends 'round there that took care of you and take you home."

He said, "Did I got to the Black Cat where all the colored people go?"

I said, "You went to the Black Cat and that ain't all. Crossin' the street, the main highway (it came through the little town) the cars stopped in order that you'd get out o' the way."

He said, "No, I didn't."

I said, "Yes, you did."

And then he said, "I want to meet the whole church. I don't want only the deacons of the church to pardon and forgive me in the study. I want to stand before the whole body on the third Saturday of the month and tell them all that I have done wrong. And all of you what is in favor and ready to forgive me for my wrong doings, I want you to stand up on your feet."

And that's what he done. That time the whole church stood up. There was shoutin' and singin'. You know, the Scriptures teaches us that a good name is better for you than riches. You may not have a dime sometimes, but if your name is alright, somebody will come to your rescue. An open confession is good for the soul.

Now I got into a fight one time with one of the clerks in the store, in the farm in which I lived. A white clerk. I was to wait on a man that night. He was gettin' married that night, but I had a toothache. I told him I didn't think I'd be able to serve on account I didn't want no cold to get in my jaw. And so, I went to town that afternoon carryin' a load of potatoes and such as that and I had to bring a load of furniture back in the wagon for the store. I worked for the man who owned the place where the farm belonged. He had a big store down there, you could buy most anythin' you want.

And when I got back it was evenin', it was night 'cause I

couldn't make no headway. Late, and my tooth was hurtin' me, and this man was waiting on me to get married. So I rolled up there to the door of the store, knocked on the door. The clerk came, opened the door. It was rainin' right then. I comes, sittin' them there boxes of furniture off at the store.

He said, "Clifford."

I said, "Yes, sir." (Always had manners.)

Said, "Don't set off no more like that. Put 'em where I can read the number."

I told him, I said, "Mr. Landy, you see it's rainin' out here, and it's cold. I'se not goin' to take time out—my time is out already. I ain't goin' to take time out in this cold for you to take the seal number off every one of these boxes 'fore I can carry them into the store. I'm goin' to put them in the house. Then you can take the numbers later on."

He said, "Well, if you put another one up there, we'll go together."

I said, "We'll go together then."

I put another one up there in the store. That time, when he jumped, I grabbed him just like that. And we went down between the wagon and the store, tied up just like snakes.

I made out just fine on that. After he found out that I was a man to be 'fraid of, and a man who believes in right. He's still down there. Now, when he meets me, him and me is still good friends. Had a correspondence with him. And here, this year that just gone by, when I go home I don't have to walk the back streets. Walk the front street, the main drag. White people on the street when they see me, they put up their hand to me. They knows I is a man who stands up and wants to be counted as a man.

6

You Got a Farm, You Get the Peanuts

I was thinkin' when I was a child, always thinkin' about the way I could make a livin' in case I lost my mother. I didn't figure I could. That's when my mother was real sick. While I was sittin' in my father's car, I used to think all those things...wonderin' how could I make my livin' in case I lost her.

I was around about twelve years old. My mother got better, but just about three, four years after then she died in childbirth. And my father died young too, in his forties. And it kinda went tough wit' us. I had six brothers and four sisters. I wasn't the oldest, but next to the two oldest ones. And I said, "Well, the biggest one can try to operate the farm. Someone's got to hire hisself out and work, so's to support the rest of them." And so, we made out all right. We worked out that year and made peanuts on the farm. Done all right, sold the peanuts and everythin'.

See, we had a farm, it was our own farm. My grandmother, she bought that farm when slavery time was. She was workin' for rich people, and she'd pay them fifty cents a day. That's the way she bought it. She got 350 some acres for fifty cents an acre. She saved her coins like that. She'd been married twice. Her second husband, he died. He was a man that liked to drink a lot. He fell out of a buggy tryin' to come up to the farm. Grandma buried him. My father told me about it. I didn't know nothin' about it 'cause I wasn't even born yet.

My grandmother separate the farm then, and give them so much, so many acres—thirty acres a piece, thirty of plain land and thirty of woodland—to each one of her children, two sons and two daughters. She had one daughter in New York and she didn't never come on the farm, but she had it in case she did get married. And she did get married and did come on. Her husband farmed there about two or three years. She went back to New York, and he worked a few years there. He'd go back to New York to see her, worked for her as long as he could. Every fall come, he'd take off and go to New York. That's the way it was.

She died in New York. All of them died out.

I went to school in Chamberlain. It was kinda way out, just about three miles from town, a small school. My school teacher's name was Lily Jasper. She married a old man, purser at the school. He couldn't see good. One day he put his hand right on a big rattlesnake, and it like to bit him up. I was lookin' right at him, and I said, "Git back, git back." He backed up, and I shot the snake with a shot gun and killed him, so naturally that old man liked me. So his wife was my school teacher. She was still there when I first got married.

I didn't get too far in grades 'cause my daddy and mother kept me workin' all the time. So I didn't get to go to school as much as I wanted. My sister, now, she went to school. My mother kept her in school. Boys, we was cuttin' 'bacca wood, 'cause at that time we was doin' our tobacca in wood. My father kept us cuttin' wood. In the winter time you had to cut wood to cure out the 'bacca in the summer time. We'd stack it up, in long cords just as high as you could stack them. Oak wood, cut it in cords, stack it all. This kept us busy for three months in the winter time. I'd go to school every now and then. Rainy days you couldn't cut wood—that's when I went to school.

I didn't feel good about not goin' to school, but I had to do what they told me. I did that way as long as I stayed with them, until they died. That's what I was raised up. My parents was the only background that I had. I was so young. I figured that I couldn't make it if it wasn't for them. But the Lord come along and took them, and He made a way for me to make it. I didn't have no dream that I could make it without them.

I 'cided when I come up here to Newark I'd go back to school. I did go for a year or two, but it was too much for me. I was workin' hard and tryin' to get up somethin'. I didn't stay in there like I ought'd to stayed.

My father had three head of mule. In summer he'd set us out on the farm for to plough. We did what he told us to do, the best we knew how. All of us brothers worked together. When chopping come, we chopped out our crop and kept it clean. Had a beautiful crop. My mother was there then. We got along good, had plenty of hogs. We raised hogs for Billy Giles. He used to bring feed down there every Saturday and we'd raise them for him. Had plenty of land to raise the hogs. And cows—we used to sell cows to the market. Sold a lot of cows and stuff, beef and stuff, in the towns and cities like that. On Sundays, my mother went to church. My father did too. On Saturdays we'd go to the city and buy clothes—stuff like that—and come on

back home. We went by car. Daddy had a car. They used to call it the
A model Ford, one spoke wheel. With my mother and father livin' we
got along good on the farm. When we was grown we didn't know how
to control it.

So when my mother died we tried to farm ourselves. And then my
sister, she cleared out and went to live in Charlottville. That's about
sixty miles outside of our little town. She's still stayin' there.

I was workin' then for Howard Bee. I was comin' from Norfolk
with a load of tin and that same day I was taken with bronchial pneumonia. Howard Bee's son got it too, only he died. Howard Bee said he
didn't see how in the world a poor man's son could live and his son die.

I was livin' there in my hometown of Chamberlain with my
mother's family—they had a home there. Still, I didn't want to walk out
there every evenin' and come back to work every mornin'. So I stayed
outside with Mrs. Henry and that's where I had bronchial pneumonia.

So we kinda had it tough. Had our own farm, but had it tough
tryin' to make a livin' from the start and bein' too young. So when we
did get up, got in shape, shaped up right, that's when I got married.
Then me and my wife stayed around there. I was workin' for the
Howard Bee wholesale house, still workin' there. I worked there for
two more years. That was when the Hoover days was. Everythin' got
tight. Job—I was workin' two days a week. I couldn't make a livin'.
Rent was steep at that time, 'cording to what you were makin'. So I
decided then I'd go out to the farm.

One of the houses burned up. I told my wife then we could build
a three-room apartment there. I'd go down to the saw mill and scrap
up some old timber. That's when I started to learn how to do carpenter
work myself. So I went back to the farm and started farmin'. I built
myself a small house back there; nobody helped me with the house. I
bought a mule, a old gray mule. And Seymore Daniels was sellin' old
furniture right there in town so I got me some old furniture and paid
for it in a year's time. He gave me a break. We lived there around
about six, seven, or eight years. I sent my daughter to school.

That first year I went to the rich man, tried to get some peanuts to
plant my crop. He wouldn't let me have peanuts. He said, "You got a
farm, you get the peanuts." So everythin' was tight long then with me.
We went to the court house, tried to borrow some money there. The
white people there knowed we had land, knowed I had property. They
wouldn't let me have no money—I couldn't borrow any. Me and my

wife had a old '41 Buick, green Buick. So me and her decided to come on back home.

I said, "I don't know what to do. I can't get the crop, even though I got the land. Always broke. Ready to plant my crop, can't get my peanuts to plant it with. I have to get my peanuts."

So then I went on and tried again. And Bud Andrews, he did let me have some fertilizer on credit. He let me have a hundred and fifty dollars worth of fertilizer, and I got that and made that crop out.

But wasn't no money comin' in that first year whiles we waitin' for that crop. So I worked at the church there in Chamberlain. That was Howard Bee's church. Every Friday and every Saturday I went and made my money then to support my wife and my daughter. That's what we'd eat off that first year. They paid me five dollars a day to work at the church. I set out the chairs for the Sunday School and the Sunday mornin' meetin'. Then I'd clean up the church, and the minister, he'd come in there and see if everythin' was all right. Then he'd pay me. He'd pay me $10 that Saturday after he'd check out everythin'. I mowed the grass too. Sometime my wife, she'd come up there and help me too, straighten out the church, dustin' and do all the cleanin'. So we worked along like that and made that crop.

We'd set the tobacco out with a 'bacca setter. We had a mule pullin' the setter along. There's two, three people that have to go out, one drives the mule and the others gets on each side of the seat. The setter, you know, sets down in the ground. You put your rows in a ridge, and that setter goes right along, and you have to drop those plants there in the holes. That's the way you set it out, like that. It takes off and goes to growing, like that. You have water and everything in the setter, so everytime it goes down in the hole, you put the plant down there and "ticky," she'll shoot a mouthful of water down on that plant. Then the packer comes from behind there and packs in that plant. All that at the same time.

My brother-in-law would help me. After I set mine out we'd go over and set his out. That's the way we did.

You've got to sew them in a bed in the winter time. First you burn the 'bacca beds off. Most of the people goes in the woods and builds the beds where warm at. You get a place where there's no grass there, leaves all the time. So you 'bacca beds won't be full of grass, and when the plants come up you don't have to be pullin' the weeds up. You clear the land too when you do that. Burn it off. Got to get all the stumps up. When you burn the ground you tears it up; sometimes you take a tractor with one of them cut plows on it to tear it up. Then you make your 'bacca bed, 'round about 200 yards or 400 yards, somethin' like that. You put a net over it, over the top of it, so comes snow or stuff it won't kill your plants. 'Cause the plants come up 'fore the winter get over. The 'bacca net keeps it warm, too.

When your plants comes up, it gets about time, ready to reset. That's in the summertime, about the time people start planting corn. Plants already come up and start growin' big. Go there and pull them. You get people to come there and pull the plants and put them in a basket. You get a lot of baskets—get those from Planters Basket Factory. They sell them all over the world, those baskets. You get those plants and put them in a basket straight. You've got to pick the largest plants, pull for the largest ones. Then you get to reset them, about two and a half foot apart.

When you get people to pull the 'bacca beds, everybody 'round in the neighborhood works together. All the colored people went together. The way they set the crop out, they got to reset them.

Then the plants start growin'. When they have big leaves on there, they grow up tall as I is, 'bout six feet, some of them grow up five feet, then you top it out. That's so the leaves will grow, spread large. So that's the way we did.

When it's time to pick the 'bacca, you go out with three persons. One would be on this side of the truck and one on this side. They would be a "luking horse" over there and one on this side too. It stands up that tall, and you put a stick on it, 'bacca stick. Now, I'm up on the truck, standing to my "horses." Well, my two handers, one here and one there, they passes the 'bacca on the truck to me. I take it and I "luke" it on the 'bacca stick. You tie your string here at the top of the stick. You put a hand of 'bacca on this side, and then over on this side you place another hand. But you've got to place the 'bacca so it can hang down on the stick. Then when you've got one out, you've got to do another one like that.

After you get the 'bacca on the stick you have a stick trotter. He takes it and places it in the rack. Then after, they hang it up in the barn to cure it. See they would have joists, ceiling beams, and hang it so far apart. It hangs down, and then you can put your fire on. Now, like you put the fire on on Monday, on Friday sometime durin' the day you cut the fire out. Let your barn cool, and you can go up there and get the 'bacca.

The fire is wood. Sometimes they would have a oil fire. There would be long joints of pipe, big, that would hold the fire to keep it from catchin' on anythin'.

I knowed I couldn't house my 'bacca with my wife and me and my daughter—I'd need some help. I didn't have no money to hire help with at the time, 'cause I was makin' so little money at the church. So my wife and me got in the car together and went to the bank to borrow some money for housin'. The rich man in town wouldn't let me have anythin'. So then at the bank, the bank manager found out I had a pretty 'bacca crop. He took a lien on my crop for the money. He let me have $500. That's the National State Bank, way out of Chamberlain, way over in the next county. When I talked to the bank manager I told him I done lost my barn, it burned up, I didn't have the money to have the 'bacca in, to house my crop. He asked me where the farm was at and everythin'. So he come back there and checked my crop and found I did have a beautiful crop. He said, "Where you goin' to cure this 'bacca at? You don't have no barn."

I told him, "A man I know got a lot of barns up there and maybe I can rent one. He got six of them and he won't fill up all of them."

So me and him got in his car and went up there to see the man and I got to rent his barn. So the manager let me have $500. I had my crops and everythin' housed that year. And the first selling I sold was $375 worth, first Saturday. So I paid all my debts.

I wasn't able to buy the clothes that I needed myself to go downtown. Other people all dressed up on Saturdays and Sundays—I couldn't do it. The little clothes that I had, I had to put them on my wife.

I said, "Well, I let her look decent. I'll wear the same clothes that I work in."

She washed them and cleaned them. I had to wear my broken-in shoes that I plowed in. I wasn't able to buy dress shoes and her dress shoes and my daughter dress shoes, too. I wasn't able to do it. But when I did get in shape to do it, I bought me some. But when I housed that crop, I went back and paid that debt off.

And come up the next year, I decided to raise me some hogs. And the lady there, runnin' a service station out there on the corner of the lane, well, she was very nice. I used to go there and get credit from her. She's dead now. I had hogs that would come out there, 'cause I didn't have no fences. They used to come out there in the road, but they was gentle pigs. She'd always yell at me. I could see her standin' in the lane. It wasn't very far from my place, just about four thousand yards.

I could hear her when she'd yell about those pigs comin' out to the road and a car could run over them. I'd go out there and get them. They was gentle and they'd come on back to the house just like gentle cats, very tame.

I used all those hogs for meat. Then someone came along and stole half of them. I knowed who it was, but I didn't say anythin' about it 'cause they was a relation to me. I checked up on the meat. Went to Calhoun's store in town. Checked the meat in there and asked him did he buy any meat in there. He said, ''The meat I bought is right over here.''

Some of my pigs was marked with an S. I marked those pigs so I could tell them from other people's pigs, branded them with my name right on the ham. So when I killed them that brand was still on them. That's the way I found out where my meat went to. I didn't get any money back. Calhoun told me who it was that sold that meat, and it was a relation to me—my first cousin's son. I told her about it, but I didn't press no charges. I just let the meat go.

I told my wife, ''The Lord made a way for us. We'll overcome that.'' We made out all right that year. I got a job haulin' peanuts. That way, in the winter time when everythin's dead on the farm, I was workin' for the peanut factory. I hauled them to the Planters Peanut Factory in Virginia, sometimes a couple of loads a day. Sometimes I go in the country in the cold rain, all around in the country there.

Then, after that I drove for a truck outfit. They'd tell me where to go get the load, and what truck I was gettin'. Drove fo' them in the winter time. That's the way I'd make my livin' in the winter time. Soon as summer come up I'd take my truck down and go back on the farm and started work.

For about five or six years we worked like that. Then I said, ''I'm not goin' to drive this year. I'll take off this year. We'll take off and I'll go to the Planter Basket Factory and work there in Suffolk.''

So I got me a job there and worked there that winter and stayed with my wife's sister there. I made a very good dollar that winter. I said, ''Maybe this year we'll have enough to support ourselves. We won't have to borrow nothin' from nobody, and we can pay for our fertilizer and stuff.''

See, I was already in debt with Daniel Hopkins. I gave him a deed of trust, a mortgage, for my share of the property—375 acres of land altogether. Yeah, everythin' got against me. When I was farmin' down there, it seemed like it all worked out against me. They didn't want to pay me nothin' for my stuff. Me and my wife, we do our own gradin'. Me and her sits in the barn and grades our 'bacca, grades the first grade and second grade, all like that. So now, we're ready to sell, and they put it all together. They doesn't grade it. But they was gradin' it for other farmers, long then when I was raisin' it.

Now, they had a 'bacca warehouse right here in Chamberlain. I go down there and gets my 'bacca on the floor, and they bid my crop down lower than they bid anybody else's. And I see my 'bacca was just as good as the white man's 'bacca. They bid my 'bacca 40¢, so I take it up off the floor and puts it on my trailer. Me and my wife then straightened it out, and we carried it to Seeman. They paid me top grade, first grade, $1.02 a pound in Seeman. That was my first grade. My second grade sold for 69¢ a pound and my third grade sold for 43 or 44¢; then the trash grade sold for 35¢. I sold 'round about $973 worth of 'bacca that day. So I went in the Seeman bank and I cashed my check. I got a good price in Seeman. If I sold it in Chamberlain it wouldn't bring anythin'.

Now, the white guys around us, on that road, some of them was pretty nice to me. One of the guys, he helped me some, lent me barn room to keep all my 'bacca from gettin' damp, but he was sneaky too. See, I was drivin' with my license "invoked," and he found out. I knowed my license was gone, but it made it so I couldn't get nowhere, couldn't even haul my crops. Sometimes you'd walk five miles to get somebody to haul my crop.

Well, this guy put Larkins, the state patrolman, on me. Every time I hit the highway he phoned the patrolman to let him know I was on the road. Well, he caught me at a time when I had to go places and didn't have nobody to drive for me. He chased me, but I outrunned him. So he sat out there in the highway, waitin' for me to come back. And when I come back out, there was three boys I picked up that was in the car. I tol' the boys, "The state trooper's out there; he chased me up here." So when he caught me, I got out of the car and went in the field. He didn't know who was drivin'. When they made the arrest they say I was drivin'. I say I wasn't. He didn't know who was drivin' 'cause he wasn't that close to me. But he knowed it was my car; he knowed the license number. And when the brake lights come on when I went up that lane, he knowed it was me, and he waited up in the field, way up in the field about half a mile.

He took me to court, but I got out of there. I have did some things wrong, and I knowed they was wrong. Well, I didn't know no one way out to get out of trouble. I had to tell a story. I had enough money, so I just bought 'em out. Way they had me jacked up, I had advantage o' him, 'cause I had three riders ridin' with me, and he didn't know who was drivin'. I had three testimonies, me and three, against everyone. I got a lawyer and got out of it.

I told my wife then, "When I get rid of this crop this year, I'm movin'. Goin' to Virginia and get me a new license. I can't make no living, don't I have a car."

One night, 'round about twelve o'clock, we moved out. I got me a trailer and moved everythin' out of Chamberlain. We moved everythin' after twelve o'clock, after the state trooper and everythin' quieten down. I was scared to come out through Chamberlain 'cause they had that road blocked, kinda watchin' for me. So we went out the other way, went to Virginia, and I got a license there.

Yes, everythin' got against me, so I went out of the farmin' business. I decided I'd go to work drivin' a truck for a coal yard in Virginia. They had a coal yard, the Mission Coal Yard, right there on Henry Street in Rummey, Virginia. We stayed there for about five years. Then couldn't find work there so I moved into Newark, and I've been in Newark ever since. Been here twelve years.

Had some ups and downs since I been here. When I first got to Newark my rent was high, so I didn't have no furniture or nothin'. I told her, "I'm goin' to work hard and try to get up enough to buy me some furniture and nice things like other people got. I'm goin' to try to get a house to myself." We was stayin' with Old Lady Jackson then. She charged us the top rent, twenty-five dollars a week just for one room and "use of" the kitchen.

But it was hard to get a job. Couldn't get no job nowhere. So I went over to Jersey City to some 'struction work. We was puttin' on a roof on a old house, takin' off slate shingles and puttin' on a shingle roof. One of the boys, an Italian guy, fell. I caught him and saved his life. All of them thought a lot of me. But then me and an Italian guy fell out. His daddy done called me some names, and I didn't like it so I quit.

I left construction work then, started workin' for a chemical factory. That man was a German, makin' lanolin, where you make hair grease and stuff out of it. We worked out there for six or seven years. Then he went out of business, quit workin', 'cause he got so old, 86 years old.

After that I got a job workin' for a oil company. They ship canning

oil, quart cans, gallon cans, fifty gallon drums, shippin' all over the
United States. They ship a lot of stuff to Puerto Rico. Canning the oil,
treat the oil, run it through the machine and clean the oil. Different
grades, thirty weights, twenty weights, all like that. Diesel engine oil
too. Shoe leather stuff, we made that too.

I worked there until they froze all the unions, started layin' all
the guys off, eighteen at a time. Laid most of them all off now. It's the
Getty Oil Company, and Getty's the richest people in the world.
They've got a lot of mens workin', but they got a lot of mens ain't
workin'.

So that's where I'm drawin' my income, 'ployment compensation, at now. I've been laid off now for about three and one-third
months. I'll pick up that check today. That'll be $144. They pay me
every two weeks. They give me nine months on account of the time I
been workin' there.

My union dues, I pay them every week. And so they had insurance
on my wife, insurance on me too, the Blue Cross and Rider J altogether. Now my wife got hurt on the job. She workin', her accident
was on the job, but I had to take care of all her responsibilities. Blue
Cross didn't have no right to pay her. She was workin' on a job, the
job's supposed to take care of her accident. It's their responsibility,
but they didn't do it.

She slipped on the wet floor at work and fell and had trouble with
her back and arm ever since. But they didn't pay; they didn't give no
reason either. They come here after I started takin' them to court and
offered two thousand dollars not to take them to court. They never give
no information, whose name it was who come. They sent a man here
and he said to my wife, "You take that offer now."

She said, "Well, I want my husband or somebody here to take
the offer 'cause I want them to be satisfied with it."

He told her he'd be back to talk with me, but I ain't never seen
him. Everytime he come in, he come in and try to bribe my wife. I told
my lawyer about it. He said, "Next time he comes in and try to bribe
her like that, try to get his name." The lawyer don't know who it is if
you don't get the name. The next time he come here to talk with her I
didn't get no details. Ain't nothin' we'll be able to did about that.

Then after I went out of the farmin' business, and I stayed up
here a couple of years, my brother come up here and said, "Didn't
you know your sister done give the map of the land to the white people
in Chamberlain? They got that land and they sold it."

Before I left, when I left the land laid out, I sent my brother. But he couldn't tend it. So he rented some of it out. But I sent my brother my share of the tax every year.

So I said, "How can they sell the land? I wasn't there. They can't sell my land like that until I agree to sell my share of the farm. Special me, 'cause I farmed there."

Me and my wife gets on the bus out of Newark, goes down there and see about it. I talked to Lawyer Smith about it. See, I give a deed of trust, a mortgage, to Daniel Hopkins and he died of a heart attack. I paid half the mortgage off. I didn't know who else to pay it to after he died; I didn't understand. His wife didn't say anything to me, and I didn't say anythin' to her. Old man Daniel, before he died, I used to do a lot of work for him and for his son, too. He's still livin'.

The original deed of trust, Calvin Smith in Chamberlain, he had it. I gave him the legal paper to keep in the safe for me in case somethin' come up before I paid the bill off. He was my lawyer; he supposed to be workin' for me. Workin' against me all the time. 'Cause he was administratin' for Mrs. Hopkins and he was the lawyer for me too, and I didn't know what was goin' on. Daniel Hopkins' girl come out of college, picked up that mortgage, and she swung it at me. My sister come in there and sold the farm and the Hopkins girl come to be a heir into my share of property. That's what she did.

That lawyer Smith, he was s'posed to give my papers back to me, and he give them to Mrs. Hopkins. She got the papers. I tried to get the papers from him for three years and ain't got them yet. He told me he was goin' to mail them to me, but he ain't mailed me nothin', not yet. He told me they got destroyed or somethin'.

See, there was my father, a brother and two sisters. All of them's dead now, so the land goes back to the heirs. I don't know how they sold it, but they sold it. I wasn't called in to share or agree to the sale or nothin'. When you sell heir property, all the heirs got to agree. Well, they sold the farm for $35,000. Fred Simmons, he's tax collector in the courthouse, he knowed the case, what the land sold for, everythin', he told my first cousin in Newark. But he didn't let me know nothin'. So I called home from Newark, to the courthouse, asked for my share of the farm and asked how did it work out like that. He said for me to talk to Lawyer Smith 'bout that, 'cause he's your lawyer. But he said, "I think he sold you out, just you."

I was stayin' in Newark when it happened. They didn't let me know anythin' at all about what was goin' on. They said they broadcast it on the radio. They didn't broadcast it on the radio in a station that has contact with the whole country, tryin' to find me. They didn't contact the whole country, just broadcast it in Chamberlain, that's all.

So I got a new lawyer now, tryin' to work out the problem for me. I been tryin' to shake it out. Still looks like everythin' worked against me. All the whites down there work against me. Fred Simmons, he's just as much in it as the rest of them. Took advantage of me all the way around.

I went all the way to Samford, got me a lawyer what's very religious. He don't work on Saturday and Sunday, only weektime. Saturday and Sundays, he says it's time for him to do his study in the church. Sundays, he's on the job for the Lord. Doesn't do no law practice on the special time he works for the Lord. Concentrates on the Lord then, can't practice the law then.

This lawyer's a colored lawyer. I got his telephone number and address too, at home. I call him; he calls me. He told me he's workin' on the problem. It's hard to work out, 'cause things down there against him. Lawyer Smith run the lawyer association around Chamberlain. He said, "You've got a whole stack against you. I'm just one, and I'm way over in Stamford." That's about a hundred miles from Chamberlain.

He said, "For one thing, you waited just a little bit too late." Course, it's not too late, 'cause the people who bought the land, they got four years to pay half that mortgage off.

So my lawyer told me I'm still goin' to have to pay that whole $550 all over again, 'fore he can take action for my share of the farm. That's what he called me about and told me two weeks ago. What money I did pay Daniel Hopkins 'fore he died, he return the checks. So I got my lawyer tryin' to check out, you know. Times back, ten years back, tryin' to check. Well, where's the checks at? Still ain't found no details yet. I don't know. They could have destroyed them at the bank. They mailed them out to me at my address, on the farm, but I didn't ever get them.

I'm willin' to pay the $550, I'm willing to pay the whole thing. But I have already paid half of it. They can't find no trace of it. So it looks like to me I'm goin' to have to pay that whole thing again 'fore he can take action.

But he has put out a suit for buyin' illegal property. They built a $35,000 house, a brick house, right in my share of the property. And now he's goin' to sue Lawyer Smith, 'cause he was administration for

Mrs. Hopkins and he was workin' for me all at the same time. My lawyer's been workin' on it three years. Hasn't made no success yet. It's cost me a bunch already. This lawyer, I done paid him 'round about $1,000. I kinda depend on him, but I don't know he's goin' to work out anythin' or not. I believe he'll give me a fair shake. That's the reason I picked him. Somebody so religious. People told me he was a fair lawyer. He's tryin' to do the right thing. That's in the law book to do that. That's what I wanted. Some people, they read the law book, but they know how to bear 'round it. Sometimes you get a fair judge, give you a fair shake down. But we got some judges right here, right in the city of Newark, will sell you out. Then you've got some you can't buy, right here in the city of Newark. I know that. I've been experiencin' that. I did the same thing with my revoked license in South Carolina.

So, I'm still fightin' against sellin' that land—heir property—still tryin' to get equal rights in the United States. I figure if anybody got any property, I don't figure anybody can take it but for taxes. Long as you keep your tax paid, I don't feel a man in the world can take a man's property away from him and sell it to somebody else.

7

They're Hypocritic

White people. . .they don't care for us, only our work. Some of them do like you enough, long as you stay in your place and don't try to get up there with them.

I'll tell you this. The South always was Jim Crowed until—what's his name—Reverend Martin Luther King came and got it to go through here now. President Kennedy. That's when the South got out of it. But you know what? It's just as bad here, in the North, just as bad as it was down there.

Those white people down there, they can do you a favor, you working on their plantation. They would help you. Some of them even would get a house for you and give it to you. You on their plantation, you working their farms, they'd give you a little land to work. They did us, you know. Course, when the end of the year come, you didn't have nothing. I couldn't dress like the other girls; I didn't have clothes like the other girls.

So, down there they would help you. Down there they'll let you know where you at in the first place, in the beginning. You know how far to go with them down there. But up here! Humph! They're just as bad! They're just like a snake in the grass. If there's a snake in the grass and you step in that grass and you don't know that snake is in there, it's going to bite you.

That's what it's like with the white up here. You don't know where you stand with them. It's Mrs. this or Mrs. that, or Mr. this or Mr. that—as long as you spend your money with them. But try to get out of the way, now, to get up there with them, and they'll let you know where you at. Up here they're two-faced, they're hypocritic and nasty. And I understand. I know. I worked for doctors and lawyers since I been up here.

I worked for a doctor out in West Orange, and that family was just as nasty as they can be. And now I worked for The Robert Treat Hotel. You meet all kind of people there. And I worked up here now in Montclair, worked for a lady there. And I thought she liked me a lot. You know, you can get fooled by these white people up here.

Honey, she got home one day and rushing me to get the dinner on the table. It was on Saturday. I only cooked one meal on week, and that was on Saturday when her husband was home. And I had a nice gravy to put on the table, and she didn't give me time to pour the grease off the gravy. And she came in there and did she...

"You call yourself a cook with all this grease? Get this grease out of here!"

So I was standing at the dining room table and I got mad too.

I said, "You're rushing me so fast, you didn't give me time to pour the grease off of the gravy bowl." Aw...me and her had it.

So I worked on there for a little while. My blood pressure was high one day, and I told her I wasn't coming in.

"If you're not coming in, don't come in at all."

I slammed the receiver down. I went up there and got my money. She thought I was joking, you know. I wasn't going to take her foolishness.

I walked out on many of them up here, because they was nasty. I worked with so many of them, I can't remember their names though. I walked out on the middle of a job. Just put the broom down. She thought I was working. She look—I be downstairs in the street with my coat and my hat and my bag, honey, and I'd be gone.

I didn't never have a nice person to work for up here. Let's see, I did have Mrs. Clay. She lived up on...she lived in Short Hills. She was very nice to me, but the real nice ones was down South, that I worked for as a teenager to babysit. My mother used to work there before I did. Then, after my mother died, then I still worked there for a while. And all those people in the South sent my mother beautiful flowers to go on her grave.

I did not associate with them down South; uh-uh, I knowed how far to go there. But up here they're only agreeing with you to get the work done. That's all. Don't fool yourself that they love you. None of them. They don't care for you. I used to be in the kitchen, listening to them talking about us. I make like I was busy, very busy, and be real quiet so I could hear them talking about us at the dining room table. About we colored people. I'm not kidding. They don't care nothing about us. They pretend, but they don't care nothing about you.

You know, down there you had to go to the back door to get what you want. And if they had anybody working around the house and you was a cook on the inside, they would tell you what to give the gardener working outside. Fix them a plate and take it out there on the steps and let them eat it. There was very few would let their gardeners come in the house and eat at the kitchen table down there. But in the long way up here you don't have to go to the back when you first get a job. You go to the front door. But after you get the job they want you to go around to the back door and come in.

And you know what? It's just because of the color of our skin. We are black. The Puerto Ricans can get a better break than we can. Did you know that? I noticed that. And they can't work, don't know how to work, like working in a hotel.

They were hiring one in the hotel, down on the first floor, that's my floor, to help me. I said, "Now, you get this bathroom, and I'll get the next bathroom." And then she'd come out of there. I go and check it. Honey! I'm telling you, I wish you'd seen them bathrooms.

I said, "Did you clean this?"

"Yeah, yeah, yeah."

I said, "Oh, no, you didn't neither. You making it hard on me."

They don't know how to clean, and they're nasty too, you know. Uh-huh. But they can get a better break than we can. You know why? Because we're black. That's right. They always can get better jobs. They don't work for almost nothing. And we will. I was only making $56 a week at the hotel.

If I would have finished school, I could have got a better job. All I did was work, slave in these white people's house. Since I been up here, this is the only kind of work I did. Work in laundries and the cleaners. That's the only work I knowed how to do. But if I could have got a education, oh, God, do you think I would have been working like that? Uh-uh. But that's all I did, all my life, you know, after I left home, off the farm. And down there, working in factories. I lived in Laurel, North Carolina for a while. They had nothing but factories down there.

I didn't get no farther than the fifth grade. I had to get out, stop school and go to work and help out with the rest of the kids while my mother got in bad health. There was six of us, and I was the oldest. I was born in North Carolina. I was growing up with my mother and father until she got in bad health.

We worked hard together. When I got big enough I started with the tobacco factory there, you know. I was about, I was around ten then. After we get the tobacco, on the farm, you know, and all that sort

of thing, then the factory open up, which will be in August. And my
mother put me up on this little box, and I just turned my back and was
packing 'bacca.

I wanted to do that to help my mother. Because when I'm ten,
that's the time she said, "You going to work this summer, and that will
save your own money and buy your own books for school." We had
to buy our books around there, you know.

So I worked in this factory with my mother. I was working ever
since I was ten years old. I used to be on the tobacco farm, too. We
would go out in Hurley County makin' tobacco. And we would draw—
make $1.50 a day. And then I would bring that home to my mother.
On a Friday we would get in 'round about eleven or twelve o'clock at
night, and we would stay home until Monday. And on Sunday we
would all get ready to go to church, because my mother was a very
religious person.

Oh, I loved my mother. She was a very sweet woman. I never
seen whiskey in the house. I never heard her curse. And my father,
they lived together until death parted.

But I didn't get much petting or nothing like that. My mother
cared a lot for me, and my daddy. 'Cause I just loved them. I always
wanted for my daddy to whip me, not my mama to, 'cause he'd just
spank me a little bit. "Now, go ahead, old gal, go away."

But mama would tear us up.

"Yeah," I used to say, "Mama, let Daddy whip us." (We called
him Poppa.) "Let Poppa whip. Please, mama, don't whip, please
don't whip. I won't do it no more."

And he didn't spank. He used to say, "Go on, get out of here."

Well, after that, my mother went, got in bad health. We had to
send her up to the sanitarium. TB ward.

Then there was six of us there, and all was small, but myself and
my brother. 'Cause my father wasn't such a good provider, you know.
He just didn't bring food in like my mother. Well, while she was out
there I had to take care of the rest of them, and I still had to struggle on
the tobacco farm and work. My sister and my brother, they was there
with the children. The oldest brother and the next older sister. They
was still there, and Poppa was there.

So when my mother died—she died in 1929—my baby sister was
three years old at that time, and I was eighteen. After she died—she
was thirty-seven the year she died—then I had to really try to take care
of them the best I knowed how. Until they began to give us, one to this

aunt, and one to that aunt, and one to another aunt. So we wasn't raised together, you know.

And finally my baby sister and I, we went to her mother, my mother's mother. And she wanted me to stay with my Aunt Dodie. So we went to stay with her, the one in South Carolina.

I had—let' see, how many aunts on my daddy's side? Aunt Violet, Aunt Laura, Aunt Ruby, and Uncle Jimmie, and Uncle Samuel, and Aunt Opal. Now, those was on my daddy's side. And on my mother's side, there was Aunt Dodie, Aunt Addie, Aunt Helen, and Aunt Sylvie, and Uncle Bobbie. And Uncle Bobbie, he died in '25. So they all dead now. Every one of them is dead. I don't have no aunts, no uncles alive now.

Oh, yes, I forgot. I had a baby sister named Jewel. She's dead. She died young.

All of the aunts and uncles dead now. There's nothing living now but the cousins. And we all get together like, you know, on Thanksgiving. All of us went to Brooklyn for Thanksgiving. But Mothers Day, I was going to have them here, but I was too sick. I had just got out of the hospital, and I was too sick to have them come over. But we always get together on Mothers Day. Mothers Day and Thanksgiving Day is the two holidays that we love to get together.

We were a very close family. And our cousins, all of us was raised together. We just loved to go to visit. I used to love to go to South Carolina to see my two cousins. I had two cousins that was the daughters of Aunt Dodie, the one I lived with.

Ours was religious people, church-going people, you know. We always went to church together. I had some neighbors that I went to school with. These girls, we all went to the same church. At that time, you see, my mother was a Methodist. So I was raised up in a Methodist Church. And after I got grown and was living with my Aunt Dodie, I got baptized in a Baptist Church and said I was converted. I don't know—I still didn't understand religion.

And then I made some friends, real good friends, you know, we was all in a youth club together. Donna and Esther and Selma and...oh, I can't name all the good friends I had.

Even when I was little, I had so many good friends. I remember playing with some neighbors, they used to live up the street from us. My mother didn't like me to play with them too much because they was bad children. They was bad about fighting. And you see, my mother had a fence built around the house, and when I was little, she didn't allow us out. But me—a little hard head—I always had to sneak out. And get all beat up. So after I found out those kids was fussy, I wouldn't bother with them anymore. Because they wasn't church-going people. At that time, you know, people always went. They wanted to cleanse themselves. Religious people, they didn't like to mess around with bad people, like drinking and all that. Well, I wasn't raised on it so I wasn't used to it.

And then we had some more neighbors. Another lady lived right across the street from us, and her daughter got dead. I was very small. One morning I was getting ready to go to school, and I happened to be looking out the window, and I saw this big ball of fire.

I told Mommy. I told Mommy I saw a big fat ball of fire going towards the ditch, and it had clothes on, and it was our neighbor across the street.

"Oh, Mommy, Mommy, a big ball of fire come running."

There's a big open ditch. And she just stood there in that ditch. And after a while somebody knockin' on the door. It was her. She came in and sat down on the chair. And she says, "Miss Lucy, please give me a drink of water."

Mommy had a little pitcher. I remember. I was a little girl then. I remember. And she'd always want to drink out of that little pitcher. And she said, "Miss Lucy, would you put that pitcher on my grave when I die?"

And I said, "Mommy, why does she want a pitcher on her grave?"

She said, "Well, maybe she just want it on there because she's drinking water out of it."

And so mother was over there one day and visited her 'fore she died. She had a lot of burns on her flesh, you know—all singed off.

How it started: she was half asleep and left the kerosene can on top of the stove, and it explode. And she caught—they was nice people, too. Very nice people. I used to go over to her house.

I had some more playmates I used to play with. You know, it's been so long I can't even think of their names. Oh, yeah, I remember Janice and Harvey Lee. We all went to the same school. And this girl who married my brother. She was a little older than I was, but we all grew up together. I remember that I used to go to the hotel with her on Sunday. Her daddy washed dishes. She would always ask my mama could I go with her and her father. She was much older than I was, but I liked her. I always did like the big girls, older than I was. I thought maybe I'd learn something.

I daydreamed and said when I grow up I'm not going to marry no boy that lived on a farm, because I was raised on a farm. And I don't want to pick no cotton. Like girls, we discuss it—what we going to do when we grow up. And I'd say, "Well, I want a good husband, and I want children, and I want me and my husband a nice home. I just want to live happy with my husband and my children, and I want my children to have a education."

And she would say, "Well, what you want them to do?"

I'd say, "I don't know what I want they're going to be." I'd say, "I just want them to have an education. You see, I didn't get any education. You know how it is. Mama, she got sick and I couldn't go back to school." I'd say, "Now look at you—you going back to school."

And, oh, I had lots of boyfriends—a-courting like, you know. We used to have friends, goin' out to dances. We used to sneak out, sneak out the window. Along that time, the evening dresses they was making then, you could make them. You know, this organdy, stiff organdy that they have. They had evening dresses with big capes, collars, you know, hanging in the back. And a big bow, sash bow. That was the style then. And we'd go to these dances, and we'd have a ball. Oh, I would just float. The boys just wouldn't leave me sit down. We just dance and dance and dance. And we'd go to the movies. See, when I was a child, my mother didn't allow me to go to movies. I remember one time when I was young, just before my mother died, I slipped away and went. To a Thanksgiving Dance. I met my husband at this dance. Used to have holidays there, and the band would come. And I met him there.

And then after my mother died I went to live with my aunt in South Carolina. I remember once when I was working there. This was before I was married. I was working for some people, did the babysitting and the cleaning up, the dishes in the kitchen. And the lady said she was going to take a nap. So her husband came in there and he tried—I was in the pantry, doing something in the pantry. I forgot what it was. But anyway, he come in there and trying to get fresh with me. You know, fumbling and pawing all over me. And I told him, I said, "You better get out of here."

So he said, "Hush, hush, hush."

I said "I'm talking loud because I want your wife to hear. And she's up in the front, taking a nap."

He was trying to get me to, you know. And, honey, I had to stop that man and throwed him in the barrel, in the flour barrel. She come running.

"What's the matter? What's the matter?"

And he had flour all over him.

I said, "You better tell your husband something. He's in here trying to get fresh with me. I don't go that side."

And believe me, he didn't know what to say to her. And did she give him a look!

So, after I stayed with my aunt a while, I got married, in 1931—no, 1930. I got married a year after mother died. I got married very young. When mama died I was 18 years. And he was so mean to me.

The first two years we got married, you see, I was happy. Well, he was trying. And he was very religious; well, he did live up to it. We attended church. And I was Sunday School secretary and I taught Sunday School, you know, a while. Then I sanged on the choir.

I always wanted a nice home, nice family, church-going people. Because I was raised up in a Christian home. I wanted me and my husband to work while we were young and try to have something. I said—I told him like this—I said, "We're young. We can get our home now, send our children to school, and we both work and make a good living. And then when we get old the kids will all be gone, and we'll have us a place to live."

Well, honey, he didn't want that.

He changed—he said he changed. And we left home, and we went to Laurel. I lived with him and had all those children. Seven children. That's all he left me with, a bunch of children.

I was around about twenty-one or twenty-two, I think when I had those two boys after about four years of being married. And then I began to have one, year after year after year. My life, my married life, was a failure. I still had to work and take care of my children. So I begin to figure, if I had to work for my children I wasn't going to work for him. Along at that time I—let's see how old I was when my Regina was born—I was around 27. Then a woman got between us, you know, right after Regina was born. She was a little bitty babe, just was toddling.

He was so mean, I couldn't even bring away the children. I had to run off and leave my children to keep him from killing me. I left, and do you know what I did? I came back and stole 'em one by one, until I got every one of them. Every time I sit down to eat, I'd be thinking about when these little children got any food. My husband was keeping them. I went back one night while he was drunk. I walked in there and stole the baby. That was Regina. And the next time I went back, I got another girl, Beverly. And I said, "Jimmie, you and Clifford, I don't want to take you all right now. I'll come back and get you later."

I stayed away then. I was scared because he was right behind me. And by that time I said, "I'm going to divorce this man." Like my niece did. She divorced her husband. Yes, she did; she got an independent divorce. She paid $500 for her divorce. So I divorced that man, I divorced him in 1941. I worked hard to get that divorce. Hmph! That was an independent divorce.

And I got married again. I stayed single three years after, and then I got married again. The last one, I met him when he was in service, and married him in 1944. The last son, the one that got killed, it's his father. And I didn't do no better. I still got a drunk alcoholic. I stepped out of the frying pan into a hornet nest.

You know, when we first got married we was very happy. He was in the service in Louisiana. He went there first, and it was around about six months before I went to him. I worked, you know, and took care of the kids. And so my mother-in-law said, "Go ahead. I'll take care of the kids." So I went out there. He was stationed in Camp Lafayette. And they were just fixing to ship them overseas, but they changed their minds and shipped him to Oklahoma. Then, after he got out of the service he came to Newark.

I came to Newark first time ever in 1944, when I married him. We came to visit, and we decided after he got out of the service we would stay up here a year. So we stayed up here a year; we got jobs. He worked in a Newberry's and I worked in a department store. I was young then. He was young. But I didn't make too much, working in the department store. I only got $25 a week at that time. And I think he got $40 a week. That was in '45. So then he got a chauffeur job, and he worked in Rahway. They paid us together $250 a month. And then they raised our wages to $350 a month. I was such a good cook. I did all the cooking, and he did all the chauffeuring. And I did all the planning of the meals and bought the food.

Then we worked way up in those mountains in the Oranges, way up. We worked for—what's the name of those people? They were Jews—Sultzbergs. They were very rich people. I did the cooking there, and he waited on the table. He was the chauffeur.

The kids were home with my mother-in-law. And we would send

money home, you know, for the kids. His mother kept the kids, they was so small, while we went around working.

And then we went to Florida. And we lived there. Then I got pregnant again with my baby son. Florida, then, is his home, where he was born. Then after he was around three months old I was pregnant again. But I miscarried that one. I lost that one, so I don't know what it was. And then we moved to Jacksonville, Florida, and that's where we separated. He went his way, and I went mine. We didn't separate by a man and a woman came between us. We separated because he and I could not get along. He was so mean. You know, he was mean to me, and I couldn't take anymore.

In the beginning, as I told you, we got along fine. Then he begin to run around when he came to Newark. He'd stay out two or three nights on me. I wouldn't know where he was at, especially when he got paid off. And he was a good cook. He made good. He was making $75—well, at that time that was good money for cooking. I wouldn't see him until he was broke. Then he come dragging in, you know. And we got along good again whenever we went back home to his mother, to visit the kids. We went to Florida, and that's where we were beginning to get along bad. You know what? Both of my marriages was bad, both of them. I thought maybe I marry again, I have somebody to help me with the kids. Well, he did help me. He was good with them. And when they went to grow up, they begin to see things. And they could not get along with him, so they had to move out by themselves. They say, "Mama, we don't want to break into your privacy and have a upset. We'll move out and get us a room downstairs."

So we separated. I only had that one child from that marriage. And I didn't intend to have no more children, and I didn't have no more, either. And I was careful who I went out with. And I just held myself up, and I said I was not going to bring no more children into the world. And I didn't. And I didn't even get that way either. No, honey. Uh-uh. Didn't bring no more children in the world. I sure didn't. I didn't intend to. You know, young people. . . I had fun, but I know how far to go. I took care of myself. It's no need to keep bringing children into the world and don't have no husband.

Both of my marriages wasn't good, so, I decided I wouldn't never marry no more. Just stay like I am. After we separated in '55, I didn't look for no more. And my baby son was only three years old when we separated. My other children were done growed up then. That one in there—the picture on the table—he was around seventeen at that time.

And my oldest son was around twenty. He got married to this girl he was in love with. Finished, graduated from high school and married her. We had a big wedding and all. Came from a nice background, was a nice girl, but they couldn't get along. He wanted to move out to hisself, but she wanted to stay with her father, hoping that she would get his house. Because she was the baby girl. But she never did get it. So my son was divorced from her.

So I lived there in Jacksonville until I come back here. I came back here again about 1958, and I been here ever since, right here in Newark. When I came back I went back to school on Broad Street. I went there for 23 weeks; when they was paying you to go to school. Well, I learned a lot that I didn't get when I was going to school in the fifth grade.

And I was living here in this apartment with my baby son before he was killed. When he was growing up he gave me a lot of trouble. But you know what I did? I did never pay him out of trouble.

I said, "You got into this trouble; now you get out of it the best way you can." I said, "My mama always told me a hard head makes a soft honkey."

So that's what I always told him. But when he was in trouble I always try to be nice. Maybe take him things and go visit him. And my oldest son, the one living in Detroit, he never give me trouble. Never. From a child he would always, you know, go for errands for people, and they would pay him. 'Cause times was hard then. And he would come in. "Mama, I got a little change. Do you need that to buy something to eat with?"

But after I married again, my baby son he gave me a lot of trouble. God rest his soul. He's gone now. He's dead. Remember the boys that got in a car wreck in Branchbrook Park? Two boys. One of those was my baby son. He gave me a lot of trouble. And my health was bad then—and it's still bad. He used to be in court, and he would tell me, "Mama, could you get me out?"

I'd say, "I cannot get you out. I don't have any money. And then, I don't know anybody up here I can borrow money from to get you out."

Then, when he'd come out, I'd say, "Now, try to stay out of trouble. Don't follow these bad boys around."

He was always a easily led child. He'd listen. You could just lead him around all the way, you know.

I said, "Think now—you're big enough to help me now. I'm

getting old and sick; you could help me.''

He always into something. He didn't do anything, but he'd always be in the crowd. When you grabbed the boys he'd be right there. He started going to this—up here—you know, the juvenile court. First time he was in there he didn't come home that night. And I cried and walked the floor all night. I called all the hospitals. Nobody knew about it. I took his picture and took it up to the precinct.

I said, ''My child is missing.''

They said, ''We'll be looking for him.''

Late Sunday night, the lady next door talking to her little boy, ''Don't tell her; don't tell her where he is.''

So his little cousin says, ''Yes, ma'am. I'm going to tell her where he is.''

So he told me he was in jail. I had time to get there to see him. When they had the trial the boy got on the stand and told the men he wasn't in it. He was two blocks way up ahead, and he didn't know anything about those watermelons, because he wasn't there when they was stolen. Well, the police got him, too. And from then on, the first time they get you, you can stub your toe and they'll grab you. Think you in it too. All them times, and he was gettin' in prison—he wasn't guilty, only for one thing. . .narcotics. They got him fooled and they got him on that.

He was on it over a year before I knew it. And one day I was cleaning his room. You know how you plump the things. And I found something. I said, ''What's this?'' I said, ''This here thing is what doctors use to give you shots and things.'' I didn't know what it was. And I said, ''It look like what the doctor used to give me shots for my high blood, when it was bad.''

Then I asked him what did he have that needle for.

''Oh, nothing, nothing, never mind, never mind.'' You know, just turned it off like that. And from then on, he was on, he got on it bad. Oh, my God.

I said, ''Well, I'm not going to give you no money. I'm not going to furnish your habit.''

I went to the priest up there. I even went to the New York Rehabilitation place, you know, when it was over here on Sixteenth Avenue. I went there. The man came here twice trying to catch him. The priest came here twice. Trying to help him. I was trying to help him. That's why I wouldn't give him no money to furnish his habit.

Now he just been out eight months when he got killed. Just been out of prison eight months. Then, after he was dead and buried, then they sent a letter that he was clear of that case. The case was all over. Well, he dead now.

And he had volunteered for the service, and his letters came back, but he was dead. What could I do?

He was twenty-two years old. Twenty-two. I loved my son. He worried me, it's true, but I didn't want him to die. I didn't want nothing to happen to him, although he worried me. I didn't do nothing but pray. I didn't run to nobody with my troubles. I stayed right here and prayed and tried to talk to him. Sometimes he'd make me so mad! He even took the television out of the house. I couldn't leave nothing nice I had. All of it was gone. That's why I wouldn't buy nothing nice in here. This old junk. This ain't nothing but junk. But now I can't afford to buy no nice furniture.

He sold the television. He sold my cake mixer. All the little things. He took my fur stole. Sold that. But he was trying to change. About three weeks before he got killed in that car wreck, it looked like he was changing.

He'd come home at night—he never would stay out at night. He'd always come home. Just now and then he would stay out at night. And I'd be worried about him when he wouldn't come home. But you see, that morning, I didn't worry. I just figured he went off to spend the night. And then I went to church. You know, I always go to church every Sunday morning. And the firemen, they had to go to church to find me.

Downstairs, Miss Harris, she told them, said, "You want to find her now, you'll find her in church." She said, "You go there right now. She's in church."

So the minute I saw those men standing there, standin' over there by the pastor's office—they was waiting for church to be over when they came in. And one of the ushers came to me and said, "Reverend Black and those gentlemen want to see you when church is over."

And by the time he was ending church, the firemen went on in the back. And I was shaking hands with different ones, you know. I took my time about going around there. So I went on around there and I sit down. And he told me. Oh, honey, I blacked out. That's a hurting thing, you know that? And once in a while, I ask God to get it off my mind. Because it's about to run me crazy. Right now he bearing down on me. That's right.

I'm all alone now. One son comes in and out. He stays here

sometimes—sometime he don't. I only got three boys living. My son in Detroit, he's very happy with his marriage. They are very happy together. They got a beautiful home. One live out in North Newark. I don't see him. I haven't seen him since he was here after we came back from burying my baby son. I haven't laid eyes on him since. He doing all right. As long as I don't see him, he's doing all right. He just don't care about coming around, that's all. He stays all to his self.

And I got two daughters. One live on Longfellow Street, married, and one live on Ashland Street, married. They're the only two girls I got. The one on Longfellow, well, she and her husband didn't make it. She's by herself. He left her with seven kids. But she says she's happy without him because he was awful mean to her. I know that myself. And the other daughter, the baby daughter, she had a happy childhood 'cause my brother raised her. And she got everything she need. That's why she spoiled now. She had a very happy marriage for a while. Then her husband began to turn. Now she's not with him. She's by herself but she says she's happier like she is, because he turned. He begin to get mean. Although he gave her anything she wanted. When they got married he already had his apartment, the furniture, and everything. They was just holding the furniture until they could get them the apartment. And they was living with me with their furniture stacked up in my house. And when they did get the apartment, they moved all that stuff in. That's where they separated at. But it's so bad, I can't take it. Anyway, now they separated. She get the four kids. And she says she is very happy like she is now. She was here Saturday. Stayed about two or three hours with me.

And Beverly, the other daughter! Hmph! You people from the Project come to see me more than Beverly. Hasn't been here yet. She go everywhere but here. She even go right down the hill there to a bar but don't put her foot on the door. She's not coming unless I tell her I got something here for her. "I want you to come over here and eat dinner with me." And I work in the kitchen all day Saturday getting it prepared. Then she'll come. She didn't even ask me for dinner on Mothers Day, and I just got out of the hospital.

She saw me just once since I been out of the hospital. And you know how she seen me then? My brother from Washington and his sister came over. They came over and spent two or three days here with me. I hadn't seen him in six years. And we went there to see Beverly. That's the only time she saw me. Other than that, she's not coming.

When I was in the hospital that time I stayed for five weeks. My pastor, he came to see me. Well, you see, I asked him—I thought it was pneumonia. But he said that my doctor said it wasn't. What I had was bad. It was a blood clot on the lungs. I'm not ashamed that I didn't know what it was. The doctor told me, "You is a very sick woman. Very sick." And he was telling the other doctors. They was all standing there. And there was this girl—colored girl, wanted to be a doctor.

She said, "Why, you know, she stopped breathing. We had to fight."

And he said, "That's why you got that cut on your neck. They had to operate in order to make you breathe again."

Oh, my health was bad ever since, way back in '61. My health has been failing me, you know. But I still try to work right on. I work, I be feeling so bad, but I kept on working. Many days I'd be sick, but I still went on to work anyway. And all the sleet and snow! And then that arthritis got set in on me! And I could work now if it weren't for my old lame knees. I'd get out and try to work. I just was raised up workin'. I worked hard all my life and don't have a thing to show for it but the kids, and they now all gone. Getting old now, but they don't care about bothering none with me too much, you know. Oh, I hope you don't do you mommy like that. That's the truth.

I sure gets very lonely at times. You know, in the summer I can get out with the other ladies and sit and talk. And on Sunday, you know, don't hardly get lonely on Sunday 'cause that's church. I come home, got that old TV, and I look at that.

I have good neighbors. I have a nice neighbor lives across the hallway. Another one there, down the next. All of us up here, we gets along fine together. And from the way things look, I'm well liked by people who live here in the building. I gets along fine. When I was sick here and I came out of the hospital, I didn't even have to worry about food. This one would bring me a dinner, that one would bring me a dinner or breakfast. They was all nice to me. Even they'd come in and work. The one across the hall, she washed the windows and put up clean curtains for me, and they was nice to me. When I was in the hospital the neighbors came to see me, and I had beautiful flowers in my room they brought me. Now, I don't worry about—like a lot of them worry about boyfriends. I ain't got time. I just don't want to be bothered with them. I'm trying to make it easy. That's right. And you know why? When you get converted you got to work on it. Just getting converted, sitting down and don't do nothing about it, you still can go right back out there, doing the same thing you was doing before. So now I'm trying to make it easy.

But I didn't get converted while I was sick. I got converted before I was sick. Long time before I was sick. Uh-huh. And I live by it. I try to live by that each and every day of my life. And I let Christ come into my life. And you know what helps you? Reading the Bible. Some I understand—some of it I don't. But that I do understand, I been cutting out these things. Things that was sinful.

Like having affair. I cut that out. It's been a long time since I had one. It's a sin. It's, say, committing adultery. Now, I don't know whether my husband is living or not. I don't know; I haven't seen him since 1955. I had a chance to get married again, but I didn't know where he was at and that would have been living in adultery, if I couldn't have got no divorce from him. You know, I got a divorce from the other one. So I stayed single. Stayed all alone. So now I'm happy like I am. Really, I am. I'm happy just like I am. And I got used to being alone so much, until it don't bother me no more, you know.

I been living here six years. I were living right here when the riots started. Could see the people, the snipers, all up on top of that building over there. I keep down low and keep the lights out 'cause I was scared. Wasn't hurt none. But my son was over on Bertrand Street, and he got burned with the powder from one of the snipers. They had to lay down on the floor. When they shot through the window all of them lay down, but he happen to get a power burn on the back.

Didn't only see the snipers. I even saw a man right out there in the streets. The police beat him down to the ground. The thing hurt me so bad. To see the police beating up those men like they did, makin' 'em all bloody. Beat 'em down to the ground with the, you know, that stick. Well now, what for I don't know. Because I wasn't close enough to hear what they were saying. But I saw them beat two men. Right out there. In that court over there, by that building.

And I never did learn the reason for the riot. And it made things worse, don't you think? I think they made things worse. Because they ought to let things go on like it was. What did they accomplish? I don't see nothing they accomplished. They just tearing down everything. Look like a ghost town.

And then the nice colored people, that want to do right and want to live right, want a clean, decent place to live, they got to put up with our bad people that don't care what they do, don't care what they say.

We have to bear with that, just like rotten apples in a barrel. That ruins the whole barrel—but not all the time. If they could kick the rotten apples out, and then the good apples will be good right on. If you let them alone, all the apples stay together, quite naturally some would rotten the whole barrel. Well, what can we do? We got to stay in. There is a lot of decent colored people, law abiding citizens; they want to do right, they want to live right, they live in the ghetto, and they can't help themselves. You know why? They don't make the money, and then they got to stay in it along with the bad ones. And then you know what? They think all of us, all of us bad. But it's not so.

Well, I'm going to tell you one thing. Both sides need to be improved. Both sides. There's hate amongst our people and there is hate amongst the white people against us. A lot of our color should wake up and try to be somebody. And then the white will help us more. Don't tear the white man down. He don't make us do all the things that we done amongst our own color. He don't hold no gun on us, to make us drink and with the dope. Because it's spread amongst his color too now. And since it's spread amongst his color, now they trying to do something about it. But it's too late.

I just don't know, honey. I'm telling you, I just don't know. This world—this beautiful world that God created for us. It's not the world that's wrong, this beautiful world that He put here for us. It's our people, both sides, white and colored.

And then we got a lot of Puerto Ricans here now. And then there's this American Puerto Rican now. There's plenty of them now. They just as bad as the colored and the poor white people—just as bad as our colored too. You know why I know that? Because I work amongst them.

I worked amongst white people all my life. I have worked with low-class white people too. They're, you know, just trying to get by. I've worked with the middle-class white people, and then I have worked for rich people, and everything. And now, in the low class of white people, they just as dirty and nasty as our colored is.

But you know, if we can cooperate together, our city would be better. But you know, the devil is busy just as the people is very evil. Oh, don't put it on the world. It's the people that live in this beautiful world. That's my opinion, you know, just my opinion.

8

Quinine and Gin, Drink It on a Young Moon

I come up in Georgia, out in the country. My father and mother lived in the country, they had a farm. Cotton, corn, potatoes. It was sharecropping. We had a lot of work to do. We had cows, we had hogs, and all three of us children had a cow apiece to take care of. Milk, feed, put them out to graze, and when it's hot, go get 'em, bring 'em in and put them into the shade. And when my mother figured it was cool enough—they was cool enough—to have water, we'd give them some water. And then we brought them back. We had to milk the cows, too. That was part of the job.

We played some too. We went fishing, and Sunday mornings better go to Sunday School, and then to church. They was children close around, and we could play with them. But I was raised the old-fashioned way. I didn't go very far out of sight. When I went somewhere, I had somebody to go with. There was always somebody to go with me. If my sister didn't go, or my mother didn't go, my brother went. I didn't like it, but I couldn't do nothing about it.

I didn't go much to school. Started when I was five. I only got half through the third grade. I learned how to read and write. I don't do it all right, but I can do it good enough. I can get by.

My brother is four years younger than I am, my sister is one-and-a-half. I was sixteen when my father moved me into town, with my sister, brother and mother. We all went, 1926. There was a section where the colored people was at. The colored people didn't stay in the white people's section. Even when you went to the town, there was certain streets that the white people didn't go on. If you walked through the streets where they was at, you didn't go in where they was at, to get served or nothing.

Well, we moved into town. My father got a job at the mill. He worked at the mill until he died. He got the job in December, 1926 and he died in June, 1927. Now, I don't know the reason he moved into the city. I don't know because I wasn't raised to ask other people questions.

I was raised old-fashioned. My parents weren't mean or nothing. The only thing I say about it is this: if I done wrong, I got a whipping. I mean, make it then. In those days, that was the way we did. I suppose it is cruelty now, 'ccording to what people think now. I knowed it wasn't.

I didn't have a chance to do what the children do nowadays. I didn't know those things. I could go and play baseball, anything like that, fishing, huckleberry hunting, blueberry hunting, blackberry. I used to go and do those things. But I couldn't get out and go nowhere in the streets by myself.

Before I married, I couldn't go nowhere. If I went to church my sister was with me or my mother was with me. I went with family. I couldn't go anywhere by myself.

Once, in February, when it was cold, I had pneumonia. I was twelve years old. And the doctor came, told my mother to dress me up warm. And my mother had me wear things all the time. So I had to wear like a sheet, and I'm wearing bloomers, down to here, and long drawers. Long underwear down there, with the shirt sleeves hung down to here. That was to keep me warm. It didn't snow down there like it does up here, but it was still cold in the ground. I never saw snow but once in my life down there, and that was in 1914.

Then I got my period. My momma knew exactly when my period was coming, so she didn't have to mark no calendar. 'Cause she knew it when I had it. Everytime I had a period I was sent to bed for the pain. I had cramps, couldn't do nothing.

Now, my uncle had married a second time. And his second wife's oldest daughter had a baby. My mother said to me, "Fanny."

I says, "Ma'am?"

She says, "Now, I'll tell you something. You know who little Richard is?"

That was that girl's baby. And she got a baby but she wasn't married.

I said, "Yes, ma'am."

She says, "If you don't keep your dress down, you are going to end up with what she's got."

I wanted to know more, but I didn't ask any more questions. Are you kidding? I knew better than to ask other people questions. I wasn't raised that way.

So when my father moved us into town we moved next door to where Al were. That's how I met him, the one I married. He was the only boyfriend I had. According to him, he said he was 18 years old. I was 17. We wasn't going out nowhere. He came to the house, him and another guy came there, a guy named Harry. They would just come to the house, and we'd sit down and we'd read, talking, and naturally ain't nobody up. My mother ain't going to bed though. But daddy going to bed, sister and brother going to bed, but my mother, she won't go nowhere.

Anyhow, Al says to me, he says, "Fanny, Harry, he's married."

I said, "He is?"

He said, "Yes, 'cause I've seen his wife."

I told my mother. I said, "Mama, Al tells me Harry is married."

She didn't say anything. All she said was, "OK." She told my daddy.

The next time the two men was there, my daddy walked in there and said, "Which one of you niggers in here is married?"

So Harry says, "May I have my hat, please?"

Well, that meant that Harry was married. Al wasn't married. I married Al. We met in February one year and married in August the next year. I was eighteen. He was the only one that asked me to. I went with him everywhere. Otherwise, he was at my mother's house, you know, with me.

He asked me to marry him in March. We had made arrangements to marry sometime in June but my father died. I couldn't swear to it that my father knew this boy had asked me to marry him. I don't know. Anyway, I got married in August at home. My pastor married me.

When we first got married we lived in the house with my mother, a whole year. And then we lived by ourselves 'cause my mother, sister, and brother come up here. When my father died, this place he was working at, they give everybody at death a thousand dollars. She put some of it in the bank, but she couldn't get it out for a year. She put some in the post office. In the post office you can get it quicker. She put half in the post office and half in the bank. Then in 1928, she took the money out and she come up here. She had a brother in Newark and one in Jersey City.

And so we stayed down there. My husband was working. He was a presser. He was working for a laundry, but he wasn't supporting me. If he brought his money home, I didn't get it. I don't know who he give it to.

So my mother left in 1928, but in 1930 she came back down and brought the two of us back here in Newark. I wasn't working when we first came here. I wasn't doing no work because I didn't know nothing to do. Down there I didn't know how to be doing no housework, excepting for working in my own house. You know what I mean? So I didn't get anything to do; I didn't know about housework until 1932.

Up here my husband found work as a presser, and he could make more in the run of a day than he made down there in the run of a week. And he was making all this money, more than he made down there. If I wanted something, to go out and buy a bar of soap to wash his clothes with, I'd have to tell him, "I want a bar of soap to wash clothes." You see down there in the South, I could make lye soap. You know what homemade soap is? Grease and whatnot. But up here you buy a bar of soap. After he got up here, made more money than he ever had in his hands before, I'd say, "Give me a nickel."

He'd say, "What do you want with it?"

Or if I said, "Give me a dollar."

He said, "What you want?"

I'd say, "We got to eat."

He didn't give me nothing that I didn't ask for. I would write myself out a note. If I wanted some meat, if I wanted some vegetables, I would always put down more money than what I figured it would cost, so I would have a few pennies in my pocket. As far as clothes was concerned, that's what I needed, so I cheated. My brother where he was working there was a woman working there and she'd give him things to give me. Even when I was down South they'd send me shoes and clothes that peoples up here had give them. So that's where my clothes came from. Al didn't support me any. I cleaned for him and cooked what I had, but he didn't give me nothing.

We lived with my momma up here, at Number 1 Statton Place. She only had two rooms. She already had two children with her, then me and my husband make five people in two rooms. Now we had a coal stove in those days. And my mother made this proposition, that my brother get up two weeks every morning and make fire in the coal stove, and my husband did the same thing. But he got up one morning, and he won't, 'cause he sees the window is swaying. He wrote "Beware," that's to say what of, so my mother asked what did it mean. And he answered the window was swaying.

It was cold that mornin' with no stove on. And my mother says to him, "Al, I got to beware of you in my house. One of us is got to go. It's my house, and I'm not home in it."

The first thing he done was pack up all his junk in a suitcase.

So then my husband left. He went to the Morristown area, to my mother's brother. But my mother's brother wouldn't let him leave his suitcase there. So he came back to my mother and asked my mother could he leave that, his clothes, in that suitcase there. And she said yes, and so he did.

I was glad. As far as I was concerned, he wasn't doin' me no good. He done me a favor by leaving. I stayed with my mother, stayed until my mother died in 1950.

So after he left I found work. I was working in the Puritan Paper Products Company. I worked there for more than fifteen years, until they went out of business.

I was only twenty-one years old when we separated. I got a divorce, and then I went back to my maiden name. Now I wasn't fooling around with no other man when we separated, but after we separated I met a fellow, in 1930. He was married, had a big family, but he was good to me so it made no difference. And that lasted up until 1954. Let's see, in 1954 I was operated on. Anyway, this guy was two years older than I was. My birthday is in February; his is in August. That doesn't make no difference, would you say, six months?

He treated me better than I was treated by my husband, the only man I ever knew before. We went places together. We got along together. I don't know if I loved him, but he treated me right. He treated me better than anybody treated me—good.

He gave me money every week. It wasn't a lot of money, it wasn't let's say fifteen or twenty dollars a week, because I was making good money, but he give me money. I mean, he give me money every week.

For instance, when my mother died, 1950, when I found out she was sick, I went to him and said, "Charlie?"

He said, "What?"

I says, "Momma is sick and down in Georgia. I've got to go down there because brother is down there, which you know a man can't do for his mother like a woman can, like her own daughter..."

So he said all right. I didn't ask him where—I didn't tell him how much money I want. I didn't tell him anything. I said, "I don't know how much it costs; go down and check it for me." So he checked it. He come back. I guess he went to the bank. He didn't carry that kind of money on him. He come back and give me fifty dollars. I went down and bought the ticket. It only cost me forty-five dollars to go down.

His wife was alive then. She died later, before he did, so did his oldest son. In the beginning she didn't know nothing about me. A particular woman told her about what was going on, but she never had anything to say to me.

Now I was pregnant in 1934, but I didn't want no child. So I went and got me some quinine, powdered quinine, and boughten gin and put it together and drank it on a young moon. And it came down, came down in great big lumps. Only took one dose and that did the job. But twenty years later I had to be operated on, because it wasn't clean. After I had my operation, all Charlie could see was that I was no good. He figured that I was no good after surgery. I tried to explain to him, I said it didn't make no difference at all, that it didn't affect me no how.

The doctor told me when I was operated on, he said, "You'll never have your period anymore after this month." I was operated on December 10 and I had my period January 5th. My period had never left me. I still had it. I only stopped it, say, about when I was better than sixty. So they didn't take nothing away from me but that tumor and my appendix. But Charlie was old fashioned. I told him it didn't make no difference, but he didn't listen. With the other fellows, it didn't bother, because they didn't know, and I still enjoyed my sex. Charlie would speak to me, but he never put his foot in my house after that.

It didn't bother me. There was a fellow named Sam Sheffield. He was married and had one child, was living with his wife. I knew him from 1954 to '57. He didn't give me as much as he should; he'd hand me a few pennies. But I was working same as I was working when I was with Charlie, so that helped me some. There was always somebody around, one at a time.

I had my own apartment. After I started living with my sister, I used to go to my friend's house, but with the others I had my own place. I had a little tramp one time that wasn't worth salt to put in his beer. He was living with me. I broke up with Sam Sheffield and this guy moved in. He was one of these guys he liked to roll dice. And anything that he could beat you out of or anybody else, he would. He went to jail twice. Two different years on the same article. He and a woman named Cora Lee, between the two of them they got that.

He had the check, that I know, because I saw the check. He asked me to go down to Swansons and cash that check for him. And I knew who that check belonged to—I knew that woman. He asked me to go down Springfield Avenue and cash that check in.

Now, according to Cora Lee, she cashed that check. And so the two of them went and spent thirty days at Caldwell. And then in '63 he had to go back to Caldwell again on that same offense. And I told him in '63, I told him, "If you ever go back to jail again, you can't come back here. I'm going to move, and when I move, you can't move with me."

And then the last one I had was Lannie Tauber. I knew him for about five years. He was married, but his wife was dead when I met him. He had two rooms, and I used to go up there. But he died, last October. So I haven't been bothered since. I'm satisfied. 'Cause the first thing they want to know, "You got a job? You got your own apartment?"

You see, I didn't do bad by myself. I don't need them. And when you get to be a certain age, you don't have very much no how.

I been in the house with my sister ten years this past April. Charlie died since I been in this house, '64 or '65. He was living here in Newark, 336 Robie Street. I went to the funeral home. I could view the body, but I didn't go to the funeral because I had to go to work.

My husband, Al, used to come around every so often when I knew Charlie. As far as I know, he's still living in Newark. I haven't seen him years and years. He lives over on Concord Street. Doesn't have no children to my knowledge.

And since the Paper Company went out of business I've been doing housework on and off. Domestic work. I started working down there in Sweeney's [a neighborhood tavern] cleaning up sometime around 1967. I been getting social security since March last year. Get $112.80 a month. I get a little more from Sweeney's, depending on how long I work. He pays me by the hour. Between that and the social security, I'm able to eat. See, when I get my social security I give my sister my check and she puts it in the bank. We pay $110 rent, so I give her that. When it's my time to pay the gas and electric, I give her the money for that.

I got my own room and she got her own room. She doesn't complain about my drinking because she drinks. We could get in senior citizens' housing; I can get in now, but can I carry her with me? There's a catch to moving there. She has a stove—I never seen a grown woman before like that with a stove. She won't leave that stove! She paid $495 for that stove. If she sold it I don't believe she would even get half the money she spent for it. I been in the house over ten years, and she had it then. I figure it like this. I only have one sister. If she was willing to move, I'd move with her. But if she won't, I can't go!

If I had my life all over again, I wouldn't get married. And I wouldn't have the same boyfriends either. Naturally you got to have a boyfriend though, 'cause sometimes you need a man.

I'd give the girls advice: I'd tell them not to have babies at fourteen years old and ain't got no husband. I'd tell them to keep it down.

See, if I had had a child and my child would have been born in 1934, I'd probably have great-grandchildren. I don't miss having that child—I missed the heartache. Children. . . the way children carry on, taking dope and all that kind of stuff. I missed all that heartache.

9

Going to Live Like My Father Lived

My daddy never did want to stay nowhere all night from us. He'd always—if he didn't get a job to go out and work, he'd come back so he could stay home at night. He always said he thought he should raise us up together. That's what he thought and always said. Everybody ought to raise their own kids, and he thought mother and father ought to be with them. And it was tight, you know, because he would never go out and be away from us.

Oh, you know, he would go fishing, and he'd go out hunting all day and come back. It wasn't like it is now that the game ain't there. They didn't mind them shooting and going on the big farms at night. We'd get up in the morning, and he'd have two bags, this one maybe full of squirrel and that one maybe full of turkey. He told us they were doing that to help us out. But, you know, he never stayed out. I don't remember one day he ever stayed away from us at all.

He had one brother, see, one brother just left his kids. His wife died, and he just left his kids on the grandparents. And he didn't get a chance to see them until just before he died. He'd been gone thirty years. Naturally, I'd never seen him up until that time. But he came in about a weekend before he died. Something told him just to go home. When he got there, my daddy was sick. Well, he been sick about, about a month or more. It was the last weekend there.

And that's the way we was raised. Daddy always said he didn't take advantage of leaving his family like Uncle Henry did.

And we was raised up to take food out there to the children, my uncle's children—like potatoes, meat, lard. We always shared with them 'cause their daddy left them, and my daddy'd help the grandmother with them.

See, we all lived at least five miles from them. They call that close, because we walk out there and same day come back, see. Get up in the morning and put the food in the sack and head out and come right back that afternoon. Wait till it gets cooler and walk on back home, and that's the way we did it. And sometime my uncle, or the old lady, she'd get somebody and they'd come down and get it. My other uncle, Uncle James, and his older sister all lived right there together, but they had children. They worked for white folks in the house, and we farmed. Worked on the farm in tobacco.

I never remember staying the night with nobody, only with just us. Once in a while my daddy would let us go out there to visit his people, five miles out in the country. But we were older—go about once a year. He'd let us go out then, stay on that farm, play around, and come back. Stay overnight on Saturday, and bring me back Sunday. He never did want his children to stay out of the house, from around him and momma.

There was eight of us, we raised eight. You could say ten, but you talking about the living ones. My mother had ten, but see the living ones was eight of us. We all, you might say, close together. My baby brother was sixteen when my father died.

I remember one of the worst things that happened to me; I got burned when I was five years old. My mama was washing, she was washing in the back of the house. I would help Mama wash every week. So this particular week my sister was here, and my little sister was walking and talking, so she said, "Sister, you go around, take the kids and go in front so they can play."

I wanted to help with the wash. Well, after I got the children playing on the front, I didn't say anything, and I came back. See, as I came back the pot was betixt me and Mama. And I saw the pot, you know, and I just jiggled it. So when I jiggled the pot, see, the stick went over and I went into the pot, just like this. Went into the boiling water, and it was colored clothes and had potash in it. So I went right over into it like this. And I didn't want to tell Mama. Didn't know how to tell her. The first thing come into my mind was to just get out of it. I got myself out and then I got a little distance—maybe, I'll say, about four or five steps. Then this floor, it start rolling up, and I fell onto it. Then she ran to me and grabbed me. She couldn't understand what it was. I had on a white wool sweater and it was burnt. She cut the sleeves out soon as she could get it, and pulled it off, and I was burnt from here to there. Being burnt, you know, I grabbed myself like this, and I also burnt this spot where I touched it, but it wasn't as deep—just this part was so deep. And it was about five months—she said around about five or six months—before it got well. Because them days they didn't use doctors. So this one remedy it, that one remedy it. Finally it was cured up. But I had got so I couldn't even walk. Just sit in the chair, you know. She had my brother and sister push me around in the chair. I got weak, I wouldn't eat, because, see, the odor of that would cut my appetite. And Mama, she started me by putting a little piece of 'bacca in my mouth. You know, just for it to bring my appetite back. I can't remember using it, though. She said that's what started me. She put a little piece of tobacco in my mouth to find out if I could eat, and I got strengthened.

And yeah, we all went to school right there. I didn't get to just about fourth grade, you know. See, we farmin' and those old folks didn't have—they didn't let their children go to school. Matter of fact, my father didn't understand that education, I would need it in the years to come. My mother, though, she could read; she always interested in me going to school. Plenty of days we'd have to stay home. Sometimes go to school two days out of three weeks. We didn't get to go but a little bit at a time, from time to time. Sometime two days out of this week, then never go back then for another month. My father would always hassle us and keep us something to do. Keep you out of trouble if you busy—that way he would see it. But Mama would say, "Well, I didn't get no schooling, and I want to give them the schooling what they give them." Lot of days he'd be going to work, and it would rain. He told us to do something. She'd tell us go on to school, come back tomorrow, maybe it would be a better day. "And that day you can do that for your daddy, tomorrow." So I didn't get too much of schooling.

My folks was farming, you know, and that was the only help they had, the children. We was never able to hire, just maybe like the crop get behind, well maybe they would hire somebody for three or four days to catch up, you know, like that. But we was never able to create enough to hire nobody. We done our own work.

And this little town we live near, Wabash, Georgia, was small. We got along, we all got along. We'd go down on Saturday evening and walk the streets and go back home. We got along with all the colored folk and the white folk down there . . . you know, friendly with one another.

Now, my brother, the one next to my baby brother, he worked for a lady there who run a hotel. She had cows and had her own milk and made her own butter and run this little hotel. And she'd make lunch for the train. Meet the train and send something. He worked for her quite a long time up until he got a good size. She always called him boy. And he didn't say nothing. He didn't want any Petersburg Nine.[5]

The big holiday, when we went out, was the twentieth of May. That was our day. We didn't celebrate Thanksgiving—no, we didn't because the colored folks didn't do that. The white folks did. And they never was told about that fourth of July. And Christmas was a day that was a home thing. So we'd have that day the twentieth of May. Like, most of the time, somebody would be in the kitchen, cooking and helping out other times, but the twentieth of May, don't care what happen. Sometime they'd be doing their job but they would go. Some of them got fired on their jobs, because they was off that day. They'd say, "Well, we going to have that day." Us is a small town, and people come all over there. We took it down there to the Baptist Church. They'd fry fish and carry their food. They'd carry trunks of food, pies and all that cooked food from home, but they had extra fish and lemonade. Big barrels of lemonade, and extra fish. Everybody paid maybe went to about fifty cents, until you buy two barrels of fish and the bread and the lemonade and the sugar. See, that's all they had there.

Then after they have lunch, 'round about one o'clock, there's a ball game up the road, about a half a mile out up, and they all go to the ball game and have a big barrel of lemonade and soda—somebody would be there to sell it. We stay up there all day. We stay right there till right 'fore sundown and my daddy said, "Go home sundown," so we said, "Well, all get ready now; it's time for us to go." Meet all— some of the relatives would come from Deusville with their kids and bring us over. That was partying time—the afternoon was partying time. So we had it good. It was very enjoyable. My daddy played ball then. He was young, and there was four brothers playing on a team. And they had a good time, playing ball. We was kids, we weren't doing nothing but walking around and looking at them and talking with other friends. And when we want soda, then go to our daddy and get us a little piece of money and go get us a bottle of soda. And that's the way it was.

---

[5]The Historian probably made a mistake in referring to the Petersburg Nine. She quite possibly was referring to the Scottsboro Boys, nine youths captured on a freight train and hauled into court on trumped up charges of raping two transient girls. The research we've carried out has turned up no other case in which nine individuals have figured.

Sometimes I think it was much more, but they didn't have no fair. No kind of fair. Nobody fighting. Now I never known a fight to come up the whole time I was raised up—never nobody got mad and fought. Like, you know, lot of people just get to arguing and fighting. One place out there on the other side of town, they had a church day over there. They'd have a church day the fourth Sunday in August, I think it was. Now, them people would mostly get out there, rough like, and they'd get to drinking and sometime people get cut. Quite a few times people got killed. But we never went there. Our daddy would never let us go nowhere like that. That was somewhere we never went.

But we had conventions, big meetings. He would let us go over there, but none of us alone. Our aunt had to take us. Didn't go by ourselves. They were, like big Methodist and Baptist conventions, you know, there. Sometimes they come to that particular town, or maybe the next little town, three miles apart. My daddy would let me go with my aunt, his older sister. And we'd enjoy ourselves like that. We never went nowhere, the girls, by theirselves.

Sometime, once in a while, there would be somebody who would have a little birthday party, and we'd go there. You see, my father was young, and they would take sides in that. But he would take us along, and I'd be running around there, looking at all the people, we had to look to see my daddy and ma. I want to go to them, I look in the crowd, and only see the foots of the ladies. It was enjoyment. They were young then. But after that, say, after the years rolled by, they didn't do nothing like that. They with us or go to church. My father baptized in 1922. My mother said she got baptized when I was a baby. My father was late in years before he come. And after that night, he just cooperated in church work.

Now, my brother, after he got in his teenage, now he was bad. That's the one older than me. He give them trouble. He got the way he would give my mother a lot of trouble. That's the one reason Mama lost her health so much. Because he went in and he had a way of taking things—he was always taking something. Now, he was the only one like that. Not another one like him. So I guess it all fell on him.

I remember when Mama used to go to a little court about my brother. He as bad, taking things, and she always trained us to tell the truth. She answered the white people just like this:

"Now, you-all in the jury and the lawyers, all I ask you-all to do—I ain't going to say he didn't do it. But that's my child," she said. "I got feeling for him just like you would have for yours. Now, all I ask you-all to do, is you just be easy on him if you can. But I ain't going to say he didn't do it. But I just want you to be honest, because he's my child.''

So she was always tryin'. Mama was just truthful. She just figured that if she would tell the truth, she will always come out more better, you know. She raised us like that. But, you know, always got to be one straying in the bunch. Now that's the only one that was strayed. But he died. Died in '54, but he was a grown man then. He had married and had a family. Him and his wife had separated, and he had married again. And that's about all the tragedy that I remember that happened with us. Sometime, you know, it can go one way or the other, and that's about all.

I try to be truthful. I never did, I couldn't tell stories. Sometimes it hurts you, but when you tell it, on the other end you will see then it will come out. Like, I said the other day, you don't get nothing out of telling stories. You can't frame up a story and tell one. They say a good liar can frame one up, do it good, but I never tried. I tell it just like it is, 'cause I've always been trained to tell the truth.

See, I was a child, I believed in my mother and father. What they told me, that's what I did. What I told my mother and father, I tried to live up to, see. And when they tell me something, it went with me. I don't care where I go, I thought about what they told me. When I was fourteen, I told my mama I wouldn't run out and get children for her to be worrying over, and I didn't want her to worrying about me being out with the boys. 'Cause she laid things plain to me when I got to be a missy.

So I said, ''Well Mama, don't worry about me. You done told what it takes, what I shouldn't do and what I should do.'' So I said, ''I don't want you sitting down there saying that Sister laid with some boy. Or that Sister did this or that.'' I said, ''I want you to understand I told truth. Don't worry about that part, because I'm not doing these things.'' I said, ''I won't be a slut. I don't want to hurt you. I won't do it. Now, I won't never drink no liquor. I will not bring a child in here on you till I get married.''

So I didn't do it. A lot of people don't believe that, but it's true. . . that's the truth. And anything that look difficult that come up, sometimes my brother, he would do a little different things, Momma would ask me if I were anywhere around, 'cause she knew I would tell her the truth. She'd say, ''Sister will tell the truth.''

One night we went out possum hunting, a friend, my cousin, my brother and me. They first had to go put the snare together. So something happened that night. This girl told her mama that she was going to her friend's house down there, and the other girl, my cousin's girl, says she's going up to Miss Loo's house. They stayed out late, and their mamas went out to look for them. And they ran up on them just soon enough to see some boys run in the river, down by the railroad tracks.

So that night Herman, me and my cousin and my brother went possum hunting down there. We went all around the fence, and we decided to sit down. We wasn't going to trace them dogs, we just going to sit there. And me and them got talking and laughing and just sit there. By that time we thought to go home. My brother said, "Aw, come on, let's go home 'cause that dog ain't going to retrieve nothing." So we went on back. And when we got home this lady and my cousin's mother, they had come over to Mama's, just come over there and they was standing up in the door.

As we got there to the house, Mama was standing in the front there, standing on the step. They just ready to go.

And Mama says, "Sister?"

I said, "Ma'am?"

She said, "Where you-all been tonight?"

I said, "We been a-possum hunting."

She said, "Where did you go?"

I said, "We went around the fence. You remember—we go around by the old Fletcher farm, right on down over there by the gate there. We went over there, and when we got over there we sit down and we didn't go hunting, just sit and wait for the dog to retrieve. Then the dog never did retrieve, so me and my brothers come home, my cousin come home."

And she say, "You sure of that, what you done?"

I said, "Yeah, Mama, that's what us done."

She stand up on the step and me standing down there. I didn't know what it was all about.

She said, "Well, Sister don't tell me no stories. Now, Sister, the boys ain't carried you nowhere and left you, and they went some place?"

I said, "I been with them from the time I left here until I come right back here now."

She said, "You sure of that?"

I said, "I'm sure of it. What is wrong, Mama?"

She said, "Well, it's just something that I wanted to know. I believe it. She don't lie—she ain't telling no stories."

So both sides went on back home, got some switches, and whup them girls till they did tell who it was. See, those girls liked the other boys and they figured to tell them it was our kinfolk, see, thinkin' they wouldn't pay it no mind. But after they got on to the ruler, they mama made them tell. I never did, couldn't tell stories. You don't get nothing for telling stories.

So, we stayed about five years in one place, on one farm. After we left there we went to Bordenville and we were doing day's work, and that tobacco. That's where I married, down there. I was seventeen, July, 1926. I remember when I was young, I was going to get married and try to raise my family and just live like my father lived, and that's what we always said. I asked the Lord give me a husband I can stay with through our marriage, and the Lord blessed me with him. Yeah, me and him never separated. You know, we had our difficulties but we never separated, and I never, never did have no hard time of living the best he could. Course he did get out of my hands before he died. He lived four years with a stroke, but that was after the kids was all grown.

So I married, then left home and went to Miami, Florida. And my husband also was raised in this little place called Bordenville, but we went to Miami, Florida, and stayed down there thirteen years. Most of all my kids were born down there. I had four kids down in the state of Florida.

I moved on to a big tomato farm. Big farm, raised tomatoes, and they had a grading factory right there. My husband was a truck driver on the job. I willing to work, but my husband didn't want me to work. So after he didn't want me to work, I decided I would wash and iron. My step-mother, she told me, she said, "Well, now, maybe you ain't got to work. If you want to do something, just take in some wash and ironing, and you could stay and keep your kids." 'Cause along then, they was charging one dollar a week for each child, to keep them, you know. I was having them pretty fast, and so she said, "Well, that's the way I started off, washing and ironing." That's why I got these leg ulcers—standing up, washing and ironing. 'Cause, see, like she say it, I'll wash and iron and stay home and cook, and I could keep the children myself to help him on the farm. You know, they didn't pay too much. He was a truck driver most of the time. My husband had flat feet, but it is fallen arches. So his father always tried to give him a job. Well, we stayed there on that farm a long time, up until us come back to Georgia.

Jason was born in '39; he was three months old when we came

back to Georgia. Raised him up in Georgia. So I was busy, stayed home and done work. I wouldn't be out too much. I never done a lot of visiting like most people, going about like most people. When I left home, my father said, "Don't get into trouble, go about your business." He told me I wouldn't get in trouble by being home and doing my work as a woman. Sometime I'd think about going to one of my neighbor's houses. Then I said, "Well, all I know is what my father told me; I was not going to get in trouble by doing my work." Then I'd be doing my work, and that time would pass over me, see, and it would be months and months before I'd think about going out any more. I'd always wind up doing something. I gets my enjoyment out of doing something mostly. And going to church. That's my thrill, is going to church. I like to be with certain people when I'm in the church. I don't like too many folks when I'm in church. 'Cause a lot of them, you know, noise and things like that, especially in these churches now. Get off to oneself, one person and me, and them would talk. So I just want another person just like me.

And my husband, he never did like to go nowhere. When we went, went together, see. That's the way we raised our children. Bible time, church time, he keep the kids and let me go. And I keep the kids and let him go. So that way we raised them up, like that. Howard, he never a man that like to go nowhere. Stick around the house, and maybe he'd go out and play checkers. He liked to play checkers. Maybe go out, stay hour or two and play checkerboard, come back and say, "Well, you know, I had a big game of checkerboard." Come on back to the house, sit around. And that way he just didn't like to go around. Time for him to go to work, he'd go to work. Then he come back.

Then we come back in '39 to Georgia. I had three children born in Georgia after I came from Florida. Some is not living though. And, well, you know, still wasn't nothing to do in Georgia but a little farm work. You know, days work. Day after day. This farm, particular farm here, was tobacco. The oldest one, he didn't get too much schooling. He was the oldest one, in and out. He didn't get too much schooling, but all the rest of them had a little bit, 'cause we was on this tobacco farm.

White folks owned it. They're just selfish. Now, that was a big place. Big tobacco company, and they have all the way from, oh, I don't know how many farms. About twenty-five or thirty farms, different farms, and the names, they were named after the letters in the alphabet. And we moved on there. My father-in-law was working down there before I married. Anyway, this big farm, they had the packing houses and they raised tobacco there. They carried it out of the barn and went to the packing house and packed it right there. They're doing that now. But there's not much there to do like it was, 'cause all the places there went down.

So me and him moved back down there. We finished raising the kids. I had but one girl. She being the only girl, see, she work right along with the boys on the farm. And after they got grown, see, they would do other things. See, now, my oldest son, he left on account of the back-breaking work tobacco was. And his back hurt. He left then and went to get him a job, first got a job into the Coca-Cola plant, capping bottles. And he stayed there about a year or so, and then he came back to where we were and got a job at the Model Clay Company. And that's when he stayed there, five years, until it make his health bad. See, the dust, he inhale that stuff until he got to the place where all he could do was sleep. And a lot of it was because the father was sick right along at the time. Got sick, and my son would try to work extra hours to try to make a living, 'cause he had to pay out money for his father's doctor bills. Then we had to travel back and forth, didn't have no convenience, paying people to take you back and forth to the doctor. So his health became a little bad. He sleeps. Put him in the hospital. He fat. They say it's his fat, but I really don't know what it is.

All the rest of them healthy. They come up, I never had no doctors. Little complaints, you know, I had. I kept castor oil. They took that castor oil, and that would get them straightened out when they get a little ill.

My father passed after we came back, in '45 he passed. Come back and he died. And the last baby I had, in '45, it was born dead. Then, my husband got sick in '51. Yeah, the fourteenth of March, '51, he fell with his stroke. He lived four years with this stroke. He got stroken in '51 and lived till '54. Then he died.

He had this radio, and everytime this, the Yankees play, during the World Series, he would always turn it on. He loved it, and that made me pay a little more attention. A lot of times I hear baseball mens, I hear the names calling out, and I know that's the same man that was running when my husband used to turn it on. Yogi Berra. Yeah. I'd listen to that because that was his enjoyment.

When he was sick we never leave him. When we worked, we carried him to work. Many times when we picking cotton, carry him in the truck, carry the food and everything, keep him in the shade.

Carry him right along with us. We never left him from the whole time, four years. I don't care where we go, we would carry him. Church, Saturday—we go shopping, take him to town with us. Drive the truck in a cool place for him to stay, and he sit in the truck. And we carry him little knick knacks and things, for him to be happy. So that's the way he went, up until about a week before he died. Stopped it. He told me he didn't want to go no more. Like, this Saturday he told me, and next Saturday he passed. . . died.

My baby was 13 years old when he passed. That's the baby, that's living here in Newark with me now. All, see, all the kids was living at home—none of them were married yet. They all went to school, the childrens, but they had that part-time work, especially time when they graduatin'. They'd pick up money to buy the graduation suits and things, to help out. I kept them in school all I could. That's the way they had to do. See, after I lost my husband, the kids worked on the farm.

Then my daughter, she married, had some kids too. She had me tied with three of her kids. I raised them up. Then she remarried, married a man from the railroad, so she took the kids back. One of them is on his own. The other two—the girl, she went to stay with her mother 'cause the mother had married, and the boy, he stayed longer with me. When I came up here, I turned him back to his mama. He had two years before he graduated. So he was with his mama, and he finished up those two years of schooling, he did graduate. So that's the baby boy I raised.

My children helped me. My boy, my oldest son that moved off the farm, he would bring up a supply of food every two weeks. Check on us every two weeks. Sometime he would stay overnight and go back. And then some nights he would be able to do nothing but just drive up there, get somebody to help him drive up there, and bring the food and go back. And he tell the rest of them now, he the father, because Daddy died. So he finish helping bring them on up, the children and the grandchildren. Saw him down the hospital the other day, telling all, "You-all done know I been your daddy."

Two of my boys went to service. The one next to the oldest, he went in during that Roosevelt time. Then the baby boy, he went in later. He volunteered and went in '62, I believe. After he got out of school, he went on in. See, something that he wanted to do, the army was helping him in that. And he didn't see no other route for him to have a good job, so he just volunteer and went on in the army. But during a period of years, that was cut out before he got out of the army.

See, some of what he wanted to get he didn't get, but he had to finish up his three years. So he went to New York, finished the last year overseas. Then when he come back from overseas, he came right here to Newark and that's where he stopped, you know. Got him a job. He said, "Mama, I won't come home. I'll just stay." He wasn't able to get a vacation after bein' in the army. And he been up here ever since. When his sister-in-law died he went down there, buried her. Hasn't been able to go back South since.

I remember it was in 1957, when I was down South livin' on this farm, the kids was workin' on it, we got burned out. That's a tragedy, but it's not a body tragedy. My son had been in the army and was just comin' out. My big son was living with us. And another boy had got married. All of us living in the same house. My brother had come up from Florida, 'cause Mama was sick and she was in my house. He came up stay with her, see if she get better or worse. So he were living there too.

It was the eighth day of March. It was a high wind that day, too. My mother was sick and in the house. And somewhere, somehow, the house caught fire, and we did not know it. Somebody call and say there's a fire and smoke. We went to see what the smoke was. You look up, you could see it seeping in.

It was about 8 o'clock on Friday morning. So I ran and got my mother out. And see, while I'm trying to drag Momma around the fire got bigger and bigger. We didn't understand where it come from or what. So by the time I could get her out like this, the house right next door, the wind was going that way, see, the smoke was so bad. And she's sick. So I said, "Well, I can't leave her here. I have to carry her further." So me and another man just picked her up and just carried her further over to another house. It was so cold that morning, it was freezing. Then a lady put her in her bed and got us some cover on and try to keep her warm. I went back to see about the house, but it was all burned down. Just this corner, I could just see that corner standing. All my things....

We just went out everything we had. I was dressed in the worst dress I had. I got up that morning and took breakfast and said I'll go and re-change, you know. You know how we womens do. Never had a chance. But the neighbors were very nice to us, very nice. So I was out, but I was able to get in a small little shack house. Come the next Friday morning I'll be in a little shack, you know. And they give me enough stuff. Had put up beds, and I had about three stoves in just that length of time. Different ones called me and asked me where I was planning to stay, and I told them to bring things to my neighbor's house, put it there. Then Monday, I got in touch with me a white man, he told me I could move in that old house to stay in it, you know, for nothing. We went down there, stayed in it, and made out all right. Stayed there a good while, too.

See, I was just surviving by my children at that time. My son was in the service, he made out a check for me, a small check. But after he come out service, that was cut off. And I drew my husband's social security. And my baby boy, he was thirteen years old when his daddy died, so I got welfare up until he was eighteen.

Now my other son had married. He's the son born in Florida, three months old when we came back to Georgia, raised him up in Georgia. And him and his family lived up above me. He left the farm, came up here to Newark. He came up here because times kind of tight, and he come up to get a better job. They didn't have any place, couldn't find a place for them to stay, so they left the kids with me. So I had their kids and my daughter's kids. So after he was up here in Newark two years, he came back on vacation. Every year he came back on vacation. So the last vacation he was down I was suffering with my leg. My leg was aching me, and I wasn't too much good then when they come down to be with me. So he said, "If you'd come back to Newark, see some of them doctors, they will do you some good."

I said, "No, I won't go now 'cause I have to do something about my stuff." I said, "Well, I'll tell you what you do. If you wait later on and send for me, I'll get things straightened out like I want. I'll come up there then."

I cashed my furniture and stuff; then I come up here in '64. They took the kids back from me the year before. And the most exciting thing when I got here was going into New York. I had to try to adjust myself to what was going on, you know. I wouldn't do too much talking, but I would just watch. See, if anything I didn't know what was going on, I'd keep conjectures to myself till I hear somebody say it. When I got to New York, it was so funny to me to see all them lights. Most of the thing was the car lights. I didn't understand between the car lights and the city lights; so much lights, you know, I didn't know what that was. You know, looked like the road coming to you. Going from you was red, coming to you was white. Seemed to me like it was just something with the red lights and the white lights. After, we went through the

tunnel. That didn't bother me. I just realized that I didn't went there
before, and I enjoyed it.

And after I got here, I went to Philadelphia. I didn't never think
I'd ever go there. See, I would always have in mind when I was coming
up in school that I'd want to go places, some place that I hadn't seen
before. And I would always say, "Well, I'd like to go to Philadelphia."
Just come to love that name when I was in class. It was hard for me to
spell, and I wrote it on my hand and spelled it, and when I missed it
in spelling class, turn my hand over and look at it. And often I'd say,
"Well, I believe I want to go there. Some of these days I hope I live
long enough to go there." Just come to love the name Philadelphia.
And so finally I got a chance to go. But see, what carried me there. My
step-mother-in-law lives there now, so I goes over there once in a
while, take a weekend vacation with her. Haven't been there now in
about three years. Philadelphia.

See, my son took me on over there. And when I saw it, I liked it
pretty good. I didn't really have in mind what it looked like, 'cause I
never have been in too many cities. When you come up here from the
South, you really don't know how things will look. But I was glad I
finally got there.

So after I got up here, was just going to stay three months, see,
going to go back home. Then my baby boy's wife died, you see, and
that what caught me right in. He said, "Well, nobody else available
but you." His sister is married and her family and all. Weren't nobody
else to be loose but me. My husband was dead and all, so I said,
"Well, I just put in to stay here with him."

I had difficulty with my own children sometime. They do aggra-
vate you a little bit, but not nothing too bad. And that's the same type
of life I'm raising my kids up now, my grandchildrens and this boy's
children. But you know, the time is not like it was when I growed up.
It's a little more, a little more complicated. The reason it's like it is
because there's so many things happening, and it keep you alert to
thinking about what would happen and what could happen here than
it was back then. 'Cause see, down South you'd do a lot of things all
day. You wouldn't even think about the children 'cause you'd know
where they was, and want nothing to be bothered. But, now, one you
got, he come to you and you tell him he come in at 9:00. He don't be
there. You start thinking, start thinking. You figure then that might
something done happened to him. Somebody's done kidnapped him

or something done happened to him. That's the difference as far as I can see in life with these kids, you know, different from the world when I was coming up. Not like when we was coming up. A lot of things you have to think about here, you didn't have to think about back there. Not as much temptation down there as it is here.

My life is with my son now. 'Cause, see, my son is supporting, doing the best things he is, and what not. So it's a little better for me now than it was then. 'Cause I don't have that bother, worrying about life, house, and all. See, that no problem of mine.

That's my life, see. Washin' and ironing. I didn't do anything but housework. Keep the children. A baby would be born, and it would two months or three months old, and I'd be going back to wash and ironing, 'cause I tried to help my husband. These ulcers come out of me in 1929. A little place on my leg, a little bit comes from a little bump. I picked it. In the beginning it would run, run, run, so I went to the doctor for this. The doctor treated about nine or ten months before he could even tell me what it really was. So he said to me, he said, "Well, you have to stay off your leg with this kind of sore. You just have to lay down, and say about three weeks, if you get in bed, it capable of healing up." At that time I was pregnant with my daughter. So I did get in bed. I stayed there nine days, and after the nine days it was cured up. It just healed. And it stayed healed. About a year and two or three months between this girl and the next boy, I got pregnant— by the time I found out I was pregnant, it broke right back out again. See, at the time, that's the way it worked. We had children so fast, I think that's what's causing it. I didn't stay off it enough. And working after my babies come. 'Cause after they get about two months and a half old, I go right back into washing and ironing. Standing on my feet, see. That's the way I lived for about nine years, doing that, time after time.

And the year was '52 when I had the operation for it. My husband was still livin'. I went to the welfare for help, 'cause he was sick with a stroke. So they said, "Well, if I could get you well, you could work for youself, help your own self out." So they gave me a operation. They put me in a hospital and operated, but it didn't last about four months. Broke right back out again. So that way, in and out, I been from this doctor and that doctor on up until now.

Been in the hospital—even been in the hospital here in Newark. I been into the clinic, Martland Medical Center. They still wanted to go cut me again, so I wouldn't set for it. Now I went to St. Matthews, and they treated it. They got to the place they didn't want to look at it. I went there the last time, and they started asking what I wanted them to do for me.

"Well," I said, "Well, I thought you was goin' to give me my dressing. If you don't give me no dressing, just give me something that I'll take it home with me, dress it home myself."

So he wrote me out enough dressing to do it. I went on over to the drugstore, picked up the stuff, and dressed it at home.

Then this lady moved down on the main street. She wanted me to try Dr. Norton. So next time I try a doctor, I tried Dr. Norton. He treated me about—I don't know—I think it was about five months, maybe more. So he just decided ain't nothing he could do. Then he had a nurse call Dr. Southfield in West Orange. And he gave me an appointment, so I went up there and started. I stopped going to him, because I told him now he got my leg doing pretty good, so I was just going to take the treatment and do it myself.

Then it began to ache now and then. And Miss Stanton, she called me about going to the doctors. I went down there one day, and she saw me, and she say, "It ain't no use you just keep going like that. Try my doctor." So then I got to Dr. Twining. He gave me an examination and everything. Then he said to me did I want to go in the hospital?

I said, "No, I don't care about going to the hospital. I go in there, at that time if you want to you cut me, and I ain't going to accept fate." I said, "I'll go back to my ulcer doctor."

He asked me who it was, and I told him Dr. Southfield. He also knowed him. He said that's as good as you could go to. So I started back to him in January. I been continue going with Dr. Southfield up until, you know, I went down South. 'Cause, see, I'm just living here in Newark for my home, but I been going back and forth down to the South. Now I haven't been back to the doctor yet, 'cause I just haven't taken time and gotten no appointment.

Going to the doctors helped me, but it just couldn't cure it. See, after some length of time not going, it would break down. Naturally, like this, I been stirring on it too much. See, when it break down, then I go get another doctor and try that doctor, and so he heal the tissues back up. So this doctor, Dr. Southfield, he is doing something I never had before. He put it in a cast, then you go two weeks. Then you go back to see him. But two weeks I wasn't home. So now I go back and see, is he going to put it back in a cast or is he going to continue with a treatment. And I do hope I'll be able to get back in there to see him

one day next week. I'll put it off till next week. And I been sufferin'
even from '29; that's the year it come out on me. '29, in October, the
middle of October.

Since I been in Newark I love to go to everything that's at church.
Church is a piece of my life; that's where I get my happiness. After I
get that, I think I got all I need. Well, since I been taking after you,
after the senior citizens, I go out on those trips and things like that. But
before then I didn't take no trips nowhere. It was just church, and my
church cooperating with somebody else's, and paying visits. So that's
the way I lived. I never was a person to go to no shows. I never been
to a picture show in my life till I come to Newark. The reason I went
then was because my son and his wife would go out on Sunday evening
and they'd take me. "Well," I said, "I'm going to go just to see what
it looked like." So I went twice to the drive-in. My son offered to pay
my way. But I didn't do a thing but go to sleep. We had our station
wagon, you know.

The time of the riot we had just left on vacation. We left on a
Saturday night. That coming Wednesday this riot happened. I didn't
know what it meant by riot. We was visiting my daughter in Florida.
She just happened to go uptown and she spoke to one lady say she had
just left Miami and heard that they raising the devil in Newark. She
said they just setting fires and burning up everything. Well, that was
something unusual for me. I couldn't understand it, you know—what
it was all about.

So I said, "Well, I'll listen to the news at eleven o'clock."

Sure enough, we were sitting there, looking at all these buildings
burning down, all the flames in different places. My little grandson
knowed that building up there.

And he said, "Mama, see that place right down there?"

I said, "Yes. You know, that's right where I was."

He said, "It might get our house."

When we got back here it was shocking for me to see everything
all bolted up. I really didn't know where I was till my son stopped out
there, in front. And he said, "Well, this is it." The food store all bolted
up. Well, we were going up to see what they done to me, you know. I
said, "Oh, I don't think they bothered us." Sure, enough, they
didn't. Nobody bothered our place. Nobody went in our place.

I don't think it was worth it. I don't think it was. It don't seem like
it's did any good. I really don't believe in my mind that you can conquer nothing being violent. If I want to conquer something, I always

try to move with, well, you know, right. Use right things, and you conquer all. Even if you had a difficult child, you should go to his right. See, if I know that you was going to be wrong, I would just cut off and go on and let your passion serve you like you want and go on about my business, till I catch you in the right attitude, see. I just don't see no sense in being violent. I just don't see it. It might be just I ain't got enough education to see it, you know. A lot say there's a need to go more schooling. I believe I haven't got that kind of education to see into such a thing. But I think it didn't accomplish anything, by doing all that.

We got to use peace, I think, to have a success. The Lord say He left peace in the world. Peace would accomplish more than a riot will. I just believe that now. 'Cause everything I do I try to do in peace.

10

Take Those Red Lights Out of Here

With my mother we was very close, but we were not so close with my father. He was tired when he come home, he was ready for bed. And if we did anything, my mother said, "I'll tell your father." We would just think that was terrible.

He loved us, but he would never talk much with us. I could hear him tell people about his sons—my brothers played football and when we got a little older we had a team—he'd be off bragging to the store about this son, his son, and oh, his daughter was in a play and oh, how she looked, but he would never tell us that.

One time I was a whole two months getting a hat, a red hat. I'm trying to get this hat—I saw it in the window and I thought it would be the most gorgeous thing I ever did see. I paid two dollars for it, and I would save like a quarter one time, a quarter the next time, and fifty cents from a woman where I would babysit. I worked all Saturday for that fifty cents. I finally got this red hat. I put it on. I thought I looked beautiful that Sunday morning. I was going to wear it to church.

My father said, "Where do you think you're going with that on?"

"I'm ready to go to Sunday School."

"With a red hat on? You're not going to wear a red hat. No daughter of mine is going to be walking the streets in a red hat!"

So I had to go and take that hat off. Do you think I could wear what I had been looking at all those months? My mother knew I was wearing that hat. But he said no daughter of his was going to wear a red hat. Or nothing else red!

So I gave it to my cousin. She gave me fifty cents for it. He told her she looked nice. She got dressed up to go somewhere, and she had on this red hat and suit with red around it.

"Oh, you're all dressed up," he told her.

I don't know if he ever knew that was the same hat. I never told him. But he was like that, you know. We put red lights one Christmas in our living room. I thought it was beautiful. We had this pine tree and it didn't have lights on it, and the red light made it look pretty.

"What is this, a red light district?" We were very hurt. "Take those red lights out of here!" And the red lights went.

When he got older he changed a little, but not too much. Maybe he just didn't say as much. But when he did say something, that was just it! But he provided beautiful for us. If we would ask to do anything, he would always say, "I don't care if it's alright with your ma; do it."

My father worked for one of the top men, chauffeur and everything. And the Southern white men was good to their employees. Most of them had chauffeurs and maids, personal maids. Didn't make much money—six or seven dollars a week. But then three dollars would feed you. They could get by on it.

In this home where my father worked there was a cook, a maid, and everything. After supper at night the cook would take all the food and put it in a basket. My father would bring this great big basket home every night, because the Southern white people, they didn't eat anything that was left over. Every day was fresh. And the cook would give him all this food to bring home at night. There was really food for the next day or food for anybody that wanted it. We were never hungry.

So we had a happy childhood, very happy. We lived in the city in South Carolina, born in the city. I had six brothers and sisters, and I made the seventh. Actually I was the oldest girl, the third child.

Our first house had three rooms, three rooms and a hall. My mother had curtains between that, and she really made a bedroom out of that. We had a woodshed built in the back, and we kept wood there. And we had a big fireplace. The house had a yard and a space for a garden. There was a little fence around it, and there was the neighbor's house—a city. We had fruit trees; peach, pear, plum and apple, I think we had. Oh, about five different trees. And at the back of the garden there was a grape vine. We canned the fruit and gave it to the neighbors. I doubt if it was ever sold. And then people that had gardens, they would share their vegetables with us. So there was always plenty of food around. We had a few chickens, but people weren't allowed a cow or a pig, because we were in the city limits. Our streets were paved and there was bus service in front of our house.

Every day we played around. We had swings from the trees, dolls, mud puddles. I played with my younger sisters and a brother. And occasionally we could play with the neighbor's children. But it was just a few that we allowed in our yard. Most of the time we went in their yard.

My father worked in a rich home, and my mother worked in a rich home also. While my mother went to work, the older children, my two older brothers, would be at home taking care of us. One went to school in the morning and one went in the afternoon, so one would be home with the younger children in the morning and one would be there in the afternoon. And the oldest one would start supper.

We had work to do around the house. I remember we had lamps, kerosene lamps. They were small, and every day we had to wash the chimney. Keep them shiny, so we could see.

And as far back as I can remember my mother had these curtains in the hallway. She slept out in the hallway, and my father had his own room. My sister and I would talk. We'd say, "How do they get more babies when one sleeps in there and one sleep in there?" Because the girls had told us that the mother had to sleep with the father to get the babies. I never seen my mother in the bedroom with him.

We'd lay there at night, and we'd try to figure it out. Because after this sister, there was another baby, my brother come along, and then another one. Well, we asked her one time. We just couldn't understand it. More babies keep coming, and she's in there and he's in there. We used to try to stay up, awake some nights. You know children; they're always busy pulling mischief. We would try to stay awake some nights, and maybe he'd get up and go in there. I never heard the door open during the night.

I would tell children nowadays they should have lived when I was young. There was so much to do. We made fun out of, oh, just little, minor things. At night in the summertime, when my father was home, we would sit on the porch, and he would tell us things that happened when he was a boy, and all types of weird tales, and we enjoyed it. And my mother would maybe make a bucket of lemonade before we went to bed. She always had something sitting around for us. And in the wintertime we would quilt. As far back as I can remember, she had a frame that she hung into one of the rooms and put a quilt on it. She would give each one of us a needle, and we'd all have to make a row, as she'd call it. And in the end we would quilt a quilt. She'd quilt one for the neighbor, you know. She had to get something, so she would charge $1 for it and we all learned to quilt, and we thought it was fun. It would be wintertime. While we was quilting she would maybe put a pan of peanuts to roast or some potatoes. Oh, they would smell so good. And we loved it. My brothers too, quilted. They made a couple of stitches too.

And then she would tell us, "No matter how clean you are, you are not clean enough." We had to wash our feet every night before we went to bed. I just couldn't see that, every night.

"No, you're not going to put your dirty feet on my clean sheets," she'd tell us.

And no matter how tired we were, or what happened, we're going to get that pan of water and wash our feet. We just couldn't go in and turn on the faucet. We had to go in the back yard and there was a faucet, and we got that pail of water and would bring it in the house. And then we would warm it on the stove where there was a kettle.

Then we moved out of there to another house, a bigger house, where we had our separate bedrooms. Three sisters, we all had a bedroom. We were in heaven because we had electric lights and a bathtub, a great, big bathtub there that you could get lost in. Huge tub. And we just going to bathe ourselves to death. But we soon got tired of that. That home had one peach tree, but the front was beautiful for flowers. My mother kept beautiful flowers. She didn't always work; she was home at times.

In this big house, everybody had their own bedroom, and we had a big front porch. And we had a big gramophone. Nobody in the neighborhood had that. I was about ten years old when we moved there. It wasn't far from a park, with a swimming pool, swings—just beautiful. We could go in the morning, because there was supervision there. Some afternoons we went, but we wasn't supposed to go alone. We had to go with somebody.

We had more than the average people in our neighborhood. My mother had two sisters that went North, and they worked for rich homes doing domestic work. They would send clothing back to us from time to time. And around the holidays or Easter time, they would send maybe five or ten dollars to my mother. She sewed at home. My father was always bringing something home. We had beautiful chinaware, glassware, and the average neighbor didn't have that. The other children would like to come down to us from school a lot of times, because we was rich—no, we lived like rich people. We had spreads on our beds. You know, they didn't have this. We just had a lot of things because even during depression times my father still worked. And my mother did a little work. Everybody was getting a bucket of soup or a loaf of bread at that time, but we didn't have to do that. Because we had food, and my mother's sisters, they still continued to send something.

In fact, if we didn't want a certain thing, didn't have to eat this or didn't have to eat that. Certain things my mother didn't cook. All this pork and pig tails and hog maws and chittlings—my mother never cooked it. Because she was brought up in homes where the people didn't cook this. In the mornings we had eggs, cereal and jelly and hot bread. In the afternoon we had vegetables, potatoes, meat, fish—we were fed very good. We always kept food, and we could always share with some of the neighbors.

When we went to public school she would pack our lunch like we were going to the man-in-the-moon. She'd put these big, baked potatoes in there, sandwiches, and pieces of fried chicken that was from my father's place from the night before. And our sandwiches would be the loaf bread, you know, and the other children, the most they would eat was a biscuit. They'd look at that light bread, light bread sandwich, and they would have biscuit and a piece of corn. My mother didn't bake the bread, she bought it. You could get a great, big loaf for a nickel, three for a dime. So she used a lot of it. But most people, they used biscuits. At ten we'd have recess and pick something out, and then at twelve we'd have lunch. We were home by 1:30, and we ate that whole lunch there. We'd eat some of it, and sometime we'd give it to the other children, give some away.

When we went to school I started at the Saunders Seminary. It was just a block from our house. At that time it was a girls' school; I think it's a college now. It was quite expensive, and I couldn't continue. They had public school, but that was quite a ways, quite a walk there, and my mother didn't want us walking that far. I think I got in the second or third grade, and I went to the public school.

The teachers were very strict, very strict. You couldn't go to school without your hair combed. The boys had to wear ties each morning. And your shoes had to be shined. You couldn't go to school any kind of way—a button had to be on, your hem couldn't be hanging out. And they made you speak with good English.

In the public school the teachers were colored. In the seminary we had white teachers. Schools were separated. We went to the colored school, and the white, they had their school. At that time you were in school to learn. You didn't go to school, acting up in school. If they send you out of school, well, your parents had to come to school. You think the worst was going to happen to you. You respected that teacher. You went to school, and you didn't play all this hookey. You either went, or somebody would see why you wasn't in school. Your mother would surely know about it.

They had straps that they would whip us with in school. And then if you told your parents, you got another one when you got home. So that was two. But the children had respect for a teacher. And a teacher was respected. She had to be qualified for a teacher. If she wanted to teach she had to be recommended for the job.

The only place we ever went to together was to church. Once a month my father would be able to go with us, because he had to work on Sunday. Only one Saturday a month did he get off. But my mother would see to it that we were in church every Sunday morning, every Sunday afternoon, and once during the week. We went to the Methodist Church. We lived just around the corner from it. And my mother belonged to all the clubs and missionaries and this circle and that circle, and sometimes she'd have the meetings into her home. And she took care of the children's programs, and she made the little costumes. We would have little pieces to say and recite, and we'd sing with the choir director, and the teacher would give us songs, and we would act out little skits. And my mother always made the costumes. They'd have like Tom Thumb, mock weddings, the Easter program, and so forth. And my mother spent a lot of time with it. But my father didn't.

Christmas was a real nice, big holiday. Always had a tree. Either the boys would go for it, or some of the neighbors would bring us a tree from the woods. We had all kinds of decorations we would put on. We made a lot of them, and a lot we would buy. In school we would make a lot of them and bring them home and decorate the tree. Then the little tinsel, we would buy some of that. Save our nickels and dimes for it. At that time it didn't cost too much to decorate a tree.

My father worked in this family twenty-three years, and there was always a turkey and a chicken from them. There was eight baskets of all kind of food. And my mother made this fruit mixture that she called ambrosia. In fact, all the families had this ambrosia. And my mother would start cooking about, oh, a few days before Christmas, baking pies and cakes and making vegetables. Everything would be about ready, and there wasn't too much company, just the family. It would last maybe a week, nobody worked for about a week.

There was a few things for the children that Santa Claus would bring. I found out there was no Santa when I was about eleven years old. Christmas Eve my father came in and told me. My mother was sick, and he came in and told me, "Your ma is sick. You have to help me play Santa Claus for the children tonight. There's nobody to help me."

I didn't know what he was talking about. And he gave me this doll, the one I had wanted. It was up in my mother's closet. She had said, "Well, if you're good, I'll see if I can get Santa Claus to bring it to you." I couldn't believe my eyes. And he had one for my sister, too.

I said, "Santa Claus is supposed to bring this doll."

My mother was so hurt because he told me. She said, "You could have let her have this moment."

You know, it was just before I was eleven years old. That spoiled everything for me.

I kept that doll, and I named her Sadie. The last time I was home that doll was still there. It was a china doll. I really should have put it away, because it is so old. I don't know if my sister threw other things out or not, but that doll was still there.

Well, I didn't tell the others about what I found out. No, I didn't spoil their moment. They learned, one by one.

I wouldn't teach a child now about Santa Claus, because now if you got a little extra money you can buy a child all this stuff every day. But you didn't see it then but once a year. A lot of children got a piece of candy at Christmas time, or certain fruits, or new clothes or something. Now people can afford to buy these things the whole year.

At Easter time, we always got little things. A hat on our hair. We could have our hair straightened, what we called it. Other than that, we did not straighten our hair. We would wash it and roll it up in curls. And Easter week there was always a big meal. Spent most of the day in church, up in the choir.

I never went to stay with a friend and spend the night with them, but a friend would spend the night with me occasionally. When school was out—my mother had a sister that lived in the country—we could go there for a week. And my father had a sister that lived way in the country too, and we could go there for a few days. Took this train. My mother put us on with a market basket full of food, and away we'd go. They would meet us with a horse and a wagon, and oh, that was so much fun. You went in the back of the wagon on the way home. They would show us the pigs and the cows and how they fed the cows. My mother's sister, she would pick cotton. They planted cotton, and all these little white balls—we would go with her, pick cotton, pick a few balls of cotton. We enjoyed that. Every summer we'd go to the country for a couple of weeks.

Course, we lived in a segregated world, a black world. It didn't have any effect on us because we lived in the colored neighborhood. There was no whites. The only white that we seen were at the grocery store, the business people. That's all white. We didn't see them because they lived too far away. We had two colored churches. In the hospitals we had part black, part for the whites. You could get on a bus that you had to start for the back of the bus, and you couldn't sit beside a white person.

It didn't bother us any, because we knew what was expected of us, and we just went to the back of the bus, that's all. And if you went into the stores downtown to get service, if there was a white person in there to get waited on, you had to wait for the white, but then they'd wait on you. So you expect those things. You know, we'd go to certain places. Some places you couldn't go 'cause the signs say "white only." Your sign "colored" points around to the back. Everybody else did it. We expected that, and we never had any problems, no fights. But the young people come along, and they began to see things a little different.

"My money is good as his money. So why can't I sit here? Why can't I sit there? I'm not going to move."

But in my time you went along with them. We knew you wasn't supposed to go there, and you didn't go.

And then I graduated from elementary school and went to junior and senior high. The graduation from sixth to seventh grade was held in this church, Holy Word Church. And my mother made my graduation dress. I went as far as the eleventh grade in school. I had a brother and a sister who finished college, but the others, they all went to high school.

I was seventeen when I married the first time. You see, I had a very strict mother and father that believed in work, work, work. You couldn't do enough work to suit them. And I was the oldest girl, and I was just like a mother with the young ones. I had to just work, work, work. And I just couldn't see going to school, coming home, working, working, scrubbing. Everything had to be shining. I don't think there was anybody as clean as she was. Everything had to be just so. And if she'd see dirt on you, "Look at that! You better get in there and scrub that neck." You know, it just got on my nerves. And the other children, I had to do for them while the other girls, my friends, would be out.

After ironing and things, you'd have to get the wrinkles out of all the laundry. Everything had to be folded. Every towel had to be just like this. The pillow cases had to be folded this way, not that way. And I figured, "How much work can you do?" And I thought I was getting away from that.

My husband was always after me to get married, get married. My mother was telling me to finish school, to be a nurse, to be a school teacher, to be a nurse, to be a school teacher. I felt like I wanted to be a nurse at the time, but teaching school! That would have been awful. So, so be it. I decided to be very smart, to get married.

We didn't know each other very much. If the boy came to your house, he had to be out by nine o'clock. That was the law. If you went out, you had to be in by nine o'clock. We would write letters to one another, give them after school, if you see them. And they could visit like certain days, like Sunday afternoon and, I think, Wednesday, after we were finished eating.

I decided it would be so nice to get away from home, and do what I can do by myself. There was no planning. A minister married us. We got the license a few days before. And I lived with my own family for two days. I waited just till my mother and father went to the movies, and I put the license on the bed. Then I went out of there, and I was afraid to go back. I was afraid to tell, because she had such high hopes for me. Well, after they saw the license they knew, and my father got up the nerve to call me to come on home. And why didn't you tell her anything? But they forgave me for that.

My husband and I lived with his sister. And then we got our own place. He was working. Then he had a car accident when we'd been married nine months, not quite nine months. I was home and he was coming from work. My sister told me. And the child was born that night. See, just long enough for a baby.

It was no insurance, it was no aid. You just had to do the best you could. Didn't I have to go back to my parents? It was harder living with them, because I was a widow with a child. I had to be a respectable widow, you know. They told me I couldn't work. I thought I was in hot water in the beginning. This was really murder! I couldn't do anything.

"You're a widow with a child and you can't be doing this, and you can't be doing that."

I still wasn't twenty-one. They always reminded me that I wasn't twenty-one. So I was just looking for a way to escape. I went to work. And my mother took care of the baby while I worked. My parents loved my baby, because that was the first grandchild. My mother would take him on long walks. My father showed the love for him that he did not show his own children.

At work I met this girl, and her brother had been in the war. He was back visiting, and I met him. He wanted me to go back with him and get married. He just felt like I would be the one for him. But I didn't know him. They were just leaving. He came back when his army time was up, and he continued to write to me and ask if I would come. I finally said yes. He sent me a ticket and money, but I stopped writing because I just couldn't marry a boy that I didn't know.

So I looked one day, and there he was, downstairs. I still didn't go to be with him, but a month later I decided that I would. I must have been just about twenty-one. I think I turned twenty-one after, and my mother lectured me.

She said, "If you go there, and if you don't send me a marriage license, I'm going down there and pick you up."

So I did go. I think I was in the city a week before we cleared things to marry. Every day I would get a letter. That Monday I got two. She was waiting for the marriage license. So I finally sent it, and I didn't hear nothing else when we got married.

I didn't know there was something wrong with that license. When he was applying for Social Security and different things, he had to show the marriage certificate, license, and there wasn't a seal on it. The social worker said that this don't mean a thing. He said, "You're not even legally considered married." It was no good. And after all those years! But I had that straightened out. They gave me a new license with a seal on it.

So after marriage things were fine. My husband was working, and I worked part-time, and we had money. I was able to travel each year, take a trip with the children. I was able to have friends in for dinner, and I enjoyed that. I was able to fix my house up nice and well, and I could keep it clean.

But after a while, things began to get slow. That was after we came to Newark. It was a struggle. My husband was disabled, just able to do light work, and then nothing at all. That was thirteen years ago. And then we got relief, later on they called it welfare. He just be able to work sometime and sometime not. I did laundry in my home. I did uniforms and shirts before all this nylon got it. I was living in the housing projects then. Yes, there was quite a few nurses around, and I would do their uniforms and that was a little change. And I did shirts, children's dresses, and I was able to pick up a little change to help out. But now I can't even hold on to a iron with my arthritis condition. There was always ways then. Occasionally I'd go out and do days work. I found out that it was cheaper to stay home than to get out and do days work. My children were small and I had to take them some place and pay to keep them. And take food for them for the day. We didn't come out too much ahead. You know, you can stay home and eat what is around and it would be cheaper. There's car fare to take them someplace, there's car fare to get them and to bring them home. So I found out there wasn't too much to gain by doing days work. But we managed; there wasn't anything to waste.

My children were real young when I took sick. That is, I had three that were young. The other two are so much older. My oldest boy is forty-one, and the next one is thirty-one. The oldest is married and has three daughters plus a dog. You'd think the dog was a child too.

They both live in the city. That is, my second oldest boy lives in another town, but he visits me from time to time. He's not married. He made a career out of the service. Occasionally he calls me and comes over. There's a lot of difference in their ages. The oldest one has seen things change. He's been to the country, you know, and he knows about country life. But the others, they don't know anything but city life.

How did I manage when the children were small? I did a lot of shopping at the Salvation Army. You know, I could go in and pick up clothes for the children for practically nothing. Now their prices has gone up just like everything else. But when the children were small I could go in with a dollar and bring out a few clothes. You could get little girls' dresses for fifteen and twenty cents that were almost new. Bring them home and do them up and pick up a coat for fifty cents and clean it. You know, I never bought shoes from there. I never cared for used shoes. But the children were cleaned up, they were attractive. Everyone told me, "Oh, you keep your children so nice. How do you do it?" But it was just knowing how to manage.

I would shop around and plan the meals ahead. Really had to stretch on food. If I got enough for today I could use, there would be enough for another day. I wouldn't have to cook fresh each time. And learning different brands. There's a lot to learn in the different brands of food. And just because there's a sale, you don't always get a bargain. You get stuck a lot of times! Try to get something on sale and then cooking it! I learned you have to have a system to cooking. And I always managed to feed my children.

Sometimes I've been very low on food. I even had to borrow from my neighbor. Then there's always my son in the service. But I hate to bother him. Still, I didn't bother too much, borrowing from anybody, because I would try to manage. Like for curtains for the home, dishes, pots and pans, I'd go in to the Salvation Army and get a stack of dishes or glasses for very little money. There were certain days when trucks would come in, and you'd run in and get there before everything is picked over. You could do quite well. You'd pick up a blanket maybe for fifty cents. It would be very good, because a lot of that stuff came out of the better homes. You could get a blanket and you'd launder it up. Maybe you would get it for fifty cents, and it would be an eight or ten dollar blanket. It would certainly be better than any blanket you'd go down and get for $2.98.

It bothered me a little bit in the beginning, when things got slow. It did seem kind of rough, when you want things for your children and you see you can't get it and have to do the next best thing. But it doesn't bother me now, because the children are grown up now, and they can do for themselves. After my daughter got old enough to sew, they began making things for themselves, and that saved a lot. My daughter made her own graduation dress. And it was beautiful. So we did manage.

You know, nobody has never known how I managed. Like, some people have been to me and said, "Oh, I don't have a thing in the house to eat. My husband didn't come home. There's no money. I don't know what I'm going to do."

I never told that. I have been without things—maybe sugar—for a whole week. Nobody didn't know it was like that. Nobody knew, because I just did without it. Or somebody would come for a cup of this, a cup of that, a onion, a potato, a little milk, a piece of bread. Nobody never knew I didn't have these things.

I made out with what I had. Didn't have a cup of rice? I'd use, I'd use a potato or noodle or something, or you did without it. I never went around saying I didn't have this or that. Nobody didn't know. Because it's not going to help if they're not going to help you. They'll just go and tell the next one: "You know, she didn't have this or she didn't have that." So I never told.

Now the young children are big enough to help themselves. School is out for the summer, and our main concern now is to get the children ready for college and prepare them for the summer. But there's not any summer jobs for children this year. Now the daughter who is sixteen has been trying to find a job because school is out, but there is nothing. Just yesterday I called the Employment Office. They said the situation is still the same, still nothing for the children. They had a few jobs last week, forty jobs. They had about fifty or sixty children to come in. There's really not enough jobs for all the children because they don't have the funds. My daughter's been all around to different places, different organizations, but it's the same story. And she was looking forward to doing something this summer. She'll just be content to stay around and babysit right here.

The older girl, she will be going away next week to a summer program, where they will pay twenty dollars a week while she's getting this training which will get her ready for school in the fall. She was accepted at Douglass College, and she'll stay on the campus. In fact, she was accepted at so many schools, it was hard to decide. And she felt she wouldn't have a chance being accepted. The University of Michigan accepted her, Stanford University accepted her, and the president even made a long distance call to talk to her if he could. He called because I have two nephews there. Well, I had one that graduated from there, and he's in his own business in Buffalo, the catering business. Now there's another nephew there, so she wanted to go there. But she was so late getting a letter from them that she had already accepted Douglass. She took Douglass because it is an all girls' school and it has whatever she wants. Then she received a scholarship from Douglass. So everything is set for the first year. I don't know about the next years. I think she'll make it—hope so anyway.

The summer program she's going to is to prepare her for the coming years at school. It will be at Rutgers, in New Brunswick, and she'll be staying there for six weeks.

My oldest girl that's in college is working now. She's found a job in a restaurant and she'll be working all this summer. She had the same kind of job last year. She had a few offers from different places where she worked. The librarian wanted her, because last year she had two jobs—she worked at the library in the day and then at night worked in a restaurant. In that way she had enough money to help her through school last winter.

She's going to graduate in 1976. And then she's going to have to go away and take some more years of training. In the beginning she was majoring in teaching. But now she's in psychiatry. You know, to me it was a little strange. I should not have been so surprised, because with all the notes and books of the mind and the brain I should have known something was in the air. That's what she wants to be.

She feels like they're going to be so much in demand.

Welfare gave her fifty dollars a month up until this year. She's going to be twenty-one. Plus she worked after school at the library until closing time at night. She always managed to make a few dollars, because she went to work about three or four and worked until they closed at night.

Tuition came through a bond—higher education—they grant like a loan and if you're an outstanding student, so much is knocked off of your tuition. There's like a scholarship for the first two years, so much. And then they have this fund for higher education. I really don't know just how that works, but there is something that she receives every two or three months, plus what she's able to earn.

Well, if I should live to see her become a psychiatrist I think it would be something. I do hope she makes it. She's doing quite well, and she's tried. We have high hopes for her.

11

Put a Handle on His Name

On the plantation, back in them days, white folks used to suck my mother's titty and all that. My mother used to cook for them, eat at the big house, like they call it. Now, a boy used to suck my mother's breast, one tit, and me on the other one. Still, when I'd go to his house, he could go in the front door while I had to go around the back. He was at the table sittin', but they feed me in the kitchen. That's the way them things was. When a boy got up, big size, he knowed he had to change his attitudes.

My father lived in Montclair and my mother in North Carolina. They was together up until the war time come. My father went in the army and come out. On this plantation where we was stayin', him and another guy took the old mules out. They kept them out all night. So they laid him across a barrel and they beat him. He left us. Just never was seen no more. My movin' around I doin' when I came to be a big boy, goin' from one to the other, from Montclair to North Carolina, I'd stay down there a while, and come back here and stay a while.

See, I was born in Lawrence County, North Carolina, and come to Newark in 1915. I had eight brothers and one sister. All of them dead, but just us two. Some of them died when we were little. That flu come along in World War I and killed out practically all my family. I lost my last brother July 10th, year before last.

There wasn't too many colored doctors in the South. There was an old one named Dr. James. When my brothers was bein' all that sickly, all through the flu, you had to go 'bout ten miles to the little town and get him. Then he'd be out on a call, and he'd come the next day, or the day after. By the time he got there, everybody would be dead and you'd be goin' to the funeral.

Didn't have no family doctors then, 'cause you couldn't afford it. People was workin' sometimes, makin' 50 cents a day. Sometimes they wasn't. Some would work ten hours for that 50 cents. From sun-up to sundown. Then you don't know whether you going to get that money or not, 'cause if the guy goes to town to sell and he don't sell, you ain't gettin' paid. But up here it was a little bit different. At least here you'd make five or six dollars.

The way we was raised up down there in the South, it was most like a plantation. Everybody know everybody. They wouldn't go through no big change. My father used to teach me when I was a kid. He said, one thing you've got to remember when you be playin' with white kids. You got to remember that you is a black boy. I always remember every word: you gotta remember one thing, boy—you is black. He never used that word, Negro. In other words, he meant for me not to prop myself too high with them. He just as good as tells me a lot of hardships and things goin' to come over. Sometimes I'd go too far. We used to play together, sisters and brothers all play together—and I'd catch myself. I'd say, "Well, I ain't gonna do that." Stay in my place, and I always got along with them. That's the only thing.

But he'd tell me, "Don't let nobody push you around." So I always got along. If I got one I couldn't get along with, I didn't fool with him. Always stayed in a hurry, cleared out quick, and that way I stayed out of trouble. You may have ten guys that were very nice, and one egg come up and spoil it all. Didn't like colored people, so he'd put mean things in the other guys' heads. But most of the time we got along, 'cause here in Newark, whites used to stay upstairs and colored downstairs, and they all got along like two peas in a pod. Never had any problems.

I came to Newark with my mother in 1915, on a visit to Montclair. We didn't know where we was goin', to tell the truth. We got into Penn Station at the time Old Charlie, the train, used to back up there. My mother couldn't read. I couldn't read at that time. My sister and brother, they didn't know nothin'. So this guy took my mother and us down to Number Five Perry Street. I never will forget it. They kept us down there two or three days before they'd show us the way. It just about broke my mother all the money she'd got up off of. They put her on the trolley and told her to go to Montclair. We went past Montclair, all way up to Caldwell. The man was good enough to put us back on that thing and bring us back down to Montclair. And that's how I found my aunt.

After then I stayed with my aunt and uncle quite some time, goin' back and forth down South. I come to like Newark, so this is where I've been all the rest of my life. I was in a Jewish section, and with Italians too, all mixed up racial. We lived in a different life than the younger people live today, you understand. We had raised up with more manners and more understandin' than young people got today. Other words, only thing I can say about it is that young people now got more to deal with than we had in those days. All kinds of children there, Jewish, Italian, colored. Most of my clan right around that vicinity, there wasn't too many Negroes on this hill. When I come here Negroes went back towards the neck, you see. Penn Station was like a chicken coop then. Course they then rebuilt it about ten or twelve times. I lived up above an old horse stable on Beverly Avenue and years and years on Donald Street. Then we lived in Montclair for a long time.

I didn't get too much schoolin'. I'd go to school a little while, and then stop and work a little while. It was kinda hard on us all the way around. I mostly had to help take the family along, 'cause I was next to the oldest. My uncle was a preacher and I wanted to be a preacher, but I couldn't get the schoolin' so I just gave it up. I never got more than the third grade in school. I had a little more since I've been around my sister. I learned how to read and write pretty good. Different old people, helpin' me, coachin' me. And I went to school at night.

I wanted to be like my father, too. He was a very intelligent man. He always kept a piece of money, always tried to hold onto somethin'. He used to teach me, if you've got a dollar, try not to spend no more than 75¢ of it. He said, "That other quarter will keep you off the hog." Anytime I asked him for something, he had that quarter or fifty cents. He'd tell me when he give it to me, "Don't you spend but a dime of it. 'Cause you may be able to ride that hog tomorrow with the other fifteen cents." That was the way he used to train us. I wouldn't spend but a dime of it, just like he said.

I wanted to be like him and my uncle. I never could. Did you ever see anybody, trying to climb? Trying to get a hold? I never could get a hold at that time.

My mother was a beautiful woman, kind hearted—they don't make no better. You couldn't ever do nothin' wrong in her eyesight, unless you mistreat some older person. Then she laid on you. She'd lay somethin' on you if you done sassed somebody. Then you'd get a double whippin', too.

Didn't have too much time for playin', too much outlets. When I did get out, mostly on Sundays, Sunday morning. But I didn't do that much, 'cause when I come out of public schoolin', I had to go to a man named Anderson, go to his store and work to make ends meet.

My first job was workin' at a bowlin' alley. I was settin' up pins and shinin' shoes there. You get five cents a shine. Get a man's sock, get a smack on the side of the head. Settin' up pins, if the guy win a game he'll give you somethin'. If he lose, he didn't. I guess I was about 14. I went to work before then, but that was first real job I had. Before that I was workin' in the store for $2.50 a week, carryin' groceries. Worked for a drug store, and used to have to ride a bike all the way up in Bloomfield, deliverin' medicine. I'm the guy in 1930 that break a leg in those big balloon pants, when they come out!

Then I worked in Newark for a clothing company. I worked around, little old funny jobs. Washin' windows for a while. Worked for a dime store. A little of everything. Kept a little old job, 'cause I liked my own spendin' money. Had to help clothe Willie and my sister—up until he died. Didn't have nobody then, but my sister. I just completely give up school; wasn't going much, every three months and then stop, see. My mother and father, if they had stayed together, I imagine I'd have been just about whatever I wanted to be. I was a big boy when I saw my daddy again. I was right here in Newark and he was in Montclair. Six miles from here, and he didn't even know it.

It was in 1936 I saw him again. I had been back South. My daddy sent me pants there, and they were for a little four year old kid, and I'm way up there. Yeah! Yeah! I had an aunt back on a visit. She happened to come back by my mother and saw those pants, and she was tellin' my daddy about it. After that, when I came back in 1936, I went to see him. I was sittin' there in the house, waitin' on him to come. At that time he worked for a coal company in Montclair.

My daddy come in, and the lady turns and says, "Do you know that gentleman settin' there?"

He looked over there and he said, "Yeah, looks like I seen him around here somewhere."

She says, "Look at him good, now."

"Yeah, looks like I done seen him sittin' 'round here in the park somewhere."

So my auntie says, "That's your son."

"Brother, is that you?" Then he grabbed me, and hugged me, and kissed me. He didn't know his own child. He'd been gone so long, he couldn't recollect. Now, in these days kids couldn't take what I went along with. But back in them days they would have taken it.

When I was travelin' back and forth, from New Jersey to South Carolina, there was a whole lot of difference. Like, if I been callin' a guy by his name before I left him down there, and came back and called him by his name, they would have said, "That nigger done went up North and got rude." They would say, "He ain't got no manners now." That guy want me to put a handle on his name, although I'm older than he is. I been sayin' James to him and he been callin' me Campbell. But when you come back, they put a handle on your name, and they want you to do the same. They call you uncle and you better call them somethin' or other. They're still that way today. If you stay in your place you'll be all right. I always got along. You run into a bad egg, you got to feel your way around till you get a chance to say, "I've got to go now." That's the only way you can stay out of trouble."

I know one particular time this man used to take his old hat in the sun, and the white man would drink out of it, he'd drink out of it, and since the white man drank first, it's all right. Then the white man'd turn right around and drink right behind you. Like, I used to carry water on the job. They had a dipper, you know. But you had to give the boss some first. He'd drink yours, and then you could drink. But all the time he's drinkin' right behind you. It's just that simple to them. They want you to get them along.

When I was a young person, I was pretty well dressed, well mannered. The girls saw quite a bit of me, sort of spoiled me. I was free hearted, good hearted all my life. Felt that way from a kid. Boys now know too much. When I was comin' up, you'd do good if you'd hold a girl's hand or get close enough to hold her hand. Or carry her books to school. Be a year or two years before a boy would get up enough nerve to say the wrong thing to her. I used to say, "Well, I'm goin' to ask her this time." But I didn't get enough nerve to do it.

I lived in New York for about nine years but I never liked the city. I'd be in Jersey about as much as I was over there, anyhow. The town is too fast for me. I worked for a clothin' factory over there, cleanin' up. Never could save no money. Never tried to hold onto a dollar there. Always somewhere to do, somethin' doin'. You're broke before you look around, if you don't know what you're doin'. In New York they've got somewhere to go every hour in the day and every minute of every night. Somethin' jumpin' all the time. They got just as many after hours joints as there is other joints. I used to be in all of them till I learnt some sense and come back to Jersey. Then I could save me money.

I was the only man that stayed in New York nine years and worked there just about the whole time, and go out of my pay every week before I get it. If I didn't go to this after hours joint, I'd go to another one. I'd owe this one tonight, and I'd owe that one tomorrow night. By Thursday, when payday is, I'd pay this one and pay that one. Then come back, borrow from this one to pay the last one. I'm right back where I started.

I'm the only man that stayed here in Newark and got put out every week. You know, the times was so hard, I had a room and got my board and my clothes washed for 75¢ a week. And I couldn't pay that. I couldn't pay that. I worked so many places, I went so many places, people knowed me. I got me a record all way cross town there. Then I met this girl here, 47 years ago, and she straightened me out. I've been straight ever since.

She's here from Atlanta and was workin' with the wife of a friend of mine, doin' domestic work. This friend told me for two or three weeks that he wants me to meet somebody.

"I want you to meet a nice girl, somebody to straighten you out. Nice and quiet."

I kept tellin' him I'd be up there Sunday, but I'd never go. So one day they come lookin' for me. I was stayin' with a preacher and his wife. I had a place up in the attic. I'd been out havin' me a couple of drams. I'd go up there in the attic, and I could cool it from the preacher. This particular Sunday the preacher called me down and said, "You've got company." I goes down there and here is that Bessie with a girl named Iola. My friend tells his wife to go get some change 'cause they had a cab with them. I was livin' a little outlawish at the time, but I didn't much want to go along with the program. But I looked, and seen a few of them brothers there, you know. I was shootin' a little bit bad, wasn't shootin' too good, so I said, "I guess I better go along with you all."

So we went on out to one of those there taverns, where you get those big mugs at, and we had a few of them. At that time, they were sellin' old moonshine whiskey, 35¢ a pint or 15¢ half a pint. We got a few of them. They had an old jerk down there, runnin' it. It was somethin' like a Greasy Spoon, didn't have but one table. So we was sittin' in there. I always have been a pretty good, loud talker, and I told him, "This is my wife, man. Fix the table up nice for her." We was sittin' there, all four of us, eatin' hog maws, and we got hooked up then.

She was living at Water Street at that time. She kept tellin' me to come down there, and she gonna fix dinner. I made like I didn't want to go, but I was real ready to go down there, you know. So I went down there, and so we got hooked up. This is about as quick a marriage as I ever seen. 'Cause she had about thirty-five or forty hundred dollars. I didn't have none. It was no use me losin' no time. I went on, and got hooked up with her, and that was it.

There was no long engagement, no, nothin'. No kind of boolsky. Come on—let's go. No wedding plan or nothin'. We just went down there and told the man to hook us up. Let's see, I think I paid $2.25 for her, that's with marriage and everything. Got everything for $2.25. Then we come back and got us a little half a pint and some beer and celebrated. That old strong moonshine made a crowd of people drunk at that time. It was 180 proof, I guess. And we've been hooked up ever since. Haven't been separated. Been together 47 years.

Before I got married I had a whole lot of foolish ideas. For one thing I wanted to meet a well-to-do girl, and I wanted a girl that would stand for somethin'. But it just didn't work that way. I look at it another way. I didn't have no education to go along with them things. I just saw it for the best and I think I got the best. After you been with a woman for 47 years and don't be separated, you got the best. I'm tellin' you, I got the best.

We lived in Newark. I was in my twenties when I got married. Tell you the truth, we were married almost ten years before we decided to get an apartment. We'd stay with these good people, stay with some more good people. You could get a whole house for $12 a month. Two-family house. Newark got packed up here just in '39 and the forties. World War I brung all these people here. You used to find a house anywhere you wanted up here on this hill without any trouble. The landlord see you standin' up, lookin' up there, he'd come down and they'd be fightin' over you.

I had one uncle here in Newark, but he passed pretty soon. That throwed me to be on my own. Now I've only got one sister and my four kids—that's all. That's my whole family. There won't be a whole lot of hollerin' goin' on at my funeral.

We always helped out my mother and her mother, too. My wife's mother is still livin'; 97 years old and she looks as young as I do. She's an Indian type of people. They all mixed breeds. They don't fade away too fast. I never had to support my father, just my mother. My father, him and her separatin', I knew he would not do but so much for my mother, know what I mean?

Say, for instance, you was my wife. You gets troubles in your family or whatever it is; when you got trouble and you're my wife, I've got trouble too. 'Cause I know you ain't goin' to be satisfied until you get somethin' done. So you can just go on ahead and do it. Same thing fly back to her. If she knows that I had trouble, know my mother needs things, she would go and get them. I never had to tell her. She'd never tell me to send her mother twenty-five or thirty dollars. I'd just stop at Western Union and go ahead and do it.

"I sent Momma some money. Here's the stub."

That's all.

She'd say, "I didn't tell you to do it."

"Well, you got the letter statin' that she wanted somethin', so I just went on and do it."

That's all. That's the way we do. We always got along.

I don't expect my kids to help, though. My oldest two kids what live down South got a little more consideration than the two here. My two oldest was raised up to a certain stage different from these here in Newark. One went wild at fourteen years. She got four babies now and ain't twenty years old yet! And my son, the youngest one, he's just twenty-one years old and he's got four or five. It's a whole lot a different stages than them other two kids. Just like every twenty years a different generation. I don't care what you do; there's gonna be change in people. They going to find more things to associate with, more environment, more everything. The world is like a battlefield. You can't get away from it.

I can call my oldest two right now down South and tell them I need so and so. Be here just like that. I don't bother them to pay that money. They want me and Momma to come there and live with them, but I won't go. I don't want to be no burden on them. I'm all right by myself.

I got friends here in Newark. The whole town knows me, white and colored. I got friends everywhere. I'm known all over. Just like I told you once before, I wasn't no house man. I gets around. Me and my wife, we understood one another from the first day we met. She knowed that she wasn't gettin' nobody to sit here and look at her. 'Cause I could find her when I come back. I knowed she was goin' to be at home. And she had enough confidence in me to know I was comin' back home. That's just the way we lived all our lives.

She'd say, "I'm goin' over to Lucy's."

I'd say, "O.K. Tell Henry to see that you get back home."

So when I get ready to go, she'd tell me to tell Julie to take care of me. "Don't keep you out too late. Tell Julie don't keep you out too late." We didn't never have no problems, no big thing, 'cept if one stayed out late. Then the other one got his mouth all stuck out.

One time I done went to work at U.S. Metal. I drawed my first little pay. Come in here and give it to my old lady. Kept me ten dollars, 'cause one of the boys around the corner been good to me. I went over to the tavern, and they drunk that up so fast that I didn't get me no whiskey.

So I come back and told my wife, "Let me have another ten, baby." There I was, borrowin' my own money.

She told me, "I didn't know you was goin' to give me this little money and come back and take it."

And she throwed it all at me.

So I went back that time and I rolled up the benches all the way around—the stools all the way around. The guy what brung me back knocked on the door and left me standin' up there. I was real tore up. My wife opened the door.

She said to my kid, "Move out of the way. Your daddy's sick."

What did she want to say that for? I drove back to swing at her, and I hit the floor. I couldn't get up 'cause I was too drunk. She got on me with some high heel shoes and started peckin' me all over the head. She just hollerin' and peckin', so somebody called the police.

When the police come she done got up off me. Kids in one corner, hollerin', and she in the other corner, hollerin'. Still got the shoe in her hand.

The police said to her, "What do you want me to do with him?"

I said, "What in the hell do you mean, man? I'm the one bleedin'. I want her arrested. I'm the one that called you."

They still tease me about that today. Yeah, still tease me. But my wife ain't never wore no more high heel shoes, and I ain't never come in and tried to swing at her no more, either. I ain't slept with her either from then on no more. She no woman she whip me. She stayed in her room—don't know when I come in. I don't know when she come in. After then, when I did come in—you be with the boys when you get paid off and you have a few drinks—when I did come in, I'd lay her money up there. Go in her room and lay that money on her dresser and went straight on in mine. Wasn't nobody that said nothin' from that day on. Ain't never had no more trouble with that. She picked me up that time. She broke me from that, but she ain't never throwed no more money at me either.

I used to come in and give her all my money and I'd have me $10 or $12 left. Before I get out the door she'd tell me, "Wait, will you stop at the store and bring me such and such a thing back? I'll give you money when you come back." When I'd come back she ain't got no change. That's the way it goes. No argument or nothin'.

I asked her one day, "Let me have a couple of bucks. I want to go to town."

"I ain't got no money."

But let my boss call and say come to work, she'll find somethin'. So we have a lot of fun. To tell you the truth, she's a sweet, lovely woman. Been that way all her life. Ain't never had no problems, you know, no big thing.

I got four children, pretty good family—'fore I give out. I got a daughter and son live here in Newark, and a son finished the University. He's a undertaker in Atlanta. I got a daughter, she married a doctor in South Carolina. I wanted my kids to take up somethin' good in school. Which they were doin' all right till I got in that trouble. The youngest ones, they were a little bit wild after that and there was nobody here. My wife wouldn't speak above a whisper hardly. She was a good hearted woman. Whatever you said, that was all right with her, and so these two young ones went a little bit wild. My daughter had to quit high school. Fooled around and got pregnant while I was gone. And my boy got with the wrong crew and fooled around with that dope and different things.

I don't know what these kids go to school for these days to save my life. I bought them every kind of book it was. Six closets are full of them. I bought them medicine book, doctor book, all kinds of books for them, and they did nothin'. After I got into trouble in '67, they went wrong. My daughter got trapped, and my youngest son got with the wrong people. Just one of those things. Was nothin' I could do about it.

I didn't have too many problems till then. In 1952 I stopped my wife from workin' when she give birth to my baby 'cause I was a foreman, come home with $241 every two weeks. That was enough to take care of them. So we was doin' good till this trouble come up. A guy put the counterfeit money off on me, knocked out all my teeth. Then I shot him. Wounded him pretty bad. I got 15 months for that.

Bein' in prison is unconvenient, you know. A 4x8 cell—can't go any place. You got to get a pass to go from here to the kitchen. You go to the yard once a day. I had a good break while I was in prison because I worked for the doctor the whole time. Make your bed for the warden

and all that, and then I was out every day. But at night, you be
worried half the time about your family. The worst thing about bein'
in prison is when you don't get a letter from home, or you don't get
no money, you don't get no visitors. 'Cause after my wife was taken
sick, she couldn't visit me like she's s'posed to do. So that was another
problem, added a little more worration. She must have taken sick in
'68—some time like that. With her heart, you know.

In prison you take your life under considerin'. It puts you in a
big notion to go back and think. What's goin' on? Was she bein' mis-
treated or what? So in all uncertainty—this was in '68—you quit gettin'
anythin' from home. That keeps a man worried and aggravated. Every
holiday you can send a card home, and you get no repeat from it.
Christmas come, or Thanksgiving—you don't get nothin'. Like once
a month I was gettin' boxes and different things from home and all that
stopped, all of a sudden. You want to know what's goin' on. Ain't
nothin' you can do, 'cause you just bat your eye wrong in there, you's in
trouble. So you've just got to set there and worry and half sleep at night.

I said, "Well, I'm here now. Just got to make it. That's all."

Just got to stay there and mind your own business, and just got
to be that way. You've got to make the best life out of it, 'cause you
know, in the first place, you done did somethin' wrong. Other words,
you wouldn't be there. You've just got to realize that.

It's twice as hard to get out of there as it is to get in there. You've
got to have a strong chest, take it as it comes. I've seen them hop off
the beds; I've seen them hang theirselves, cut their wrists—do everything in there. Baddest thing about it—you'll see a guy tonight, you
be talkin' with him, and the next thing you know, they got to go out for
breakfast in the mornin' and he's dead. Done bled to death in his cell.
Or you'll be talkin' to a guy tonight, and he blow his top 'fore day.

You can't let those things bother you. There's two things about it.
A old timer told me this here when I first got in there. There's two
things you got to give up when you get in them places. Got to give up
the streets, see. Can't worry about the street, what happens. You got
to worry one thing: how you're goin' to get out; how you're goin' to
do the time. That's your biggest problem. That's where you got to
live. That's your life you got to live all the time. You can't live no other
way. That's what's wrong with the average young man right today.
He'll get in there and try to press this thing. But he don't never think
if he hadn't ever did wrong, he wouldn't be there. It's no honeymoon.
This is capital punishment. Other words, it's there to make you *don't*

do wrong no more. Make you think before you do wrong.

There's another thing about it. If you got a guy got as much time as you is, you got to try to get with him. You can't get with a guy got more time. 'Cause the nearer you get to the end of your time, that's the harder he try to be on you. He make it bad for you, if you and him get real tight. You've got to stay away from them people. You got to stay with somebody in your category all the time, if you want to get out of those places. You can't get in that neighborhood with a guy got ten years or fifteen years or twenty years, 'cause he's goin' to do somethin' wrong all the time. He gets to where he doesn't care. And if you gets that way, you'll wind up doin' all your time, not gettin' parole. That's the way them things go.

I made parole—I knowed I was goin' home on such and such a time—and I got with guys like that. Like, he's goin' home a month or two before I do or a month or two afterwards. Them's the kind of people you gotta hang around with. 'Cause you can get in trouble there with the bat of an eye.

What makes evil in those places if a man don't get no visit or his woman don't come to see him. He don't get no money from home, don't get no letters—he stays evil. There be a fight there every minute during the day. Any man. Don't take much. The dangerist part about it is the mess hall. You liable to get killed in there anytime. You settin' here with the benches lined up, you settin' here with your back turned. If a guy get somethin' sharp and throw at the other guy, it's liable to hit you when he ducks. You've got to stay on the 'lert. You've got to keep your eyes doin' this all the time. I seen them get hit in the head with rocks. A guy take a rock and put it in his sock and walk up the line and knock another guy's brains out. Seen all that while I was there. So it ain't no play bein' in prison—it's bad.

Even goin' to jail is bad. The way they feed you in jail, that slop and stuff. When I was in jail I had a little tin pan and they'd dump everything in there. You'd begin to eat it all. Look down there and they'd be a long hair in it, or there's a big roach—a big roach after you done finished it all. It's the same way down there in prison. They don't put no seasonin' or nothin'. They just dump it out. You eat it or leave it. But they don't throw away nothin'. They put it back. If you don't eat it on line today, you eat it next time.

I got sick while I was in prison. Matter of fact, I was sick before then. But after that little trouble I had—it just got on my nerves. See, everything gets wrong with you whenever you don't get no letters and things from home. You have to go to bed and sleep it off. You got to be careful about anything you do in there. You're tryin' to get out, and anythin' you do in there, it's a charge. You go in there with a little old folder with two pieces of paper in it; when you come out it's about six inches thick.

They used to have a wing there for you to stay in, sit out and play checkers all day. After they had a riot about food and stuff, everybody be locked back so nobody never got out. You go in, you just got to stay in. No checkers or recreation. The younger peoples runs all those things, not the guys who have been there. You can't fight city hall. You can't force those people to do anything. You—the easier you be, the more careful you be, the better it is.

I wasn't here in Newark when this big riot was. I was in Trenton at the time. You could see it up in the rec. room, on television. I don't think they accomplished a bit more than what was goin' to happen anyway at the time. What it takes here in Newark is just people with mother wit and will power. It doesn't take all that fightin' and goin' on. What the hell! You hurtin' your own people. Just like they go around here, hittin' you on the head. They holler, "Soul brother," then turn right around the corner and knock you damn brains out. But you see, that's most of these jail house guys that join up with the movement. They come out of jail actin' that way. And the movement don't know no more about them than man-in-the-moon. They nice people in the movement—go well dressed and well cleaned. Yeah. But these guys go to jail, to Caldwell or Trenton or Rahway somewhere, and they join up with them when they come back out here. Then they holler, "Soul brother," and stuff and that's a mess.

So, after I went to prison the state taken over my wife. They give them about 200 and some dollars a month the whole time I was gone. I came out of prison sick. They had to put me on the state too, on account of I was the bread winner, the man that did all the work. So they take me.

I could have went back to my old job, but I wind up with the shiver and things like that. My doctor won't let me work. I felt bad. It's a whole lot different a man comin' home with $241 every week, you know. I got to come out here beggin'. I had a slip from the doctor. The welfare sent me everywhere. Every doctor I went to, they advised me not to work no more. My boss wanted me back, but I couldn't go back to my job. It took me about six or seven months to get on the state after I got out.

I don't know why it took such a long time. You've got different investigators and different things. It's hard to get on welfare. You got to tell the history of your life, when your momma died, what she died with, and all that to get on it. Here a young gal can pop up and get a baby and walk right down there and get help, but it's hell to get help for an older person. I'm not kiddin' you. It's hell. They don't give a damn about the old peoples. Don't care nothin'. I was twenty years on one job, and it took me six months to get help. And my wife worked about fifteen years doin' domestic work. 'Fore they give both of us help, they cut her off completely and put me on. We only live off $200 a month. That's all we gets—$200 a month. You can't get any more. I have to pay my rent, buy clothes, buy food. Everything.

Here there's a woman go down there with a baby, they start her off at a hundred and seven dollars a month. She get another baby by a different daddy, she get another raise; another baby, another raise. All of them kids got different daddies. When I moved in this apartment seventeen years ago, I had to have a birth certificate, marriage license, and if I had a dog, I guess I had to have him registered. They tell me we got to take care of these babies and things. I said what about people that done worked all their lives? You all care nothin' about them. Young girl—sixteen years old—never done a lick a work in her life—get a baby and head right down to 1006 and get right on the state. But a person done worked all their life, helped build the town up, a taxpayer—you go down there and it takes you nine months to get on. You got to go through the history of your life, and you've got to be almost dead. Got to go to four or five doctors, and they all got to pronounce the same thing. If one says it different, it's a problem. I'm tellin' you the truth.

All that money they done tax you for when you workin', what you gettin'? What happened to that money? I hear your white people. They get on TV and holler about the welfare. But when you workin', they tax you. They take forty some dollars out of my pay every week. And it was for twenty years. But that don't mean nothin' to them. It ain't nothin'. You ain't paid no tax. All that money they done tax you for, what you gettin'? But they talk about billions and billions—they send billions and billions of dollars up there to Viet Nam or somewhere, some other place. They fight an unknown war for nothin'. But here, the po' peoples here, the older people, starvin' to death, worse than they is overseas.

I see a need for po' peoples—white, black, blue, brown, yellow or pink. Puerto Rico or anybody. For all po' peoples. I see a great need for improvement. After all, they human bein's. There's a lot of things we could do for po' peoples. Like Roosevelt. He started that RFC, PWA, and all that. Just to give people work. Cleanin' the streets up, doin' everything. But I don't see nothin' none of these presidents doin' now. They talk about welfare, that they gonna do this and do that. But, hell! Look at all these cities, all these slums. They could clean all that up easy, givin' people jobs.

I still got plenty faith in politics, because I been a big-time Mason all my life. I got plenty of faith in a way, and then, one way I don't. Because I used to do that same thing when I was head of all the lodges. I'd get up and tell them big things and make big promises. It's to keep the people happy, as long as they vote me back the same thing. Some of the things I promised, I'd go to doin' some of them. I could have did them in the first place. So that's why I don't like politics. Politics ain't nothin' like it used to be. It's like Nixon. He didn't start tryin' to do nothin' 'bout the war until election time, but he could have done all those things in the first place.

On the radio they talkin' that they don't want the war to end. They talk as if a man's life is nothin'. "We don't want to give up. We don't want to surrender." Hell, it's better to surrender 'fore you get over there and stop a bullet.

Just like I said down there. Now they draft my son to the army. Call him to go. I goes down there to get his marriage license for him. They told me I had to bring his marriage certificate.

I said, "You didn't have to have nothin'—you didn't ask for his birth certificate when you all put him in the army."

"Do you know somethin'? What in place of killin' out all these young people, they should take me, you, and all us old peoples and put us over there and get us slaughtered? Let them know how it feels and they won't be back here dictatin' no more."

That's what I'm prayin' for. Get us hell out of the way. You raise up a son, and he got to go over there and get killed. Eighteen years old, and he ain't seen no part of the world. Ain't seen nothin' in his life. Take him over there and he stop a bullet. And he think that's somethin' if he make it back. But the first bullet he stop, that's it. I tell you, I just ain't for those old dictators, settin' back in the White House. I tell you the truth, I'm not for any kind of politics.

Fact, when I got this age, there ain't nothin' for me to do now. I been healthy all my life until this time here. I come to be 62, almost 63,

and run into my bad health now. Ain't nothin' much in life I can do
but just take it easy. I got a sick wife. I'm sick myself. I come back from
prison and I had a place here, but I come back and my place got destroyed. My kids took advantage of my old lady while I was gone. They
went on dope—one of them did—and he took the place. I had to come
back here, scrappin', pickin' up a piece here and a piece there. I
haven't been able to get my stuff back like I wanted—get my house
lined back up. We just livin'. We not livin', to tell you the truth. We
just hangin' on.

My wife was sick before I come home. When I got home from
prison, I find her here. She was sick before, I guess, about my gettin'
into a little trouble. Then my daughter—they're pretty close together—
she flew out and got pregnant. That was another thing. Then my
youngest son went on dope. That was another problem. She worried
about me too. It don't take too much to make a person sick. Mean-
while, while I'm gone, she lose a brother and a sister. So her heart went
real bad. I have a problem. I don't know. I just sit here with her
everyday.

You know, you get married and meet the right girl, if you got any
kind of heart at all, you're goin' to try to do a few things right. But
each year goes along, and a man get to thinkin' that he's gettin' older.
I got to try somethin' before it gets too far. So then, afterwards, you get
up in a certain age where you don't think about it. You get to lookin'
at one another. You come to favor one another 'cause you be with that
person so long. You get so, you don't want to be out of one another's
sight. After you come a certain age, you ain't got nothin' else to do but
set up here and look at one another. You ain't got a lot of energy. Now
a lot of old men runnin' around here, doin' things they ain't got no
business doin'. But you really got to be up to it, you know. Now, I had
a good wife; I didn't have no cause. I went out and did a little everythin' in the book sometimes, and come in here and tried to make her
mad, but nothin'. You can't hurt a person like that long.

She just come out of the hospital, and I stay here with her night and
day. I just went off parole in December. I ain't had too much freedom,
in a way of speakin'. I walks out a little bit in the mornin', get bread
and different things. Come back here and fool around the house—mop
up, sweep up, straighten the house up. Now I been doin' a little cookin',
somethin' I ain't never did. I make broth, different things like that.

We didn't tell her when she lose her last brother. We tried to keep
it from her. Then an old lady come by here—you know, one of them

see everything, been everywhere and then, to tell the truth, never been nowheres.

So she come in here and asked, "Did you go to the funeral?"

"What funeral?"

"Your brother's funeral."

"Is my brother dead?"

"Yeah. Buddy's dead."

Then, she just went like that. She quit eatin'. Got pains in her chest. I felt like runnin' the woman out of here, but you got to think before you speak or say anything. I felt like it, but I just caught myself. Now, the lady come back here last Thursday, and she begged my pardon. So I told her mistakes is made everywhere. It's just one of those things. You got to forgive. God forgives and you got to forgive. You can't go around puttin' evil chips and things on your shoulder.

Like, many times a man brings things about hisself. Now, the average colored man gives whitey a hard name, but he made hisself the way he is. Read your history and things, and you'll see. The average Negro Jim-Crowed hisself. He does it right today. You go to a public place and when you walk in there, you've been so used to goin' to the back, you go all the way back there. Even if there's a seat right here, twixt this man and the next. You notice it?

They say to me one day on a crowded car, "Why don't you come back on here with us? What do you want to be, white?"

I said, "No. I just want to let that man know that I'm just like he is. We both his equals."

I said, "Color is only skin deep. If you act as a gentleman around those people, you'll be a gentleman. They'll treat you like a gentleman."

As long as you act like a yard dog, waiting for them to throw somethin' to you, you'll never get yourself nothin'. When I was young, I used to go downtown to Broad and Market. Used to be that they wouldn't let no colored down there, but I used to be a pretty well sported-up guy. Nice, clean every day; pocket full of money. I'd walk right in their bar, sit in their bar, almost push them off the seat to get in there. They'd all look. Take me a drink and walk right out of there. The bartender got to know me. When he seen me comin', he'd set the same bottle up there and the same glass. I didn't care if a white woman was sittin' there—I didn't care who it was. I'd go right in there and get a drink. I'd get me a drink everyday at 12 o'clock, just for meanness.

I see a lot of things. I see a lot of mistakes I made in life in different areas. I could be a wealthy man today, but I wasn't doin' bad as it was. We done saved up some dollars, but we had to spend it all when I went to prison. We lived good. I can't grumble about my life, my whole career. I'm still hangin' on. I come up with a crowd of guys, all of them dead and I'm still around. All of them gone and I'm still hangin' on. So God keeps me here for some good purpose.

Always want to stand up on my own. Never wanted to do leanin' on nobody. Always wanted my own thing, all my life. Always wanted to help people. I didn't care how poor a guy was or who he was. As long as he was nice, he was my friend. My mother always taught me, "If you can't get along with a person, stay away from them. Deal with the nice, not the trash." So that's my motto all my life. I had time, I don't care how low you get or how well-to-do you is. I've got time for conversation or anythin'. I ain't never seen a person too low to talk to. That's the reason I say God keeps me around.

12

I Whipped the Socks Off o' Him[1]

There wasn't a day I didn't have a fight. Yeah, every day I'd beat the kids up, but they still liked me. If they wouldn't bother me, I wouldn't bother them. They called me kindergarten baby. I had long hair, and they pulled my hair or picked on me, and I didn't like that. I didn't mind them calling me kindergarten baby 'cause that was my pet name to them. But they didn't have to pull my hair. I didn't take none o' that.

We moved up here to Newark from Georgia when I was about a year and a half. First we lived on Grotto Street, then we moved over to River Street. The first day we moved to River Street, Johnnie Marshal, he was the leader of the gang of little kids on River Street, he challenged me into a fight. He beat me that day, but the next day I whipped his socks off o' him, so I became the leader of the gang! And every night we used to go up on Plum Street and play and have fun, and the cops would chase us. We would run down, around the alleys, and hide.

One night we went up and we turned all the garbage cans over on Plum Street and the cop Patsy chased us. My mother was sitting out on the stoop and all the mothers were sitting out. And I was hiding behind my mother's chair. Patsy came up.

"Mrs. Johnson?" He knew me and my mother. "Julie and all the kids of River and Donaldson and Swanson Street turned every garbage can on Plum Street over."

"OK, Patsy, I'll take care of her when she comes home."

When I went into the house, (my mother used to make us all come in between 9 and 10) my mother said, "Julie, why did you take all the kids up on Plum Street and turn all the garbage cans?"

I started to lie to her and she knew it.

She said, "I'll show you how to turn over all those garbage cans!"

---

[1] This Historian did not wish to talk about her years after high school, but her gang tales are so interesting that we decided to include the material even though it is incomplete.

She had a leather belt hanging behind her door. She never took none of our clothes off to whip us. She'd whip us on top of our clothes. I had a good mother and father, too. I loved them both dearly. So she put my head in between my legs and turned my behind up to her and gave me a good licking on my behind with that leather belt. I never did turn another garbage can over. We'd go over on Plum Street and play, but we didn't touch no garbage cans. And all the kids, you could hear the kids screaming and hollering all over River and Swanson and Donaldson Street that night. Their mothers were tearing their behinds up.

On another occasion we went up Mulberry Street, the Chinese part, where the Chinese restaurants and Chinese lived. One night we went there and we got in the middle of the street and hollered, "Chinky, Chinky Chinaman, eat dead rats."

The Chinamens didn't like you to call them Chinky, Chinky Chinaman. So Chinamens stick their heads out the door, and a big fat one came running with a butcher knife in his hand.

"Come on, kids, let's run."

And we ran down Mulberry Street and all them Chinamens were chasing us. They couldn't catch us—they couldn't catch one of us. We ran in back of the alleys and hid. They came as far as Swanson Street and they stopped, because that's where the colored people started at. And so they didn't come no further. We ran on home and hid in the alleys and didn't tell our mothers about that.

And once I got hit by a car on Mulberry and Swanson Street. I was about eight years old, between seven and eight. And I had a facial stroke when I was seven or eight years old. My face twisted to one side one morning. My mother got up and had gone to work. My sister was fixing breakfast for me. I was sitting down at the table, eating breakfast, and I was talking. My sister said, "Say something to me."

I talked, and my face twisted.

She said, "You're not going to school today."

"Why?"

"Because your face is twisted."

"That don't stop me from going. I'm going to school."

But she kept me home. And my mother came in from work, and I was outside playing.

My sister said, "Call Julie and look at her face."

So I came in when she called me.

"Tell her to say something."

"Hello, Mama," and I went up and hugged and kissed her.

She looked at me. "There's nothing wrong with her face."

"Tell her to say something."

"Where you been, Julie?"

"I been outside playing." And my face twisted up.

My mother screamed. My mother screamed so loud the little colored man who had a grocery store down in the basement over on 54 came running over.

"What's the matter, Sylvie? Why you screaming so?"

"Look at Julie's face."

My father hadn't come in from work yet. So this man looked at me, and he said, "I'll call a cab. You take her right up to the ear and eye infirmary up on Central Avenue."

He called the cab and it came right down. My mother had changed me. I wasn't dirty, but she put a clean dress on me, clean underwear and everything. So they rushed me in there. They took me to Emergency, and the doctors looked at me. I had around fifty doctors and I don't know how many nurses around me that afternoon. They all was looking.

"Say something."

I was talking to them, and my face twisted. One of the doctors looked at me, layed me up on the table, and examined my knees, elbows, thighs, pressed every bone in my body. He slapped me in the face, and it didn't hurt. They stuck pins and needles all over my face. It didn't hurt me.

"Don't feel no pain?"

"No, don't feel no pain."

They kept me overnight. My mother came back the next morning, and they wouldn't let me go home. Told my mother to come back for me about four o'clock. So four o'clock my mother came back, and the doctors had me in the examining room. They didn't know what was the matter with me.

One doctor, elderly doctor, he said it came from a fright. Another doctor said it came from a spider bite. Another doctor said it came from sleeping in the rays of a full moon.

So the doctor who said it came from a fright went out and gave my mother a solution to use on my face that would bring it back to normal. And it did. He let me go home.

My mother asked, "Can she eat anything she want?"

"Yes, she can eat anything. No special diet. She's OK, just don't let anybody hit her in the face. That's all."

And he told me, "Don't let no kids hit you in the face."

So I was very active. I played. I went to school and everything, and none of the kids laughed at me or made fun of me or nothing in school. Because all the kids knew me, and they were nice and I liked them.

And the doctors told my mother that that stroke would fall somewhere in my eyes. Somewhere that facial stroke would fall, on my eyes or somewhere in some part of my body. I thank God that it didn't fall in my eyes. But it affected my whole right side. He told her whatever part of my body it would fall on, it would build worser each day and I would notice it every year that I grow older. And it does get worse on me.

And then we moved to Wall Street. And the boys and the girls down there, we had fun. We played in the playground and all that. I was in the seventh grade it was, yes. This little Italian boy Anthony, he had called me a Nigger. I came back to school after lunch, he called me a Nigger, and I chased him. The teacher caught me.

"What are you chasing Anthony for?"

I said, "He called me a Nigger, and I'm going to get him for it, too."

I didn't like nobody to call me a Nigger. So when school let out that day we went down in the playground. He was standing on the sandpile in the playground, near the wall. I walked up to him.

"Why did you call me a Nigger this afternoon?"

"Because I wanted to," that's what he told me. There was a pile of bricks on the wall. He reached down and picked up half a brick.

So I said, "What are you going to do with that brick?"

He knew I was a good fighter, because I used to fight every day. So he picked up that half a brick and said, "If you put your hands on me, I'll hit you on the head with it."

So I stopped down in the sandpile and grabbed a handful of sand in my left hand and threw it right in his face. I got it all in his eyes, his mouth, his nose, everywhere. He's screaming! So I ran home.

The next day the principal, Mr. Watson, called my teacher and told her to send Julie down to the office. Anthony's mother is in there using the chair. So I walked up to the desk.

"Julie, why did you throw dirt and sand in Anthony's face? Don't you know you could have blinded him?"

I said, "Mr. Watson, yesterday afternoon I wasn't bothering him, and he called me a Nigger and ran upstairs. I ran up the stairs after him. In the school there was a teacher that stopped me from catching him. If I had caught him up those stairs I would have threw him down the stairs.''

So he said, ''Why would you do that?''

''Because he called me a Nigger, and I don't like no one to call me a Nigger. That's what all my fights are, around the school. They call me a Nigger. No, I'm not a Nigger.''

So he said, ''Do you know the meaning of Nigger?''

I said, ''Yeah, I know. A dirty, low-graded person, that's what it is.''

So he said, ''Who told you that?''

I said, ''Never mind who told me. I know that's what it is. And down on the playground when I approached him and asked him why he called me a Nigger, he said because he wanted to. And he reached down and picked up a half of brick. He said he was going to hit me in my head with it if I put my hands on him. So the best thing for me to do was defend myself. I reached down and got a handful of sand and threw it in his face.''

So Mr. Watson said, ''That's good for him. He got no business calling you a Nigger when you weren't bothering him. And he had a brick, and you had a right to defend yourself. I can't do nothing about it, Mrs. Bon Giovanni.''

''You can't do nothing about it?'' She was real mad. ''I'm going to the Board of Education.''

So she stormed out of his office. I don't know if she went to the Board of Education or not. Never heard nothing else about it.

When I was a teenager, I had, oh, a lot of girlfriends, boyfriends. I wouldn't call them special boyfriends, just boys that would hang around with me and my girlfriends. They all liked me. I know all the girls were jealous than me, because the boys would cling around me more than they would around them. I don't know why, but any of their boyfriends, they'd come up and talk with me before they would talk to them.

Every Sunday we went to church. Sunday School at 9:00; 9:30, morning service; then afternoon service, B.T.U., and night service. I joined that church October the thirteenth, 1928, and I was baptized Sunday, October 15, 1928. We didn't have no pool of water in our church, so the pastor had us all—a lot of children joined that night—he had us all go up to Zion Hill Baptist Church that Sunday to be baptized.

We were having choir practice on a Wednesday night in the church, and all the teenagers were out in front of the church and Hazel started it. I don't know what came over her. She came up to me and said, "You're nothing but a dirty little slut."

I said, "Why did you say that? You never seen me do nothing, have you?"

"No, I ain't never seen you do nothing, but that's all you are."

I said, "I dare you to call me that again!"

And she called me that again, and I tore into her. And my best girlfriend's father, he couldn't separate us. I beat her! Calvin Brown and all the boys are out there, and all the young girls, and her brothers and sisters—all were out there. And my girlfriend Carrie said, "None of you better not jump in there."

So they backed back, because Calvin and all the boys there were on my side. She had only her sisters and her brothers on her side. So they didn't jump in. We busted the church door open fighting, and all the senior choir what was inside tried to separate us.

She had a hold of my hair, but I had one of my hands on her, and I was beating her all in the face. Had my knee in her stomach. I beat her right down on that busted door.

My mother was up in the choir standing, and she didn't know we were fighting. She looked down and saw my dress and she said, "Lord, that's my child fighting down there."

She pulled me up off of Hazel.

"What you fighting in this church for? You got better sense than that."

I said, "Mama, she called me a no good slut, and I don't even know what that means. I asked her why she did it, and she said just because she wanted. I don't know why she done it. I told her you never seen me do nothing wrong. So she said no, I just want to call you that. So that's why I was fighting."

One Sunday after Sunday School, my girlfriend and I were going to my house. So these three boys, Ralph Ottley, and Smiley Harris and I think Sonney Thomas were sitting out on their stoops.

"Come on, now. You and Carrie come on in and have some ice cream with us."

I said, "Is your mother there?"

They said, "Yeah, she's here."

My mother told me never to go in any boy's house, especially when their mother's not home. So I said, "You sure your mother's home?"

"Yeah, she's in the kitchen."

So we went in. And I said, "Where's your mother? I don't see your mother in the kitchen nowhere.''

"Oh, we just told you that to get you to come in.''

So they locked the door. Carrie, she wasn't such a fighter, but I was a fighter, and I went to open the door. They grabbed me, and I knocked them boys around in that living room. And Carrie, she was screaming and hollering. I beat all three of them boys, and she was just standing in the middle of the floor, screaming and hollering.

"Come on. Help me fight 'em.''

"I can't fight them boys.''

I said, "You see me fighting them, don't you?''

So she started fighting along with me, and we beat those boys up.

"Run and open the door. Stop standing there like a stupid dumdum. You got no sense. Open the door so we can get out.''

She run and open the door and we ran out. They ran out after us, but they couldn't catch us. So the next day at school we laughed at them.

"I told you you couldn't beat me. I'm not afraid of you.''

Carrie said, "I know you couldn't beat Julie, because she's a good fighter.''

And I said to her, "You didn't help me none, just a little bit.''

So she said, "I don't care. I opened the door for you.''

It was funny though. Edmund Carter, he laughed. He always laughed. He was nice looking, dark brown, pretty wavy hair. He said, "Julie, I'm going to marry you. You're so pretty, I love you to my heart.''

So I said, "Maybe if we live that long, we'll marry each other. God sees fit that we should marry each other, we'll do it.''

But I never married him. He moved away and went back down South.

When I was in grammar school I didn't make my mind up to be nothing. But when I went to high school I made up my mind that I wanted to be a nurse. And my best friend Carrie—she's older than me but I graduated grammar school before she did and I helped her graduate from summer school—she didn't know what she wanted to be.

I said, "Be a nurse like me. I'm going to be one.''

So we wanted to learn nursing. How to make beds, and doctor on the patients and all, and help patients, and all like that. But in high school they didn't teach that, just typing, mathematics, and all that. And not knowing that you had to know all that to be a nurse, one day she said to me, "Julie, we're not learning nothing about nursing.''

I said, "No, we're not."

We were in our third year of high school.

So she said, "Let's quit. We're not learning nothing about nursing."

So, not learning nothing down there about nursing, we quit school in the third year. And we got us a little job, and we worked from then on. I brought my mother my money, and she would give me what I asked her for.

I said, "Mama, just give me $5 out of it, that's all I want, to buy myself a little dress every week or a new pair of shoes or something like that."

Clothes and things were cheap then. So she'd give me $5 every week out of my salary. Some of it she'd keep for herself, and then she'd buy food and like that. Most of it I know she spent on food and paid the rent with it.

And my sister got married while I was still going to high school. She had a beautiful wedding in that little four-room bungalow house on Robie Street. She got married there and the house was packed. She married the man who roomed with us. My mother had gone to the grocery store up on the corner one day, and this tall, nice looking, brown-skinned man was in the store there. He walked up to her and he says, "Miss, what might be your name?"

So she told him. And he says, "Mine is James Turner. Do you have a room to rent?"

She says, "No, I just got four rooms, one for my daughters, and one for myself, and the living room and kitchen."

He says, "Well, I'm from Philadelphia and I build roads. If you would just put a pad on your living room floor, I'd sleep on that." And he says, "I'll pay you good for it."

So she says, "Well, you don't have to sleep on a pad on the living room floor. I can buy a little couch, and you can sleep on that. One of those daybeds, you know."

He said "OK. You don't have to buy it. I can buy it myself." So he went to some furniture store and bought a nice little daybed and set it down.

My mother didn't have to buy no food after he moved in. He kept our icebox full of food and everything. And one Thanksgiving we went up to the market and bought a live turkey and put it down in the cellar a week before Thanksgiving.

I said, "I'll go down. I'll cut his throat."

"You're not afraid?"

"No, I'm not afraid." So I took a big, sharp butcher knife. He had sharpened it just as good. I went down in the cellar and I caught that turkey by the neck, and I sawed, and sawed, and sawed. I came back upstairs.

He said, "You killed him?"

I said, "I cut his throat. Yeah. He's dead."

And he said, "Alright. I'll go down and bring him up, just him in a tub of hot water and pluck his feathers off."

He went down and said, "Julie, you did nothing to that turkey. That turkey is still walking around."

I didn't even dented his throat or nothing. Ain't no blood on the cellar floor or nothing. I just sawed and sawed on that turkey's neck! And the knife was good and sharp!

So the man went down and cut the turkey's neck and brought it back up, put it in a tub and we plucked it. And that Thanksgiving we ate. My mother was a good cook; oh, she could cook. I used to love her biscuits and tea cakes.

We used to make all kinds of wine, too. Elderberry wine, grape wine, cherry wine, dandelion wine. The roomer used to make them, and every night he'd go down in the cellar and siphon a barrel or send my sister down or my mother down to siphon a barrel, any kind of wine they wanted. Put it up on the table, and we'd have a glass of wine before we eat our supper. It was the best wine.

And my sister married our roomer. He was a nice, brown-skinned man. Like me, you know, I'm very proud of my race, and never wished I was born white. I love my color. It's a nice color. I'm not black, I'm not light brown—I'm a nice brown. I don't like the word black but they use it often, and I don't care for it.

One day a caseworker came up to see me and every word that came out of his mouth was black, black, black.

So I said, "Don't use that word in here no more. Because I do not like it and do not use it in my house anymore."

"Oh, all the young people like it."

I said, "I do not care for it."

So he says, "Even my friends up in East Orange, they like it."

I said, "I'm telling you now, do not use it in this apartment anymore."

I do not like it at all. I don't care for the word black. I love my color and I'm proud of it, yes.

13

Newark Was a Beautiful Place Then

I wasn't born in a house but in a hospital. That was in Newark, New Jersey, in 1895—quite a few years ago.

Newark was a beautiful place then. It got all of everybody, and everybody got all of it. Just like, if you thought I didn't want you, you wouldn't come here.

I lived on South Broad Street, and those days Broad Street was a very nice place, and further up on Broad Street were rich people and millionaires. At that time, it was a residential area. There wasn't any stores like Bambergers, Orbachs. There were houses along that area.

Being black never affected us. We never noticed it. We never had any trouble with our neighbors. Most of them were white. And if the children got to fighting amongst themselves over various different things, you know they're children. We never knew any color line. Color was no difference. And if you didn't think you were wanted some place, you just didn't go. There were very few blacks in Newark then.

My parents expected us to live a respectable and a religious life, and they saw that we done it. So my childhood was just routine. Your parents told you to do something, you done it.

As far as I can remember my childhood was very pleasant. My father and mother took special interest in us, taking us to places of pleasure such as circuses, and things of that kind. You see, it was only the two of us, my brother and I, and my father and mother always took us places, especially on boatrides, because that's what I loved. Anything special, she taking us. Like when the United Nations or the Port Authority or anything special, she taking us, or big shows of any kind. When we were growing up my mother took me when she had time, and when my father had time, he taking us.

I had to take piano lessons, and that was from my mother because she was a piano teacher. When they told you to do something, then you did it. I started playing at five. Not professionally, you know, but I started. You see, my mother was a music teacher and a church organist.

She taught me until—you know, the teachers when I became a pianist only went so far. Then she sent me to an efficient teacher.

And we went on—we got along very good. We had no trouble in the family, as I can remember. Only when we disobeyed, minor things when we were small. They didn't punish us too much. Sometimes when we became bad we were punished, which they should have done, but otherwise I have nothing to complain about.

My father was working at clothing stores, different things of that kind, and he provided for my mother and us. Then, later years he was a superintendent of a white church. And my mother taught at home.

I'm Catholic now, but as a child we were Protestant, and we all went to church. We were very religious. In fact, my father was a deacon of a Baptist Church in Newark. He had to stop when he got the other position in the white church as a superintendent, because he couldn't go any more on Sundays. I liked it. . .in a way. I couldn't say we didn't dislike it—you were raised to do as you were told and they never sent us to church, they took us to church.

We had a time to play out and a time to study. When I was small I was afraid when I done something wrong. We were told to be obedient, and when our mother told you something, whether you liked it or not, you do it. My brother and I got along fairly well. There was only the two of us, and so we got along.

We were always in church concerts when we were small. We had quite a good teacher, Mr. Smullen. Well, my brother played the violin so well that when they had a big affair, over 2,000 people, they gave my brother that job. His teacher walked up on the stage, and he broke the bow of his violin and said, "I'm prouder than I've ever been in my life to know that a student can take my position." See, Mr. Smullen was a main musician. My brother took his place, and he was very proud that he could teach him.

We didn't move around much, very little. We moved each time to improve ourselves, and then we bought our own home. Buying our own home—well, it put us in a different status, I think. People then owned their home. I wouldn't say people were snobbish, but when you own your home they thought you were better in a way than those that didn't. Yes. Our home was a fourteen room house. It was on South Seventh Street. At that time it was a very nice street, because we were the only colored that lived there. Near the corner of South Bedford Avenue.

When I was growing up, you were supposed to be eighteen before boys could come see you. Not many girls got pregnant, like they do today. No. Because it was really made a federal case. And the families— which wasn't very nice. And you were afraid. It kept you from doing things. And I think that was alright. Yes. I saw the results. It wasn't any good to get pregnant without a husband. But nowadays they tell the girls things they don't want, but the girls get pregnant anyways sometimes. Nowadays people talk about these things, expect these things, and they're no better off.

My mother didn't talk about these things, but if anything was wrong, she would know. They kept strict supervision over you, but they didn't like you to know it. But you knew you were being watched.

I went to grammar school then, up 'til the eighth grade. And then from there to high school, three or four years. I had taken a three-year commercial course. And in those days you had to learn typing and shorthand somewhere else; you had to pay a business college. I went there and when I graduated from there I went to work, doing shorthand and making out all those legal papers and everything.

I also learned to be a hairdresser. I learned that in case I needed that, see. I had that; then I was a legal stenographer. We studied more than one thing. Yes. I went to Juilliard, not for a very long time.

Now you see my brother started out as a doctor, but he couldn't on account of—they had to take him out because he couldn't stand it. Music was secondary. But he started an orchestra. We became so popular that I had to resign as a stenographer, because we became in the big business. The music became so big that he never went back to college, and I had to give up the other. You couldn't work until three in the A.M. and go to an office the next day. I was the only one playing the piano. Sometime I'd take the whole band out if my brother had two jobs on one night.

There were ten or twelve pieces in that band. We played all over; we did what they would call "gigging," that's one night stands. Philadelphia tonight, and maybe we'd be in New York tomorrow night. All over. We played in the band over five years.

We were doing dance work. We'd play waltzes, two-step, and tango, and all of that. You know, people in those days had to go to dancing school to learn how to dance. My brother was a dance violinist and a show drummer. The show drummer has got to catch everything that they are doing on the stage. Then the drummer shows. And the dance music supposed to be all there, to be read by the violinist. You got to know all the different dances. That's the difference.

I got along alright in the band because I never had any friends in it. You see, it's a tricky business, and you got to look for the tricks. You can't get angry with the players. You either play, or I report you to the union. We weren't allowed to have a player out of the union.

My brother never was married. Brothers are very protective, over protective. My brother was the head of that band, and the players was kind of afraid of him. When I got out of the supervision of my mother, although my brother was younger, you always mind your brother. Oh, nobody didn't dare bother me much, because they would be discharged from the band.

In a way we always worked amongst white people. See, my mother did. She was never no domestic—no reflections on being a domestic. See, in them days when you married you didn't work, and before then she was a music teacher, so we never come in contact with whites only as neighbors or something or when we went out to play. In those days they had large homes and the white people entertained, and they had us to entertain in their homes as musicians. Well, then, I went in the same dressing room as the others did, see. Whenever you thought there were limitations, then you never overstepped them. We were only there for business. So I never really had any trouble with them. Unless you get a nasty individual, sometimes black or white, and you have to put them back in their place. But I couldn't say that I ever had any trouble with colored.

I tell you, in the entertainment world black people and white people generally work together. It's very hard to say that we were treated differently 'cause we had so much to do amongst ourselves, I don't think we ever paid any attention, and the white people in the entertainment world, they didn't bother. You know, they treat us just like—we're working with them, and then we're not. We never had much trouble with them. One would be on a personal standard.

And you notice amongst professional musicians, they don't make difference in marriage or anything else. But, personally, maybe I'm a little prejudiced. I prefer marrying my own color. But if I had to marry the other, I wouldn't be in a home like this—look at Pearl Bailey. No. I'm not sorry I was born colored. It never made any difference.

As a young person, then we didn't have much time for fun. You were playing; you were working. But we enjoyed that. I had pleasure, but not to exaggeration. You see, my brother was always with me. Naturally, if anybody in the band did more than look at me, he would dismiss them. I always had someone over me. I was well chaperoned, even in later life. Later, when I worked in a theater, the manager was my friend, and they didn't bother me. So there I was. And I liked it.

See, when you are in the music business, you're up on that stand, up on the stage, you don't have contact or time to contact the people on the floor. And when you go home, my brother was with me most of the time. And I liked it, because you see, he was the head of the band. You don't have much time to become acquainted with people when you work in public like that. You talk to them, being friendly, but not very intimate friends, no. I have girlfriends, but when I get girlfriends I don't have a lot. I get one or two; one girlfriend I have now, I've known her for fifty years.

And then I married. My husband came from Barbados. He was West Indian. I can't remember how I met him. That was so long ago. I knew him about a year before we were married. He was a very quiet man. We got along very good because he was a tailor and I was a musician and he accepted my career. I wasn't married too long before he enlisted in the army. Because you cannot draft a person that's not a citizen. When he went down, they told him he couldn't be drafted but he said, "As I make my living in this country, I fight for this country." I always appreciated what he done.

So he was an enlisted man. He was with the regular army in France during the war. Then when he came back—he was a tailor of men's suits—he had his own shop with another Italian fellow. As far as I'm concerned, we got along very well, because we never argued. Because he was a grown man, and I was a grown woman, and any misunderstanding that we had, we sat down and discussed it and ironed it out. When he and I got ready to argue he walked out until I didn't say any more, so we never argued.

After I married I continued to work at my profession and my husband worked at his trade as a tailor, and later on, if we saved money enough and I became older, he said I could retire. But he never lived that long. I didn't want any children. Or maybe later we would have it, he said, later on. But I was prospering at my profession, we would do nothing to hinder that. We were trying to make money and get a start in life.

So no, I never had any children. I didn't wish any. My life was too filled with my work. See, some people, the first thing they do when they get married is have children. There they are. I see other people with children. I'm independent now. I seen a few people that go to live with their children. They don't have freedom. Children tell them what to do. And you never know how they are going to turn out.

Well, we stayed together after the war until they sent him over to the hospital. He had a problem after the war. He was what they call a shell shock. He was very nice to me, but sometimes he threatened me. Ordinarily, he wouldn't put his hand on me. He acted funny like that. And he told me, "Tell them the truth when they come so they'll put me in a hospital." Then they took him, and they sent him to his home in Barbados.

I tried to get in contact, but up to now I haven't. He is declared legally dead. All my papers belong to the government, and they said everything is perfect. It has to be with the government. They said the only thing I'm lacking is a birth certificate. I really don't know if he is dead now; he was mental before he left.

And then, when I became older—nobody, no matter how popular they are, can last for a certain length of time. Their popularity dies. So after that I became a church organist. I went into New York and trained to play the electric organ. And then I played in various different churches, sang in choirs, and trained choirs. I played for various denominations. I never cared what their denomination was. I was trying to form their choir so that they could be proud of it. That's what I did. I conducted choirs and directed them. If you do what I say, you'll have a good choir. And if you don't then I'll leave.

Yes, I played moving picture organ at the theater, pipe organ in church, trained choirs and trained singers. And young groups, young chorus groups—I always done very well with children.

My family's health was good, because they all died of accidents, different ones.

During prohibition, my father was a guard at a factory, I think. And a person broke in and struck him several times. A few days after that he died. Yes.

We had a house downtown other than the one we were living in. Although my brother was a musician, he done slight repairs on the house. He was fixing the canopy over the door, and he fell off. And then, like, he neglected to tend to that until it became too late. They take him to the hospital and they had to amputate his leg, and it had gone up in his body. A month after that he was dead. I don't know whether it was gangrene or cancer. I think they termed it as a blind cancer, which I never heard of.

Since my husband left I always lived in the house with my mother. I have separate beds. It was in 1943 when my mother died. We had two doors in our dining room. One led to the cellar and one led to the hall. As she was sitting, dozing in the chair, the bell rang and she got up, took the wrong door and fell down the cellar steps. And the doctors said the shock killed her more than anything else.

Well, I sold that house. When you sell a house you have to move to an apartment. I roomed for one year, then kept house in various different apartments. I couldn't tell you all of them because I was terribly upset. I put my things in storage. I moved to Mrs. Davisson's apartment house. I moved from that one block over. Finally, when I was old enough I moved down here.

Then, as I became older, they said, go down to the playground and work, because when you're working for yourself, you have no social security. I don't know what they do now. So at one time I worked for the County Park Commission, and I did general office work.

But before, I belonged to the American Legion. And they went down to play at different places and the Lions Hospital. They take their cars to the Lions Hospital since it is quite a distance. I went there, to play for the inmates there, the patients. It wasn't very nice to see those men like that. Of course I had the best group. And the other people had the bingo. And they want you to forget about those men, if you didn't see them for yourself.

I was the only colored. I played at the convention in 1954 for one year, and then I was Vice Chairman of the music committee. I was the only one to dissolve their music committee. See, the way it was, it wasn't a matter of prejudice. In those days the majority of them were white, and they know it. Well, we have our self-preservation.

If I had my life to live over again, I'd go back to music, back to teaching. But I'll tell you one thing I wouldn't do. All those children I taught—once a year I would take them to Coney Island or on a boat ride. In fact, I spent more money than I got.

Some students still call me. Mrs. Edith Jackson. I taught her when she was eleven years old. She became an organist at the church. Although she's sick she calls me up when she's aching to do it. And Mrs. Hardy. She's another one that always calls me, and I done less for them than I did for the others.

You know, you lose children after they grow up. Parents ask if you can keep them. Five years. That's about as long as you can keep them. What I give them—they have to practice their lessons. If you practice your lessons, do as you're told, then I'll let you have some dances.

Not to children but to parents I say, pay more attention to your children when they are young and train them from one year old up. You cannot train a child after he gets ten or eleven. Really train him from the time he's born. When a baby gets mad, he has a temper and he'll show it.

I tell you as a teacher, all a teacher can do is teach that you have to do the work. These children now don't care about learning, and their parents don't have anything to do. When the teacher tells them the child has done something, they tell the teacher that she is wrong. They didn't do that in my days. I think the parents should cooperate more with the teacher and not listen to what the children say.

Now I have retired even from giving lessons, piano and vocal lessons, on account of my health. Owing to diabetes, heart condition and high blood pressure, I can do very little for myself. I don't have any relatives, only one cousin and he's 83 years old, so he can hardly help himself. Most of my friends were four or five years older than I am. When you get as old as I am now, they are practically dead, most of them, or they are unable to help themselves. Very few friends left, and they cannot do much for me. I must say, the only friends I have is from the Rutgers Aging Project; they're very good to me. They take me on different trips, arts and crafts and things. That keeps you from being lonesome.

There are a lot of children in the Hayes Project where I live. I was trying to avoid them one day and I fell. I did not know until two years after that there was a torn cartilage in my knee. I had to have a major operation on that, and today I walk with a limp. With diabetes, I'm lucky that I got a leg. And I fell two or three times, and I had stitches. I was in the hospital five times in two years. But I don't worry even now. When I know I can't go out, I ask the girl, the homemaker. I say, "Now, you take me to the clinic and bring me back. I'm going to try to get better." Some people sit down there in the yard, worrying. I think we should do what we can. If you don't try, you'll deteriorate.

I've been a Catholic now for ten years. I've only been with the church since it moved over here. I didn't go to the church for what I could get out of it. As long as I was able, I did go to mass. I've been to that church with crutches, to answer the telephone and take their calls. I knew Father Donohue and he was very nice to me, like all the other priests. When I was so sick, in Intensive Care at St. Michaels, the priests kept running in, they saw me ailing there. The sister came there and kneeled on her knees all night long. But you can't tell some people. They are so hard headed.

Most of the priests are so very nice. I would be in a nursing home today if it hadn't been for Monsignor Lawrence. That's where they wanted to put me. I wouldn't even be there today, because I'd a been dead. I didn't want to go. And Monsignor saw to it—he sent me to Mrs. Wilson who come down and paid my rent, and then when I was able I was sent home.

You see, I want to do everything I can for myself. I want to get well someday. I don't want to just sit like this forever. Of course, everything takes a lot of time on account of this leg.

My income now is solely social security plus old age assistance which I get every month. That's my sole income. This month they said there would be a difference—just $59.00 this month. So it seems it would have to be reduced. The caseworker told me that. But I don't see why—everything's gone up.

They only gave us things during the riots. Our church and different places, they brought food, and the stores got food out of their warehouses and brought it here to give to us. Not just senior citizens, but everybody. They put it in the churches and places for people to come and get it. But the senior citizens couldn't get out, and the sisters and the priests of my church came here. They took their lives in their hands to get the food in here to the senior citizens.

The riot was started near my home and it made me very nervous. When you have guns from the rooftops, aiming down at you.... There is a bullet hole in my bedroom window now. I don't think they accomplished anything, only tore the place to pieces. That's all.

Some people were caught short with food. Two ladies just moved into the sixth floor. You know how they felt. They came up and said, "Oh, we have no bed or nothing." I said, "Listen, I don't belong to those bums in the street. Come in here and get some food." I said, "You take it on home. Put it to good use; it's no good to me."

There used to be some white people in this project; used to be half and half. But they died out, just like our people. I remember one Jewish man in here. His wife died and he moved away. Most of the older ones that moved, they all died. I know about twenty in here that died. Very nice people. Most of them Polish. There is a couple upstairs is Polish. I go there every once in a while when I'm able, to see how they are. The man in there is very nice. They used to go up to the supermarket for me. They were held up so many times. When checks come, it is so bad that you can't go across from here to the mailbox. And they prey on older people.

Anyway, I go to see these Polish people. A lot of times we draw the line. We say we don't want them. You see, I never could draw that line. I never hated a person on account of his color. I never did relate to one about his color.

14

A Song Opens Up Down into My Heart

There was a big crop of us children, ten of us. And my father had to work hard to try to support his family. So when I was pretty good size, why, I had to quit school and go to work, to kind of help out, you know. It was kind of tight, because there were many mouths to feed. It took something. At that time, you know, everything was kind of cheap. You had to work hard, and you didn't get nothing much for what you work for.

So my brother was older, and I was next to him. Us older children had to quit school early. I didn't get no further than the sixth grade in school. So I had to quit to kind of work out. Got to work and help out with the other children. I had to work away from home; helped the white people.

This was in South Carolina. My father worked a farm on halves. We were growing cotton, and corn, and cane to make molasses, potatoes, and things like that. I helped on the farm, Lord, yes, I reckon I did. I helped on the farm until I got to be a good size. And then of course my father felt that I could be more help working out. And so I started working out.

We didn't do too much playing. Because my mother had children so fast—then she was a sickly woman, you know. So she kept us busy all the time.

And the first time I cooked, I wasn't tall enough to stand at the table and make up dough. My brother lent me a box and I sit up on the box and made up dough. You see, my mother was sickly, and all of them children were hungry. And my father didn't leave enough bread from breakfast to carry 'em over until night. So they was crying for bread. My mother was in bed sick and couldn't get out.

I said to my brother, "Sam, you make me a fine sauce. I'm going to cook supper for these children."

So he laughed, he laughed at me, you know.

He said, "Sister, you know you can't cook that—you're too
little."

I said, "You make the sauce."

When my mother was well, whatever she did I was always around
her, watching. And I learned a lot of things that they didn't know I
knowed how, by watching her. And so he made the sauce. I cooked
some bread, and I fried a chicken, and then I smothered it, and made
gravy, and I added milk and butter and served it. I churned too, but I
didn't take up the butter after it's been churned. I thought maybe my
father would do that.

When my father came back home that evening I done cooked
bread for them children, and then had supper ready and on the table,
and the table covered over. So when he come, he said to my brother,
"Sam, make a fire so I can get some supper cooked." So my brother
didn't say nothing. And my father came in the kitchen.

He said, "What's this table all covered up for?"

And he grabbed the cloth and throws it off the table. He looked.
He said, "Sam, who been here?"

And my brother said, "Nobody."

And he says, "Has Irene been here?"

Sam says, "No."

"Has Maude been here?"

He says, "No."

He went in the house to my mother. My mother's name Ellie.
He says, "Ellie, is you been up?"

My mother says, "No."

"Well, has Irene or Maude been here?"

She says, "No. There's nobody been here."

"Well," he says, "supper is cooked and on the table. And the
table is set."

She says, "Well, if it's cooked, Sister must have cooked it."

So he come back in the kitchen, and says, "Sister, did you cook
supper?"

I told him, "Yes."

And after that, oh, my father was the proudest that you ever seen.
Because he hated cooking, but my mother was so sick, and he had to
cook for his children. He said, "No more cooking for me." And so,
after that, why I had to do all the cooking. And from that day on, I
cooked for them until I married.

I liked to cook, all right. Then I learned to make cakes, too. And after I married, why my father, he'd pretend that he couldn't eat the rest of 'em's cooking. I would have to fix his meals and bring it over to the house to him. And I lived a good piece away. I did that till I was too far along with my older son, and so he had to eat their cooking. Yeah, he thought nobody could cook but me.

When I was little I was taking care of the whole family. Had to get them ready for school, then the washing and ironing. I'd tidy their clothes, I'd fix them the best I could. That I didn't understand fixing I'd take it to the bed get help from my mother. She'd show me how to fix it.

Well, my mother finally got better. Got up out o' bed, but she was always sickly.

We lived so far out in the country, most of the time we spent with brothers and sisters. Never went to nobody's house, never had anybody come to visit, not until after I were grown. I don't know whether or not you know anything about the country or farms or not, but people on the farms, they don't live too close together, some few do, but not many.

We used to play ball and pitch horseshoes. We used to play a game they call goosey gander and turkey lurkey. I really forgot the game myself. Or hide and seek, and all that kind of stuff. And every Sunday, we went to Sunday School. My daddy seen to that.

On the farm we had plenty of chickens, and my father killed hogs enough to do, from one killing to the other. And we had lard. Sometimes the lard would give out, and he'd have to buy more lard, but most of the time it'd last from one killing to the other. And we had plenty milk and butter, 'cause we milking from three different cows. So we fed pretty well, and our garden stayed green winter and summer.

And we had all kinds of flowers in our yard. All kinds of flowers, and the house in the middle of it. And the flowers was all around the house. It was the beautifullest thing you ever looked at. And my daddy would plant my flowers just like he'd plant corn and things. It was so pretty he had to like it, you know. And he'd get out there and help me to work it. So I had some lovely flowers. And on the porch he made me some steps and I had flower pots from the bottom up to the top. They would always bloom all colors, and they was so pretty. Oh, my mother was crazy about them. People would come out to the house just to see my flowers. Sometimes I would cut out a bouquet for different ones, cut 'em a bunch.

We were so far out in the country, we had to go off a long way to get to the store and the school. We had to walk a long way. I didn't

enjoy school too well. It's so far, and it was so cold, and I didn't enjoy
it too well. Some of the other children liked it, I think. You know,
when you had to walk so far to get there in the cold, and when you get
there, you sit in that cold house, air coming up from them cracks in
the floor, you can't enjoy that. But you just had to make the best out
of it, you know.

We moved several times. I remember twice we moved, but it was
on the same man's farm. I don't know how they divided up the crops.
I was too little, too small to know all of that. We had mules, but later
on, the last time we moved, my daddy bought us horses of his own.
And I could ride one as good as any man. I don't care how fast he
run, I sat up there.

The people were very nice to us. In fact, I stayed with these people
for a while. I even slept in the bed, between the two girls. They had two
girls, and I slept between them girls until one of them was married.
They'd come and get me every evening, and we'd play out there in the
yard in the sand until it time to go to bed. Her mother would give all
three of us a bath. Strip us naked and plop us in the tin tub and give
us a bath and put us to bed. And I remember one night, children, they
got to fighting. But they don't fight like Nigger children do. They pull
the hair and scratch you. The mother would put me in the middle, between the two. Well, the oldest one, she got mad at the other one, and
wouldn't let me get in the middle. She put me in by her, to keep me
from being beside the other one. Did that for spite. And they, they
would go to fighting. And her mother would come in there. She'd
straighten them out, and she'd spank 'em, and make 'em get over,
and put me right back in the middle. Yeah, I slept in the middle of them
two girls until they was great big girls. They loved nothing like me.
Slept there till one of 'em get married. After I was married and my
oldest son was born, I visited my sister once and I saw one of them
girls. She come running and put her arms around me, and hugged and
kissed me, kissed me, kissed me.

She said, "Mattie, Mattie, Mattie. If you ever leave me, don't
forget to call on me. For anything."

They thought lots of me, and I thought lots of them. You know,
when you're raised up with a person, don't have no trouble, naturally
you think a lot of them.

So, after that, our house got burned up. My mother's baby was
one week only that very same day. It was twelve o'clock. I had the
children in the field, hoeing cotton. I was trying to get over, I was

hoeing on very hard. I was in the last spot of brown, and it's time for us to quit, but I was determined I was going to finish that spot before I quit. And I happened to look up, and I see the black smoke, and Lord, when I see'd the smoke I knowed it was the house. And it weakened me so I couldn't do a thing but stand there and look at it. And the children at that time, they all looked up and saw it. And they start running toward the house, and I was the last one to get there. My brother, he was in the bottoms, plowing corn. He saw it, and my father. They all got there before I did.

I had washed the day before then. You know, people in the country, always, when they wash, they wash all their best clothes, and then mostly put on their worst clothes. And I had washed the day before that. So all their best Saturday clothes got burned up, 'cause I had washed and we hadn't got 'em on.

Well, people was very nice. They give the children quite a few things. But regardless of what people gave, not like your own. But children, they kind of make out. There was a lady that didn't live too far from us. She taken my mother in and some of the children. And they was building my father a house, and they didn't have it quite done, so we slept in that house. And when it got done, we all moved in.

Furniture—my father had a good credit. In fact, he could get more credit than he could get money to pay. You know, when you honest, you can get more than you can pay for it sometimes. It's a kind of like now. I can get more credit than I can pay for it right now. That's true. And so that's the way he got it. And then the people that lived on the plantation, well, they brought a lot of stuff, plenty of their things.

When I was nineteen I got married.

I'm going to tell you the truth—it's been so long, I forgot how I met my husband. I think I met him in church, in Sunday School. Anyway, we went together a long time before I got married, because I didn't marry until I was older—nineteen or twenty. I loved to get married, but I didn't much want to leave the rest of the children. Because we had been together so long, you know. After I married, I kind of got used to it. I was the first one married, out of the ten.

I tell you, it's lonely. I was kind of sad. Alone in the house all by myself. 'Cause I was very small when I married. I was a little bitty thing. My brother used to almost meet his hand in my waist, I was so small. I begin to pick up after my children begin to come. And so I was very small when I married, and if I seen somebody coming, I was so small sitting in the house, I would hide. If I see them before they see me, they would never find me, 'cause I'd hide.

Course I knew pretty much about a house, setting up a house, because you see I was the oldest girl. My mother was a sickly woman, and I was the head of everything in our house. I was just like the woman of the house, you know. So I understood very well.

And then, after the first baby came, well, I was the happiest soul. I was the happiest soul after my baby got here, 'cause, Lord, beforehand! I couldn't hardly do anything but take care of that baby. I was so proud of it. Everybody saw it, white and colored. That was a beautiful baby, and I don't say it because it was my baby—it was the best looking baby in that community, anywhere. That's the truth. And he was so fat. I just thought it was a doll. I wouldn't care if he had never growed no more. Yes sir, that was a wonderful thing to me.

I didn't trust my baby nowhere. I wouldn't let him go home with my mother and my aunt. It seemed like I just couldn't stand it. I don't know why, but that is just my idea. And my mother and aunt, they begged me and begged me let them take the baby home with them a while. They'd bring it right back.

My mother says, "You know I know how to take care of a baby. I had so many childrens."

But I just couldn't see it. And that child never did get to spend a night in his grandmother's house until he was a great big child. And I mean, he spent the night time, the next morning I was there! That's right. My children never did spend a night out of home like other children. No sir, indeed. I don't know—I just want to see them all around me. You know, if anything happens, I wouldn't know what's going on.

And a lot of people said I thought they was better than everybody else's. But I didn't. I just wanted to keep a eye, a watch over them. If anything going to happen to them, well, I could keep it from happening. Don't you know? And that was all right. I didn't think my baby was no better than nobody else, but I just couldn't bear for them to go over and stay. That's all.

And my oldest one was a year and six months and in come the other one. Both of them was boys. Well, I didn't think it was too hard, taking care of them. I used to take my children to the field, and I would take a blanket and put it down, spread it down under a big tree in the field. I would always take two blankets, if they went to sleep, so that it would be kind of thick—it wouldn't be too hard. Because they have something to lay on. And that tree would shade them from the sun.

And I would go backwards and forwards, to see how they was.

I guess I like the old way of bringing up children better, because I don't believe in this turning children loose like they do now. I couldn't do that. I couldn't loose my children like that. Maybe I could get used to it, but I don't know how I could. It's just different in the people, that's all. You know, everybody's not alike. Some people just don't have time, just not interested in children much. I was more interested in mine.

So I worked hard all my life, from a child on up. I didn't hate nothing like a lazy person. Well, I made a honest living; I didn't have to run to neighbors for money. What little I had, I worked for it. That's right.

When I was young I had in mind to be a nurse, but I didn't get enough schooling for that. After years were passed and I came up here, I worked in a hospital, tuberculosis hospital. They tried to get me to go to school. And I could become a nurse then. But, you know, I felt like it was too late. So I didn't. I just kept on like I was. If I had been younger, I wouldn't have minded. But as I was that older, I didn't bother. So I worked in the hospital here about fourteen years, maybe fifteen.

I'm going to tell you the truth—I don't remember how old I was when I went to work in the hospital. It was when I first come to Newark. Some people that I got acquainted with, they was telling me about this place, maybe I could get on there. At that time this hospital, they didn't work colored. You know, they didn't hire colored people. No colored mans, nothing. So when I started there, there was one colored person working with me. And I didn't think I'd get the job, but by luck I did. I was there a long time before any more got there.

When I first got on there, to tell you the truth, I was kind of nervous. There's so many dead people. People was dying so fast there, you know. But time, I got used to it. So after I got used to it, why, I worked this place, and I liked it, because I like to help a person when they're sick.

I was what you call a nurse's helper. Whatever the nurse had to do, I help them to do it. I don't care what it was, I help her to do it, and so that's what it was. And I had quite a few that died in my arms after I got used to it. I had them laying in my arms, and they been calling me when they can get their breath.

They called me, "Mattie, I can't breathe."

And I said, "Well, you will." That's all I knowed to say, you will. I had to hold them down in the bed. They'd be running, trying to get out of the bed, so we had to strap them. There was a man once—oh, I had a time trying to hold that man down. This man, pulling me up in the bed on him. He was as tough as—you know, they're strong when they're dying. And trying to holler. He got halfway out of that bed with me holding on to him. You see, if you don't hold them, they liable to get out of there and fall on that floor and break some of their bones.

So it ain't no fun being around a person who's dying. I mean, it takes a person with—I don't know what it takes. And so I wrestled with that man, and he didn't get to the floor, and he died. There he was, dead, holding on to me. I was hollering for the nurse, but the nurse had been scared. Anyway, poor soul, she done left the floor. Not a soul on the floor but me and them sick people and the dying man. And she done run off the floor, hunting the supervisor. And when she found the supervisor, the supervisor comes. They came on in the room where I was.

I said, "Where on earth have you been?" I said, "Didn't you hear me ringing the bell for you?"

She said, "Well, I told you I'd be right back."

But I said, "But I told you not to go...Oh, my God."

So somebody—I wasn't going to tell on them—you see, they'll fire you for that—somebody told the head supervisor that morning. But I wasn't in on it. If I had been in on it, they would have fired me. I don't believe in making trouble for nobody. So they called me downstairs that morning. And the head supervisor asked me about it. I said I was in the room with the dead man, but I still didn't tell them that she did leave the floor.

She was nice, but, you know, when you get scared you can't take it, you just can't take it, no how. And she had a nervous heart. She just couldn't take it, that's all. If that a'been me, she'd a'turned me in for that, but I wouldn't turn her in. The whole time I was there, I didn't tell a soul. I could have turned her in many, many, many, many, many times. I could have turned her in for stealing and everything else. Now then, that ain't no lie. I seed her going away with blankets, sheets, milk and everything else. That's just as true as you sitting in that chair. But I didn't open my mouth. If they don't catch her, they'll never know it.

Some of them nurses was good with the patients, and some of them wasn't. I had several times I had been off. You know, they give you a day off. And I would go back and my patient—somebody had to do my work while I gone—they would tell me how they treated them while I was gone. Sometime they would take their money, and sometime they wouldn't give them a bath, and you know, they just wasn't nice to them. But still, I couldn't let anybody know that.

A lot of the patients got better. They was a lot of them that got better, and a lot of them got married. Some of them got married to the help that was working there. But I wouldn't marry one of them for nothing.

I like hospital work the best of the work that I did, because I like to help people. I made some of them happier, I certainly did. And then, there's some that's thankful. There's some like people is out here in the street. Some people regardless of what you do for them, they don't appreciate it, you know. Just do your best and go on about your business. Just be sure you remember the right things. You know, when God was here on earth, He didn't believe some people. And what do you think He will do? He sure was in your heart; then you done the right thing. You see, if you hadn't done the right thing, your heart will let you know. So I love to make people happy if I can.

Well, I can't get around none now. It's very dull. I can't even get to church. Last week, week before last, I got a lady to come take me to buy. Well, we went in a cab. I was needing some everyday slips and quite a few little things. And the man in the store, he was trying his best to get some of the other things for me to buy, and he was just trying to out-talk me, you know. I said, "Listen, I couldn't buy those. It takes money to buy things."

He said, "Miss, I been knowing you for so many years. I know you. Go ahead and take it.

I said, "Listen."

He said, "Money or no money, forget about money."

"You can't tell me that. Got to come a pay-day sometime." And I said, "Maybe when the pay-day come, I may not be able then, I'm a sick woman, and I'm living now from medicine."

I don't go no further and I can see my way out. Because I don't like to go head over heels in debt, knowing that I can't get out. You know, there's some people that do that, but not me. I don't go no further than I know I can get out. Because I don't like a bad name, a bad reputation. I never had it, and I don't need that.

Sometimes my son comes over and takes me to do my shopping. I often get telephone calls. I don't have too many visitors, because I'm not very much of a talker. Never have been. And I tell you the truth, I never, from a child, I never did take to people. I don't know what it is. There's some people that talks a lot, and there's some that don't talk much. Well, I'm one of them kind. It's kind of what you talking about. You know, there's some people that yap, yap, yap all for nothing. Well, I can't. Now, you see, you talking about the Lord or something is worthwhile, I can talk with you a while. And if you're not, I ain't got nothing to say. And so, a person like that, why, most of the people, they say to you you're funny or something. You know you're old enough to tell them something, but they thinks you never know nothing, so you just don't want to be bothered. So they really don't suit you, and you don't suit them. So that's the way it goes. And I don't care for gossips, because I can't be responsible for them. So gossips don't take.

Only one of my sons living. He takes me to his house, and he comes over and takes me out for rides. 'Cause I tell you, I can't get around none now. My son wants me to live with him, but I won't live with him, because I think a house is not big enough for two women in it. Because it comes a time in life, a man and wife will have some mis-understanding. Ain't that right? Well, maybe it may never happen, as I know of. But it might happen. She might think maybe his mother, mother been the cause of this. Well, if the mother wasn't there, she couldn't think these things. You understand what I mean?

Now, he has a sweet wife. She's a friend to peoples when they get sick. And she seem to think the world and all of me. She always begging me to come and stay with her.

A person with a heart like me. She liable to come in any morning, and I may not speak to her. You understand that? See, I don't want to make it unhappy for them, and me gone, to find me one day like that. I'd rather for them to find me here. You understand that, don't you?

You know, I'm sort of alone, staying here with me night and day. I don't get nervous or nothing. That's the truth. Sometimes I get kind of lonesome; I used to get my Bible and read, but I don't see to read now like I used to. Now, when I get lonesome, the song opens up down into my heart. I was singing that this morning...I can't remember now. Maybe it will come to mind before you leave. And when I get lonesome, that mostly comes to me, you know. But it's a very sweet, touching little song. I sing that so much, and so...it goes away.

15

Backdrop for Our Historians' Lives

Following the Civil War there was a brief period in which this nation moved toward recognition of southern blacks as full citizens, entitled to the social and economic benefits of democracy, including suffrage and protected civil rights.

By 1900, this direction had been reversed, and a rigid system of white supremacy ensured the continuation of the status order that had characterized Southern slave-holding society. In some states, elaborate Black Codes defined the structure of the system, while in others racist practices without legal sanction came to be accepted as inviolable custom.

THE SOUTHERN YEARS

Black children in the South between 1880 and 1910 grew up in a society that demanded their meek acceptance of a lower-class position, withheld all privileges and rights on the basis of color, and struck with terrifying violence if racial codes were violated.

Violence. Lynchings, floggings, castrations and other corporal violations of civil rights reinforced white supremacy (Ginzburg, 1962). A 1919 study by the National Association for the Advancement of Colored People documented that 78 percent of the lynchings in the United States between 1889 and 1918 involved black victims (NAACP, 1919). Blacks accounted for over ninety percent of those lynched in Georgia, the Carolinas, Virginia, Alabama and Florida during the same period (computed from figures in NAACP, 1919). Georgia's record was the worst: for thirty years an average of one black person per month was lynched there (NAACP, 1919).

Lynchings were terrifying to watch. They took any number of brutal forms—hangings, burnings at the stake, shootings, and fatal mutilation. One of our Historians, seventy-one at the time we talked with her, recalled her early Southern life as "a tragic living" and shared her graphic recollection of an early twentieth-century lynching in her native Georgia:

> "I was living in my home place when this terrible incident happened about Paul Reed and Cato Smith...they burnt them to death there...burnt them alive. They were supposed to have killed a white lady or something. I was about four then....being a little girl, I could stand out there and look at them—well, it's something you'd never forget...I watched them tie the men...they tied these men to this stump. And then they pulled a lot of the knots from the tree. They piled them up on top of those men, then they drenched them with coal oil and put a match to them. And they burnt them alive."[6]

Despite denunciations from the black leadership, black churches and the black press, violent racial oppression remained a dominant theme of Southern life in this period (Ginzburg, 1962; Franklin, 1947). *Racially-prescribed social custom.* Many forms of deference were required of blacks, from tipping the hat or taking it off to standing at the end of the line. Whites were always taken care of first.

Whites were not to be contradicted by blacks. If, at the yearly settling up of agricultural accounts, a black suspected a white person of cheating him, he could never complain. No action could be taken by a black man if violence were done to him or his family or his property. Any deviations or omissions from these codes of behavior placed blacks in peril.

A black did not come into a white person's home through anything but the *back* door; he did not sit on the front porch; he did not eat at the same table. Black men had to carefully avoid looking at a white woman. There were some towns where a black person would be challenged for appearing on the street dressed up during the middle of the week (Dollard, 1957). A black was always addressed by his or her first name; the title of "Mr." or "Mrs." was never used. Such racial codes of conduct made no concessions to prominent or accomplished blacks— so far as the system was concerned, such individuals did not exist.

---

[6]This lynching is probably the same as listed on page 60 of *Thirty Years of Lynching in the United States*. According to this NAACP report, Paul Reed and William Cato were lynched at Statesborough on August 17, 1904, for murder.

Civil and political rights. Many states practiced exclusion of blacks from juries; West Virginia legalized that practice. In Atlanta courtrooms, Jim Crow Bibles were used. Unequal punishment was the rule of the day, with the laws punishing blacks much more severe than the laws addressed to similar white offenders (Bardolph, 1970).

As the Southern black attempted to vote, there was economic pressure, violence and intimidation. Complicated voting laws were written to disfranchise the black population, and fraud and trickery were perpetuated upon black voters. In Virginia, for example, a voter had to vote *against* a candidate by drawing a line three-fourths of the way through his name, and the ballot could be discarded because of length or straightness of line (Bardolph, 1970).

Literacy and understanding tests (controlled by white bureaucrats), poll taxes, property ownership and "good character" qualifications all but terminated black participation in voting. After 1898 a "grandfather clause" restricted voter registration to those persons who had voted before 1861 and to their descendants, or to persons who had served in the Federal or Confederate armies or state militias and their descendants (Bardolph, 1970). Those not so qualified (i.e., blacks) could still register if taxes were paid and literacy and understanding tests were met. Few blacks slipped through the qualifying process, and those with white ancestors could not formally claim them (Myrdal, 1944).

The effectiveness of disfranchisement is illustrated by a comparison of the number of registered black voters in Louisiana in 1896 and 1904. In the former year, 130,334 blacks had qualified to vote; in 1904, only 1,342 had been registered. In 1896, black registrants were a majority in twenty-six Louisiana parishes; in 1900, they were a majority in none (Woodward, 1955; Myrdal, 1944).

Government in the post-Reconstruction South was not the only institution to set up legal barriers for blacks. Legalized segregation evolved in marriage laws, education, housing, transportation, public accommodations, health facilities, factories and public services.

Marriage laws. Of all the racial laws, none were more universally enforced than those against intermarriage. By 1910 the laws of thirty-five states forbade unions between blacks and whites, nullified existing marriages, and sometimes sentenced the partners of such marriages to penitentiary terms at hard labor.

Education. The first segregation statutes dealt with education. By 1910 the separation of the races in public schools was required by both constitution and statute in twelve Southern states and by statute alone in three of them (Bardolph, 1970). Illustrating the lengths to which segregationists would go, the laws of both North Carolina and Florida required public schools to keep separate textbooks used for blacks and whites—even while in storage.

The quality of instruction and the physical facilities of black schools were vastly inferior to those provided for white students. In 1910, ten states spent three times more per capita for whites as for blacks, and in Mississippi and Georgia the ratio was five to one. Black schools paid their black teachers less, had larger classes, and provided shorter terms for black students (Myrdal, 1944).

Black children often had to buy their own books and supplies; white children usually received theirs free. Black schools were often very far apart, and cases were reported of elementary school children having to travel up to eighteen miles every day (Myrdal, 1944).

Whites sometimes spent twice as many months in school as blacks. In 1908–09, South Carolina whites attended school for 25.2 weeks, while blacks attended school for 14.7 weeks. Black students attended school only when they were free of agricultural work of planting, cultivation and harvest (Franklin, 1947; Dollard, 1957).

In 1940, when individuals born before 1915 were asked by the Census Bureau to indicate the number of years of schooling they had completed, it was found that the average black in the United States had completed 5.7 years while the average white had finished 8.8 years. Fifteen percent of Southern blacks of this age had no formal schooling; 60 percent had never reached the fifth grade. Only 5.5 percent of rural farm blacks had received any high school education, while almost six times as many rural farm whites had attended some high school (Myrdal, 1944).

Residential segregation. Residential segregation was almost complete in the South in the early part of the twentieth century, regardless of income or education of homeowners and renters. This arose through social custom, and was enforced by the same means. Legal residential segregation was attempted by many states and cities. The Supreme Court struck down these laws, but efforts were still made to circumvent the decision, the most effective being the restrictive covenant. This was a private contract limiting the sale of a property to certain purchasers (Woodward, 1955).

Transportation. The South's entire transportation system—railways, street cars, buses and steamboats—were segregated. A black passenger

traveling by public conveyance in the South after 1910 not only rode in
a segregated vehicle but was forced into using a whole network of segregated facilities that developed around the transportation arteries—
segregated waiting rooms, ticket windows, toilets and drinking
fountains. Laws specified that the facilities be substantially equal for
the two races; however, no one maintained seriously that the Blacks
received equal accommodations.

Other public facilities. Segregation policies were enforced by theaters,
hotels and restaurants. The mere entering of many Southern buildings
was a segregated affair, with exits and entrances clearly labeled
"Whites" and "Colored." Jim Crow elevators were operated in many
of Atlanta's large buildings. Oklahoma law required separate telephone booths for the two races. In Mobile, a 1909 law established a
10:00 P.M. curfew for blacks, while in Texas, Oklahoma and Alabama, entire towns were closed to blacks.

In Mississippi and South Carolina there were laws for general
segregation in hospitals, applying to medical personnel as well as
patients, and many other states practiced such separation without le-
galizing it. Thirteen southern and border states required segregation
in mental institutions, while ten specified that separate penal institutions be maintained for the races. Segregation was practiced in institutions for the aged and the handicapped, all according to numerous
state laws, as well as in recreational facilities, tent shows, fraternal
orders, etc.

In the workplace. There were laws dealing with working conditions, including the segregation of black and white employees, although in
many cases separation took place without the aid of statutes. Jim Crow
unionism in the crafts and trades prevented blacks from qualifying for
certain types of employment since they were not given the opportunity
to learn the necessary skills (Woodward, 1955).

Family life for southern blacks. The actual nature of black families and
family life at the turn of the century is still a matter of scholarly debate
and conjecture because of the paucity of information, the probable
shortcomings of census data, and the possible subjectivity of the
sociologists who have examined black family structure during the
early years of this century. However, it is probable that by the beginning of the twentieth century the black family structure had begun to
throw off the twin influences of slavery and the initial period of
Emancipation.

Under slavery, the master could, if he wished, breed his slaves like cattle or sell them individually without consideration for family ties, and many stories attest to heart-rending separations of wives from husbands, of children from parents, and of siblings who never met again (Bernard, 1966; Frazier, 1967). There were some owners who were very solicitous about the moral character of their slaves and their sexual conduct, supervising their alliances and inventing marriage ceremonies—some religious in character and others whimsical—although slave unions were not recognized by law (Botkin, 1945). Even in those instances where a master recognized and encouraged life-long commitments between slaves, so that organized family life existed, the family members lived under the shadow of great insecurity, for the master's death often meant the dissolution of the family unit. In short, the family life style of slaves depended entirely upon the desires and practices of their owner.

The slave mother, needed by the master to provide physical care for the children, often remained as the mistress of her cabin. The slave father was forced to a more peripheral status, having neither an assured position of authority in the family nor the opportunity for economic responsibility toward the family unit. Mothers, therefore, were more often able to assume a sustaining and protective role toward the children, a development that continued into the period of Emancipation.

Emancipation was followed by a period in which there was a great deal of wandering, resettlement and upheaval. Scholars seem to agree that the folkways of slave life were modified but not obliterated. The importance of sexual unions based upon sympathy and attraction rather than legality remained. The white community took a number of steps after the Civil War that were designed to make the marriage patterns of the former slaves conform to prevailing norms. Efforts were made to register marital unions; the military insisted upon formal marriage documents; and child welfare and public health programs required documents proving legalized relationships. Bernard believes that a great deal of family stability was achieved by 1917, with 89 percent of black infants born in wedlock or to stable parental relationships (Bernard, 1966). The Census Bureau's 1904 edition of *Negroes in the United States* suggests that the conjugal condition reported for Southern blacks did not differ markedly from Southern whites.

Economics. Life was harsh for black families. Homes were squalid and crowded. Light and ventilation were usually inadequately provided by the open door and a few small holes in the wall, roofs leaked, and

sanitary facilities for bathing and the disposal of waste were lacking.
One of our Historians described rural black housing in Georgia:

> They would have what you call a shanty, an old house
> where there was just maybe one room or two rooms. And
> four or five families, or mothers and their children, would
> have their mattresses, and they'd put them on the floor. Or
> they would pull hay or straw and we would sleep on that.
> And they'd cook outdoors.

Hard physical labor, poorly compensated, formed the backbone
of daily living. The feudal-like systems of tenancy and sharecropping
absorbed the largest number of black families, while many others
were landless farm laborers working for as little as ten dollars a month
(Franklin, 1947).

There were different types of tenancy, resulting in varying degrees
of economic status and dependency. Highest on the economic ladder
were cash tenants who rented the land outright for a fixed sum and
themselves provided tools, seed and fertilizer. Other types of tenant–
planter relationships were based on varying degrees of sharing the
main crop. Those who farmed "on halves" were known as sharecroppers and usually contributed nothing but their labor (Myrdal, 1044).
Very few blacks owned farms or shared significantly in the returns
from agricultural production, and those who did own land were very
careful not to attract too much attention from the white community
(Frazier, 1967).

Farming demanded the efforts of the entire family. A 1908 Atlanta
University study described the work habits of a Southern black family:
everyone worked in the field; the mother and daughter left just in time
to cook dinner. Hours were from sunrise to sunset, with an hour off at
noon. If there was no farm work to be done, all were obliged to report
to the landlord for other unpaid service (DuBois, 1908).

Some blacks did become skilled workers and artisans, primarily
railroad workers, carpenters, millers, smiths, dressmakers and masons,
and in the cities of the South there began to be a sizeable group of
middle-class blacks—undertakers, school teachers, realtors, news-
papermen, bankers, insurance agents, caterers, ministers, lawyers
and physicians (DuBois, 1902).

The church and other institutions. The black church was the focal point of
the community. Black leaders and individuals with creative abilities
found room there for self expression. Most church-goers belonged to

either Baptist or Methodist congregations, geography rather than social class determining denominational affiliation (DuBoic, 1903).

Other social outlets for the Southern black community were the black fraternal and benevolent societies, with the Odd Fellows leading the secret orders in size, having over four thousand lodges in 1904 (Meier and Rudwick, 1966). The Masons and Black Knights of Pythias gained in numbers after 1880, with over a third of the black Masons in the U.S. in 1904 living in the southeast.

Black Southern society spawned a number of newspapers; in 1900 Georgia and Texas had twenty-three each and North Carolina had ten (Franklin, 1947).

Social life. The Southern week revolved around the anxiously-awaited Sunday church service. It was both a religious and a social gathering, held once or twice a month, and lasting from nine in the morning until one in the afternoon. The congregation would usually linger at the church grounds until late afternoon, gossiping, feasting, holding christenings and baptisms. Generally the services themselves were alive with hand clapping, foot patting, shouting and "soul-stirring" preaching, most churches measuring the abilities of the preacher by the "rousement" of his sermons. Once a year, usually in late autumn after the crops had been laid by, the churches held revivals, a series of nightly gatherings that drew large crowds for the purpose of recruiting new members or saving souls (DuBois, 1903).

Saturday was also an important day in the rural black week, for it afforded a trip to town. These visits were used for marketing, to chat and drink with friends, and to gain a respite from back-breaking work (DuBois, 1903).

Other occasions for celebration were found. Sometimes families would give a "frolic," gathering neighbors and friends at a cabin for games, feasting and drinking. The circus was a great occasion, visiting the county seat once a twice a year, and the closing of school was also a time for socializing, for shared food, and for a night program that attracted a large audience. One of our Historians tells of the twentieth of May celebrations to which the whole black community turned out despite work commitments and possible layoffs, because it was "their day." Another recalls a "sing," at which her family and relatives entertained themselves on a lazy summer Sunday night.

Another break in the routine came in the week before Christmas and New Year's, an especially joyous period. This was the time of the annual accounting—with the hoped-for small cash balance—as well

as the end of the work year for black sharecroppers, and thus was an
added cause for jubilance.   ◆◆◆

This was the South our Historians left to seek a better life in
Newark, New Jersey.

THE MIGRATION YEARS

Between 1910 and 1930, rural Southern blacks were experiencing
even more difficult times because of the cotton boll weevil, disastrous
floods, and the low price of cotton in the commodities market.

The North needed workers. Northern industries sent labor re-
cruiters to the small towns of the South, and the black press stirred up
the "Northern fever" by graphically contrasting the racial atrocities
and proscriptions of the South with the growing economic opportunities of the North. Northern industrial pay—sometimes as high as $135
for every two months—was especially attractive to farm workers
making an average of $120 a year. Thousands left Southern farms for
the economic promise of Northern cities (Spear, 1967).

The city of Newark became the destination of a significant
portion of the migrants. From 9,475 in 1910 the black population of
the city grew to 38,880 by 1930.[7] Through letters and visits "back
home" the newcomers encouraged the continuing trek to the urban
North (Cunningham, 1966).

The city expressed a tolerance toward the new residents, if not a
welcome. A *Newark Evening News* editorial of July, 1917, hailed the
city's ability to absorb the black workers with the caption, "No Negro
Problem Here." However, many difficulties awaited the migrant.
The diet was strange; clothing and heating needs were different; the
way of life was new; and disease rates were unusually high in the black
areas. Housing was scarce and racially segregated. Some white land-
lords refused to rent to black tenants while others collected unconscion-
ably high rents for miserable accommodations (Cunningham, 1966).
Before the great Southern migration blacks had lived throughout the
city, but after 1910 they became concentrated in a few wards. The rise
of the black ghetto had begun.

The migrants found jobs in the chemical, hardware and muni-
tions plants and with the government. But not all were factory hands.
In 1920 there were over 300 blacks who had gone into business for

---

[7]This was calculated by comparing population tables in the 1910 and 1930 census.

themselves; most of these were in hair-dressing and beauty salon establishments and trucking firms, but others headed restaurants, furniture stores, and mortuaries, and there were caterers, physicians and dentists (Bureau of Negro Intelligence, 1920).

In the burgeoning black areas the church filled much the same function as it did in the South. Scheiner's profile of black urban churches emphasizes the social as well as the religious character of the institution, the fact that it was a social center, a promoter of educational and cultural activities, a conduit for aid to the needy, a meeting place for benevolent, cultural and fraternal organizations, and often a force for social control as well as social reform and protest (Scheiner, 1969).

A network of community organizations attempted to ameliorate problems in the ghetto. The National Association for the Advancement of Colored People, founded in 1914, led a silent march of over two thousand down Broad Street in 1917 to demand decent housing, reasonable rents and political recognition (Eldridge, 1966). Chapters of the Young Women's and Young Men's Christian Associations were opened in the black areas in the twenties, and the Friendly Neighborhood House, in the settlement house model, was founded in 1926. A black hospital with thirty beds served the black community from 1927 to 1953.

The Depression. The Great Depression tore apart the fabric of life in the city of Newark as it did throughout the country. Machines were idle; factories were dark and deserted. Over 600 plants had closed their doors by 1933, and in that year payrolls that had been as high as ninety million dollars in 1925 slid to a low of four million. Blacks in Newark, as elsewhere in the country, were victims of the "last hired, first fired" policy, and at the worst point in the Depression they represented one-third of all the relief cases in the city although they were only one-tenth of the population. At one point in 1931, the executive secretary of the Urban League reported that he had 112 black men in his office who claimed they had not eaten for between one to twelve days (Cunningham, 1966).

Tuberculosis, the main health problem, was seven times as high for blacks as for whites, and was related to the poor diet, the overcrowding and the inadequate hygienic conditions.

Crime rose. Blacks were both victim and victimizer. Wide status discrepancies in the eyes of police, judge and jury worked to the disadvantage of the black accused, as did great differences in the ability to hire a trained defense lawyer.

A new political awareness began to grow, and the twenties through the forties saw the beginning of black political power on the local scene. Randolph, the first black Assemblyman, was elected in 1923; Reverend Hayes became the first black to head the Housing Authority in 1942; and Jackson became the first black member of the Board of Education in 1943 (Eldridge, 1966).

World War II era. With the attack on Pearl Harbor and the subsequent entry of the country into World War II, the Great Depression came to an end. Newark's industrial production soared, "help wanted" signs reappeared, night shifts were instituted at many factories, and once again large numbers of black migrants came up from the South. Newark's black population grew by almost 30,000 in the ten-year period before 1950 (Cunningham, 1966).

Although jobs existed due to the war, blacks could not always find employment, for racial discrimination in hiring practices was prevalent in Newark and throughout the state of New Jersey. The *New Jersey Afro-American* wrote in 1941 that "while contracts for nearly a billion and a half dollars in government defense orders have been placed with firms in New Jersey, the Urban League finds that these firms have steadfastly refused to hire colored workers." (*Afro-American*, 1941)

Blacks, however, did not limit their participation in the war effort. They served as soldiers, volunteers, and (when allowed) as factory workers.

Ghettoization continued. By 1940 the Third Ward alone contained more than 16,000 black residents (U.S. Census, 1940). By 1944 nearly one third of the dwelling units in the black areas were below the minimum standards for health and decency. Outside toilets were still in use in many homes, and defective stoves and oil-soaked stairways made the wooden tenements burn like torches if touched by a stray match (Lucas, 1946; Queen, 1941; Wright, 1968).

Churches thrived in the forties. As white residents fled to outlying districts and the central city became increasingly black, solid and dig-nified houses of worship were sold to black congregations whose membership soared. At least two of the established churches initiated community progams that had great appeal to members. St. James waged an aggressive campaign against the spread of tuberculosis, and the Metropolitan Baptist Church initiated a home and missionary relief program and offered members an opportunity to invest in the

Metropolitan Realty and Investment Association (*Afro-American*, 1947).

During the war years a certain racial harmony existed in the city, typified by integrated housing ·policies of the Newark Housing Authority and the existence of some stable racially-mixed neighborhoods. Unfortunately, this was a temporary phenomenon. In the spring of 1943 a near "race riot" presaged events to come (*Afro-American*, 1943).

THE POST-WORLD WAR II YEARS

With the return of the veteran and the subsequent move of many G.I.'s to the suburbs, the Newark center city began a rapid deterioration. It lost its dominant economic place in the state; property values declined; the city budget decreased while the tax rate increased; industry was leaving the city; school, roads and hospitals needed extensive repairs and renovations, and the slums were among the worst in the nation (Cunningham, 1966).

At a neighborhood conference held at Fuld Neighborhood House in 1956, conditions in the now all-black Central Ward were discussed. City services had become increasingly inadequate; there was a shortage of police personnel with increasing incidents of police brutality; schools were overcrowded and inadequate; sanitation reforms were urgently needed; rents were outrageously high; housing was dilapidated, and recreational facilities did not meet the needs of the residents (Fuld Neighborhood House, 1956).

The urban renewal program of the 1950s added more disruption to community life, and by the sixties the city was distinguished by a long list of firsts in urban pathology. It had the highest crime rate; the highest tuberculosis, syphillis and gonorrhea rate; the highest maternal mortality rate; the highest proportionate urban tax rate; the highest population density adjusted to usable land; the highest proportion of land set aside for urban renewal clearance; and the highest daytime population turnover in the nation (Wright, 1968).

The sixties also marked a turning point in population, for it was during this period that the black majority in Newark was reached, although political power still eluded the now dominant group.

But the black community was on the move. The NAACP and the Urban League were joined by the Congress of Racial Equality and the Student Non-Violent Coordinating Committee in their fight to improve conditions for Newark blacks. Two new organizations, the Black Man's Volunteer Army–Negro-American Labor Council and the Committee for a United Newark, joined the battle at the end of the decade (*Afro-American*, 1967; Cook, 1971; O'Shea, 1967). The black churches of Newark, enjoying the continued support of the older Southern-born population, took on a new social consciousness, emphasizing religious orthodoxy less and civil rights and social philosophy more.

In spite of the increased community organization of the sixties that helped lead to the election of a black mayor in 1970, Newark's black population could not finish the decade without a violent outburst. In the summer of 1967 the city witnessed one of the worst urban riots in the history of the United States. Bands of rioters and snipers terrorized the city. Twenty-three blacks and two whites died as a result of the terror, and an estimated thirty to forty-five million dollars in property damage was attributed to the rioting, looting and burning. Many of our Historians tell of the violence that surrounded them as they cowered in their apartments until the streets became quiet once more. *The Seventies.* The seventies have brought a mixed share of hope and sorrow to our Historians.

In 1970, the city elected its first black Mayor.

Supplemental Security Income replaced welfare as the primary supplement to meagre Social Security benefits for most of Newark's elderly.

More older blacks have moved to public housing, where rents are controlled, and services are more accessible. Nutrition programs, health clinics, and social services have been established at high-rise senior citizen housing. Neighborhood improvements are slow, however, and crime against the elderly continues to be a serious problem.

Mayor Gibson, elected to successive terms, has been extremely vocal and often successful in his attempts to get more support for his city. However, state and federal governments have not come forth with the massive aid that Newark leadership believes is needed to save the city. With a slowed economy and high inflation, the nation has diverted its attention from the solving of social problems to economic retrenchment. The interest that once was shown in redressing the wrongs done to minority groups has now been redirected to the more immediate economic difficulties affecting the majority groups.

The years ahead may be difficult ones for our Historians and for the city in which they have grown old.

References

Bardolph, Richard, ed. *The Civil Rights Record*. New York: Thomas Y. Crowell Co., 1970.

Bernard, Jessie. *Marriage and Family Among Negroes*. Englewood Cliffs, New Jersey: Prentice Hall, 1966.

Botkin, B.A. *Lay My Burden Down*. Chicago: University of Chicago Press, 1945.

Bracey, John, Meier, August and Rudwick, Elliott, eds. *The Rise of the Ghetto*. Belmont, California: Wadsworth Publishing Company, 1971.

Clark, Kenneth. *Dark Ghetto: Dilemmas of Social Power*. New York: Harper, 1967.

The Classified Directory of Negro Business Interests: Professions of Essex County. Newark, New Jersey: Bureau of Negro Intelligence, 1920.

Cook, Fred. "Newark." *New York Times Magazine*, 25 July.

Cunningham, John T. *Newark*. Newark, New Jersey: New Jersey Historical Society, 1966.

Curvin, Robert. *"The Persistent Minority: the Black Political Experience in Newark."* Ph.D. Dissertation, Princeton, 1975.

Dollard, John. *Caste and Class in a Southern Town*. 3rd ed. Garden City, New York: Doubleday and Company, Inc., 1957.

DuBois, W.E.B., ed. *The Negro American Family*. Westport, Conn.: Negro Universities Press, 1908.

———, "The Negro Artisan." *Atlanta University Publication No. 17*. Atlanta, Georgia: Atlanta University Press, 1902.

———, "The Negro Church." *Atlanta University Publication No. 8*. Atlanta, Georgia: Atlanta University Press, 1903.

Eldridge, Douglas. "The Negro, A Place of Hope." *Newark Evening News*, 16 May 1966, p. 14.

Franklin, John Hope. *From Slavery to Freedom*. New York: Alfred A. Knopf, 1947.

Frazier, E. Franklin. *The Negro Family in the United States*. Rev. and abr. ed. Chicago, Illinois: University of Chicago Press, 1967.

Ginzburg, Ralph. *100 Years of Lynchings*. New York: Lancer, 1962.

Gutman, Herbert G. *The Black Family in Slavery and Freedom*. New York: Random House, 1977.

Henri, Florette. *Black Migration: Movement North, 1900–1920*. Garden City, New York: Anchor, 1975.

Johnson, Daniel M. and Campbell, Rex R. *Black Migration in America: A Social Demographic History*. Durham, North Carolina: Duke University Press, 1981.

Kilson, Martin, Huggins, Nathan, and Fox, eds. *Key Issues in the Afro-American Experience*. vol. 2. New York: Harcourt Brace Jovanovich, 1971.

Kusmer, Kenneth L. *A Ghetto Takes Shape: Black Cleveland, 1870–1930*. Chicago: University of Illinois Press, 1978.

Lucas, Curtis. *Third Ward Newark*. Chicago: Ziff–Davis Publishing Company, 1946.

Meier, August, and Rudwick, Elliott. *From Plantation to Ghetto*. New York: Hill and Wang, 1976.

Myrdal, Gunnar. *An American Dilemma*. New York: Harper, 1944.

National Association for the Advancement of Colored People. *Thirty Years of Lynching*. New York, 1919.

O'Shea, John. "Negroes Move Towards Power." *Atlantic Monthly*, July 1967.

Osofsky, Gilbert. *Harlem: The Making of a Ghetto, 1890–1930*. New York: Harper and Row, 1966.

Palen, John J., and Flaming, Karl H., eds. *Urban America: Conflict and Change*. New York: Praeger, 1972.

Price, Clement. "The Afro-American Community of Newark, 1917-1 1947." Ph.D. Dissertation, Rutgers University, 1975.

_____. *Freedom Not Far Distant: A Documentary History of Afro-Americans in New Jersey*. Newark: New Jersey Historical Society, 1980.

Queen, Bob, Jr. "Vice Conditions Stir City." *New Jersey Afro-American*. 29 March 1941

Rainwater, Lee, and Yancey, William L., eds. *The Moynihan Report and the Politics of Controversy*. Cambridge, Massachusetts: M.I.T. Press, 1967.

"A Report of the Findings and Conclusions of the Central Ward Neighborhood Conference." Newark, New Jersey. Fuld Neighborhood House, 1956.

Report of the National Advisory Commission on Civil Disorders. New York: Bantam, 1968.

Scheiner, Seth. "The Negro Church and the Northern City: 1890–1930." *Seven on Black.* Edited by William C. Shade and Roy C. Horrenkohl. Philadelphia: Lippincott, 1969.

Spear, Allan. *Black Chicago: The Making of a Negro Ghetto, 1890–1920.* Chicago: University of Chicago Press, 1967.

Weinstein, Allen, and Gatell, Frank O., eds. *The Segregation Era, 1863–1954.* New York: Oxford University Press, 1970.

Wolters, Raymond. *Negroes and the Great Depression: The Problem of Economic Recovery.* Westport, Connecticut: Greenwood Press, 1970.

Woodward, C. Vann. *The Strange Career of Jim Crow.* New York: Oxford University Press, 1966.

Wright, Nathan. *Ready to Riot.* New York: Holt, Rinehart and Winston, 1968.

Bibliographical Notes

DOCUMENTS

United States Census Reports: In addition to the census reports (1880 to 1970) which were used for this study, a number of special reports by the Bureau of the Census were also useful. *Negroes in the United States, 1920–1932* (Washington, 1935) was especially valuable for the research on migration. Two of the Bureau's reports on religion in America also proved beneficial: *Religious Bodies*, Volume I (Washington, 1926); and *Religious Bodies*, Volumes I and II (Washington, 1936). Other reports used were: *Negroes in the United States*, (Washington, 1904) and *Population and Housing Statistics for Census Tracts, Newark, New Jersey* (1942).

State of New Jersey documents used include: *Manual of the Legislature of New Jersey*, 1941; the New Jersey State Municipal Aid Administration's *Who Is On Relief in Newark*, (Trenton, 1941); The New Jersey Division on Aging's "Local Planning for Housing the Elderly," (New Brunswick, 1964).

City of Newark documents used were: The Newark Housing Authority's *Progress Report on Integration*, (1952); Housing Authority *Annual Reports, 1968, 1969* and *1970*; The Newark Human Right's Commission's *Newark: A City in Transition* (1959); *Construction Report*, Newark Housing Authority, 1956; "Annual Report of the Division of Tuberculosis," *Annual Report*, Department of Health, City of Newark, 1929; and *City Alive*, Newark Housing Authority, 1966.

NEWSPAPERS

The newspaper used most extensively in this study was *The New Jersey Afro-American*. Other papers used were: *The Newark Evening News; The Newark Star Ledger*; and *The New York Times*.